Robots in Education

Robots in Education is an accessible introduction to the use of robotics in formal learning, encompassing pedagogical and psychological theories as well as implementation in curricula. Today, a variety of communities across education are increasingly using robots as general classroom tutors, tools in STEM projects, and subjects of study. This volume explores how the unique physical and social-interactive capabilities of educational robots can generate bonds with students while freeing instructors to focus on their individualized approaches to teaching and learning. Authored by a uniquely interdisciplinary team of scholars, the book covers the basics of robotics and their supporting technologies; attitudes toward and ethical implications of robots in learning; research methods relevant to extending our knowledge of the field; and more.

Fady Alnajjar is Associate Professor in the Department of Computer Science and Software Engineering in the College of Information Technology at United Arab Emirates University, UAE.

Christoph Bartneck is Associate Professor and Director of Postgraduate Studies in the HIT Lab NZ at the University of Canterbury, New Zealand.

Paul Baxter is Senior Lecturer in Computer Science (Autonomous Systems) and Founding and Steering Group member of the Autism Research and Innovation Centre (ARIC) at the University of Lincoln, UK.

Tony Belpaeme is Professor in the Faculty of Engineering and Architecture at Ghent University, Belgium, and Full Professor in Cognitive Systems and Robotics at Plymouth University, UK.

Massimiliano L. Cappuccio is Senior Researcher in the School of Engineering and Information Technology at the University of New South Wales Canberra, Australia.

Cinzia Di Dio is Researcher in the Faculty of Education in the Department of Psychology at Università Cattolica del Sacro Cuore, Italy.

Friederike Eyssel is Full Professor and Head of the Applied Social Psychology and Gender Research Lab at Bielefeld University, Germany.

Jürgen Handke is Professor in the Department of English and American Studies at the Philipps University of Marburg, Germany.

Omar Mubin is Senior Lecturer in Human Computer Interaction in the School of Computer, Data, and Mathematical Sciences at Western Sydney University, Australia.

Mohammad Obaid is Associate Professor of Human-Computer Interaction and Head of the Interaction Design Unit in the Department of Computer Science and Engineering at Chalmers University of Technology, Sweden.

Natalia Reich-Stiebert is Research Fellow at the Department of Social Psychology at the University of Hagen, Germany.

Robots in Education

An Introduction to High-Tech Social
Agents, Intelligent Tutors, and
Curricular Tools

Fady Alnajjar, Christoph Bartneck,
Paul Baxter, Tony Belpaeme,
Massimiliano L. Cappuccio,
Cinzia Di Dio, Friederike Eyssel,
Jürgen Handke, Omar Mubin,
Mohammad Obaid, and
Natalia Reich-Stiebert

Routledge
Taylor & Francis Group

NEW YORK AND LONDON

First published 2022
by Routledge
52 Vanderbilt Avenue, New York, NY 10017

and by Routledge
2 Park Square, Milton Park, Abingdon, Oxon, OX14 4RN

Routledge is an imprint of the Taylor & Francis Group, an informa business

Library of Congress Cataloging-in-Publication Data
A catalog record for this title has been requested

ISBN: 978-0-367-69651-1 (hbk)
ISBN: 978-0-367-65539-6 (pbk)
ISBN: 978-1-003-14270-6 (ebk)

Typeset in Sabon
by KnowledgeWorks Global Ltd.

Contents

List of Illustrations		*vii*
Abbreviations		*ix*
Acknowledgements		*xi*

1 Introduction **1**
  1.1 Teaching Technologies: The Digital Turn in Education *3*
  1.2 A Brief Definition of and Introduction to Educational Robots *6*
  1.3 Science Versus Fiction *9*
  1.4 Outline of the Book *13*

2 Theories of Learning **15**
  2.1 Learning Theories *16*
  2.2 Social Learning *22*
  2.3 Tutoring *23*
  2.4 Cooperative Learning *24*
  2.5 Project-based Learning *26*
  2.6 Educational Robots *27*

3 The Interactive Mind **29**
  3.1 Cognitive Underpinnings of Human Learning *30*
  3.2 Cognitive Underpinnings of Social Interaction *34*
  3.3 Demographics *44*
  3.4 Are you really "Like Me?" *46*

4 What Makes a Robot? **51**
  4.1 The Robot *52*
  4.2 Input Technologies *55*
  4.3 Output Technologies *59*
  4.4 Processing Software *62*

5   The Robot as a Tool   71
    5.1   *Why Are Robots Used in Education?*   72
    5.2   *Computational Thinking*   74
    5.3   *Hardware*   75
    5.4   *Software*   83
    5.5   *Robotic Competitions*   85
    5.6   *Challenges*   86
    5.7   *Outlook*   88

6   The Robot as a Social Agent   93
    6.1   *What Makes a Social Robot?*   93
    6.2   *Roles of Social Robots in Education*   94
    6.3   *Outlook*   111

7   Deployment Requirements   115
    7.1   *Selecting a Robot*   116
    7.2   *Financial Issues*   117
    7.3   *The Infrastructure*   120
    7.4   *Development/Programming*   124
    7.5   *Outlook*   127

8   Applications   129
    8.1   *Learning*   130
    8.2   *Assessment and Feedback*   143
    8.3   *Perspectives*   146

9   Attitudes Towards Robots   149
    9.1   *Attitudes Towards Robots and Technology Acceptance*   149
    9.2   *Measuring Attitudes Towards Robots*   150

10 Ethics   157
    10.1 *What Is Ethics?*   158
    10.2 *Ethics for Robots*   160
    10.3 *Ethical Concerns in the Classroom*   163
    10.4 *Conclusion*   166

11 Research Methods in Educational Robotics   169
    11.1 *Short-Term and Long-Term Investigations*   170
    11.2 *Research Process*   171

Bibliography   183
Index   223

List of Illustrations

Figures

0.1	The authors	xi
1.1	Mindstorms robot	7
1.2	Raspberry Pi	7
1.3	Pepper robot	9
1.4	Aibo robot	10
1.5	Geminoid HI-4 robot	11
2.1	Example of the Logo programming language	22
3.1	Overall organization of human memory	32
4.1	The robot in the context of an educational scenario	52
4.2	Attention capturing and reporting by Pepper	62
4.3	LEGO mindstorms IDE	63
4.4	Handwriting	67
5.1	Valiant turtle	72
5.2	The WeGoSTEM robot	74
5.3	Scratch	76
5.4	Choregraphe IDE	77
5.5	Ozobot Evo robot	78
5.6	PiStorms robot	80
5.7	Thymio robot	80
5.8	TurtleBot 3	82
5.9	3D Printed LEGO	83
5.10	inMoov robot	83
5.11	Virtual robotics toolkit	85
5.12	Opsoro	89
6.1	A social robot during second language learning	98
6.2	A robot in the classroom	101
6.3	Teaching a robot fine motor skills	102
6.4	Pepper as a classroom assistant	104
6.5	Pepper as an examiner	104

6.6   A KeepOn robot acting as a mediator   107
6.7   Pepper as a learning advisor   109
6.8   Pepper in class supporting university students   111
7.1   The specifications of Pepper, the humanoid robot   117
7.2   The specifications of NAO, the humanoid robot   118
7.3   The BuSaif humanoid robot   119
7.4   The Robotikum makerspace   121
7.5   A standard transport box for Pepper robots   122
7.6   Transport devices for NAO and Pepper robots   123
7.7   Pepper with wireless microphone   124
7.8   A sample Wizard-of-Oz interface for Pepper   127
8.1   Cellulo robot   131
8.2   Empathic robot   135
8.3   The NAO showing emotions   136
8.4   Rehabilitation   137
8.5   The therapist communicates with the child through the robot   138
8.6   Pepper in class supporting university students   ·141
8.7   Components of a CAP at work   142
8.8   The Quizmaster-App in class   144
8.9   Pepper identifies human via QR-Code   145

Table

2.1   Learning theories   20

Abbreviations

AI Artificial Intelligence

API Application Programming Interface

ARS Audience-Response-System

ASD Autism Spectrum Disorder

ASR Automated Speech Recognition

CL Collaborative Learning

CAP Classroom Application Package

DARPA Defence Advanced Research Projects Agency

HCI Human-Computer Interaction

HRI Human-Robot Interaction

ICTD ICT for Development

IDE Integrated Development Environments

LED Light-Emitting Diode

LTM Long-Term Memory

MIT Massachusetts Institute of Technology

MOOC Massive Open Online Course

PBL Project-based Learning

QR Quick Response (Code)

RIS Robotics Invention System

ROS   Robot Operating System

SDK   Software Development Kit

STEM   Science Technology Engineering Mathematics

STEAM   Science Technology Engineering Arts Mathematics

STM   Short-Term Memory

T&L   Teaching and Learning

TLG   The LEGO Group

ToM   Theory of Mind

VLC   The Virtual Linguistics Campus

WM   Working Memory

WoZ   Wizard-of-Oz

ZPD   Zone of Proximal Development

Acknowledgements

This book represents the outcome of a week-long intensive writing retreat held in Al Ain, Emirate of Abu Dhabi, at the turn of January and February 2020, as part of the research activities promoted by the AI & Robotics Lab of United Arab Emirates University (UAEU).

All co-authors have actively participated in this retreat and collaborated to design, draft, and revise the structure and the original contents that compose this book.

Figure 0.1 The authors in Al Ain, UAE

They were facilitated by Ms Faith Bosworth Booksprints.net in implementing the Book Sprint workflow format. The retreat was associated with the 5th Joint UAE Symposium on Social Robotics (JSSR2020), to which the co-authors have participated as speakers immediately after the end of the writing retreat. The retreat and the symposium were made possible by a generous contribution from the College of Humanities and Social Sciences and the College of Information Technology of UAE University. JSSR is part of the activities that UAEU holds annually for Innovation Month under the patronage of its Chancellor, H.E. Dr. Saeed Ahmed Ghobash, to whom we are grateful for supporting our initiative. The authors of this book would like to thank also Dr. Ghaleb Ali Alhadrami, Dr. Hassan Naboodah, Dr. Taieb Znati, Dr. Meera Alkaabi, and Dr. Munkhjargal Gochoo for supporting the organization of this initiative. We also would like to give special thanks to Dr. Munkhjargal Gochoo and Dr. Fiona Baker for offering helpful suggestions and insights during the initial stages of the retreat.

1   Introduction

If we teach today's students as we taught yesterday's, we rob them of to-morrow.

John Dewey, Democracy and Education,
New York: Macmillan Company, 1944

What is covered in this chapter:

- The changing nature of education;
- A short history of educational robots;
- Real robots versus fictional robots;
- What is covered in this book.

A modern learning scenario: Sarah attends a computer science class and works with Ozobot today. With Ozobot (see Figure 5.5), she catches Pokémon and thereby playfully learns about basic coding concepts. Ozobot is a small programmable robot designed to support lessons ranging from maths and science to art, offering a hands-on approach. At the same time, Ben attends a Spanish language class and interacts with Pepper, a robot that looks quite like a human with arms and a face that is intended to be perceived as friendly and cute (see Figure 1.3). They are talking about the lives of street children in Latin America. Pepper speaks slowly and without accent, and repeats patiently when Ben has not understood him. Pepper is available to support teaching and learning across different disciplines. Pepper speaks 27 languages and is able to recognize human emotions and interact socially.

The use of educational technologies to support learning and teaching has progressed from computer-aided presentations and online learning environments to one of the latest teaching technologies, that is, educational robots such as the Ozobot or Pepper presented above. Several schools and universities all over the world have already started to test the use of robots in the classroom. Rapid technological innovations that are categorized under the keyword "digitalization" are a reason for this development. Against the background of the digital transformation, the competent use of digital media plays an increasingly important role in the current educational discourse. Ever more frequently, the so-called 21st century skills come to the fore, which encompass, for instance, information, media and technology skills, collaboration and communication skills, as well as learning and innovation skills. The mission of education is, therefore, to provide new knowledge and competencies and support new forms of exchange in an increasingly interconnected world. Robotics is a driving force in this technological change and its importance in our future everyday life will increase steadily. For this reason, students must be given the opportunity to approach this topic and acquire knowledge about it to be prepared for present and future living and working environments. Even more importantly, research tells us that learning with robots is engaging for students of all ages and promotes students' interest in subjects they never thought they would be interested in. Thus, the use of educational robots can help to create a learning environment that keeps students engrossed in the content due to the novelty of the interaction medium.

In this book, we will outline first the various learning paradigms that underpin educational robots and then the potential of robots in education and the roles they can play in the transfer of knowledge. Further, we will discuss technical requirements and application potentials as well as possible associated challenges. Finally, we will consider how a robot's visual, social, and behavioural cues affect learning, and which research methods are appropriate to investigate human-robot interactions (HRIs) in the educational setting.

1.1 Teaching Technologies: The Digital Turn in Education

As mentioned above, education in the 21st century is changing. The role of robots in the future of education cannot be considered in isolation, but needs to be understood in the context of the digital changes that are currently being implemented. The central idea of this new approach to teaching and learning (T&L) is that knowledge delivery and knowledge acquisition are now largely mediated by digital technologies. A central way in which these transform education is that they enable educators to personalize learning and give students the ownership of their personal learning process.

One trend in the digital transformation of education that is experiencing immense growth is online learning. Instead of a text-based, static learning experience in a classroom or in a lecture hall, students work with the online learning elements that have been compiled for them in studios, workshops, or outside of the learning environment. These contents are usually delivered on the Internet using learning management systems (LMSs). One of the greatest advantages of this is that students can choose their own learning intensity and the speed at which they progress. Courses that are offered in such customizable formats have the potential to be scaled up dramatically in that a large number of students can consume the digitalized content in so-called massive open online courses (MOOCs).

In fact, there are many education institutions that consider MOOCs as a key to T&L in a modern world. However, it has become obvious that this format suffers from extremely low accomplishment rates, often below 5%. Khalil and Ebner (2014) mention lack of time, lack of learners' motivation, feelings of isolation, and the lack of interactivity are the central problems in such online T&L scenarios. The promise of scale, in which one tutor teaches thousands of students and even non-academics for free, has not been fully achieved (Neubök et al., 2015). The high production costs of professional online courses resulted in the need to charge considerable enrolment fees (Hollands, 2014). These problems also persist in closed online courses that are being offered by established universities to earn micro-certificates (Handke and Franke, 2013). Therefore, online courses are unlikely to be the solution to the problems of traditional T&L. We need an additional component, where the knowledge acquired digitally is deepened and practised. This opens up new opportunities for onsite teaching, where in-class scenarios become competence-oriented and no longer primarily focused on knowledge transfer. Therefore, a two-phase T&L scenario has been proposed: self-guided online content delivery and content acquisition and guided depth of knowledge. Not only does this scenario, which has for a long time been associated with the term "flipped" or "inverted teaching" (Baker, 2000; Lage et al., 2000), allow students to apply their own learning style and their own time frame, but also a high degree of individualization in the online phase. Even more so, it relies on a subsequent in-class phase where the newly acquired knowledge is deepened and practised.

A big enhancement to online education that can be used both in class and online has come with the emergence of virtual and augmented realities, allowing learners to get an immersive learning experience. Virtual reality (VR) is a computer-generated simulation of environments in which users can interact in a three-dimensional and realistic way, and in which they feel present using electronic equipment such as helmets or clothing equipped with sensors (Biocca, 1992; Steuer, 1992; Zhou and Deng, 2009). Current prominent VR systems are, for instance, the cave automatic virtual environment in which projections are displayed on the walls of a cube (CAVE, Cruz-Neira et al. (1992)) or head-mounted displays equipped with LCD screens (HDM, Santos et al. (2009)). Augmented reality (AR) combines real-life objects and elements with VR components (Azuma, 1997). Compared with VR, in AR virtual elements co-exist in real-life environments allowing for merging education in the virtual space and the real world (Bower et al., 2014). Mobile devices with GPS increase learners' mobility and interaction with each other, and enable the user to experience the real world authentically supplemented by virtual elements such as images, texts, or videos. AR textbooks are an example for such applications in education. Lecture notes are supplemented by visualizations, 3D models, or simulations creating a new interactive way of learning. A big advantage of VR and AR applications in education is that they allow for real-life experiences in an immersive way. Recent work shows that the use of VR and AR systems in education can have a positive impact on learning outcomes such as increased motivation and interest, or higher performance and creativity (Alhalabi, 2016; Bower et al., 2014; Makransky and Lilleholt, 2018; Wu et al., 2013). However, pedagogical issues and challenges arise from the implementation of both online learning as well as VR and AR applications in education. Innovative instructional approaches compared with conventional teacher-centred, delivery-based methods are required.

Consequently, the teacher's role has changed from a deliverer of knowledge to that of an academic assistant, or as King (1993) put it: "From Sage on the Stage to Guide on the Side". This new role is challenging. It involves answering questions, supervising research in class, group work with the students, and controlling technology, such as Audience-Response-Systems (ARSs) or learning-apps, that is, a number of activities where several competencies are required, such as content-specific competencies and media/technological competencies. A single academic is often not capable of sufficiently taking over all these roles, especially in classes with more than 25 students (Handke, 2017). But even in smaller classes, the permanent switch between content and technology may distract the academic guide from cooperating with the students. As a consequence, we need more assistants to take over these tasks, ideally one for each student. This would approach the ancient ideal of Socrates wandering the streets of Athens while conversing with a student.

Today, however, there is a new option. One of the latest teaching technologies that will shape education in the not-so-distant future, and what is to be discussed in this book, is the rise of robots for T&L. Among all these technologies, we believe that robots have a particularly great potential to shape the future of education and lead students to success. Relevant learning experiences with educational robots (be it robots as tools or as social agents) such as coding, programming, or collaborating through and with them, can, for example, inspire creativity, train problem solving, and empower self-regulated learning—skills students need to be successful in today's and tomorrow's working life. Educational robots as social agents can, at least to some extent, take over some of the tasks which humans have to perform, thus giving the academic guides new freedom for individual advice and consultation. This use of robots, which does not replace humans but where robots become their new assistants, is an essential part of the digital turn. While the roles played by the teacher and that of the robot will change the learning experience, robots will not make teachers obsolete. The programming of the robots, content creation, and maintenance will even result in many new jobs.

One could argue that virtual agents that are based on screens or mobile applications could accomplish this task as well and would not require expensive hardware. In this book, we will argue that the unique physical embodiment and the interactive capabilities of social robots are key to forming a social yet empathetic bond between the learners and the robots, and that this bond improves the learning experience. Other mechanical robots may not be able to converse with a human, but through their form factor or manipulative modular structure, they provide a platform to learn about engineering and sciences. Therefore, in this book we include chapters on both types of robots, as a social agent and as a tool.

What about the past? Have there been examples of robots that accompanied human teachers in education before the digital turn? Furthermore, are there examples of using robots in T&L environments beyond the ones described? The following passages will first provide a general overview and will then look at the potential of robots comparing science and fiction, and precisely, what belongs to the imaginary and real world.

1.2   A Brief Definition of and Introduction to Educational Robots

Educational robots subsume all those robots that can be used in the context of education. Depending on their interaction styles with humans, they can be classified into robots that can be used as tools or as social agents. In their role as tools, they are used either to teach students about robots per se, or to impart technical and programming knowledge through the manipulation of robots (Eguchi, 2012). This category includes robots like the LEGO Mindstorms or the Aibo robot (Sony). In their role as social agents, robots are regarded as learning collaborators (Miller and Nourbakhsh, 2016) that offer support and assistance through social interactions, and can be used in a cross-curricular context. These include, for example, humanoid robots such as the NAO robot (SoftBank Robotics) or telepresence robots such as the Beam robot (Suitable Technologies). As we will see in later chapters, this subdivision is a continuum rather than a binary distinction.

Educational robots have been around for many years. Because robots were first introduced into factories, teaching revolved around building and programming industrial robotic arms as part of mechatronics curricula. The complexity of these machines (such as the KUKA robotic arm) made them inaccessible to non-engineering university students.

The Massachusetts Institute of Technology (MIT) started to work on an education robotic platform as early as 1987 with their "Logo Brick" which was further developed into their "Red Brick". The LEGO Group (TLG) was interested in this development and started to collaborate with MIT in 1996, which resulted in the first LEGO programmable brick called the "Robotics Invention System" (RIS) in 1998 (Martin et al., 2000). It was marketed as LEGO Mindstorms. The original design was improved with the Mindstorms NXT and EV3 (see Figure 1.1).

LEGO Mindstorms is arguably the most widely used robotics teaching tool today (Kubilinskiene et al., 2017). However, several new platforms that are based on advanced micro-controllers have surpassed LEGO Mindstorms from a technological point of view. Two such computing devices used are the Raspberry Pi (see Figure 1.2) and the Arduino. All of these sets are intended to teach robotics and programming. While they can also be used to teach other topics, their main focus remains in computer science and engineering. We will introduce these systems in more detail in Chapter 5.

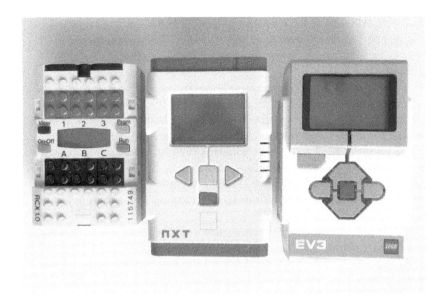

Figure 1.1 LEGO Mindstorms robots (from left to right: RCX, NXT, EV3)

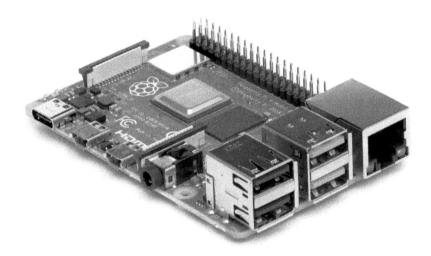

Figure 1.2 Raspberry Pi

Source: Michael Henzler

In 2008, Aldebaran Robotics (now Softbank Robotics) developed a fully integrated humanoid robot called "NAO". This was no longer a set of bricks, sensors, or actuators that needed to be assembled, but a fully functional
ready-to-use robot. It quickly became a popular research platform (almost a de-facto standard) and it has been used in many studies on using robots in education. While NAO can also be used to teach about robotics, it has been used for many other teaching areas, such as second language acquisition (Kennedy et al., 2016). After SoftBank bought Aldebaran Robotics, the robot "Pepper" was developed and launched in 2014. Pepper, through its emotion recognition capabilities, tablet integration, and suitability for multi-user tracking and interaction, is also tapping into the domain of education (Figure 1.3).

Other types of educational robots are zoomorphic robots, that is, robots that are shaped like animals, such as dogs and cats. Sony released their Aibo robot in 1999. While Aibo was not originally designed for education, Sony did provide tools to program the robot, which enabled researchers to build custom programs for Aibo so that it could be used in educational curricula (Yamamoto et al., 2006). The first versions of Aibo were produced between 1999 and 2006. In 2018, the company released an all new version of the robot (see Figure 1.4.)

All robots described so far can either operate autonomously, that is, when programmed, they act without further consultation with the programmer, or through the Wizard of Oz (WoZ) technique, that is, which implies the robot acts autonomously but is actually operated by an unseen human. Another approach for using robots in education is telepresence robots. Here, a distant teacher is remotely controlling a local robot that interacts with students. The Geminoid robot series (see Figure 1.5) of Hiroshi Ishiguro are examples of highly human-like telepresence robots (Nishio et al., 2007). Less human-like shaped telepresence robots are, for example, the Beam robots created by Suitable Technologies. It is possible for a single teacher to operate multiple remote robots and thereby enable long distance learning.

The robots available today for education have become more powerful and feature more natural forms of interaction. We will discuss the makeup of robots, their functions, and the underlying technology in more detail in Chapter 4.

Figure 1.3 Pepper robot from Softbank Robotics

Source: Softbank Robotics

1.3 Science Versus Fiction

In the field of robotics, it is very difficult to distinguish between what is scientific fact and what is mere fiction. Not only is the general public ill-informed about the state of the art in robotics, but it is also constantly mislead by fictional representations of robots and their abilities (Mubin et al., 2016; Sandoval et al., 2014).

Figure 1.4 Aibo robot from Sony 2018 (©Sony Corporation)

Endless times, science fiction writers have represented robots as companions (e.g., buddies, co-workers, life partners) or servants (most often employed as butlers, nannies, or bodyguards). Very often, in science fiction, when an educational function was assigned to robots, such function is subsumed under the role of caregiver: recall the Netflix movie "I am Mother" (Sputore, 2019), and Grace in "Umbrella Academy" (Way and Ba, 2008), or the famous robot M3 B9 in the *Lost in Space* series, which acted as companion and bodyguard of the youngest member of the Robinson family. Perhaps significantly, when robots are represented lecturing or teaching in science fiction, that is often because those activities are part of the rearing or protective behaviour that was programmed into them. Science fiction has also offered inspiring representations of robots serving

Figure 1.5 Geminoid HI-4 robot developed by Hiroshi Ishiguro in Osaka University

in the professional role of teachers and educators. Without any presumption of exhaustiveness, we would like to recall two fictional depictions of robot teachers, highlighting how both of them seem to contain unflattering and perhaps unfair judgements about the prospect of entrusting education to machines.

The first is "The Fun They Had" from 1951, a classic of SciFi literature. In this memorable short story, Isaac Asimov writes of a girl of 2155 who, after her neighbour found an ancient schoolbook in his attic, discovers that children used to learn in groups from human teachers before they were entirely replaced by mechanical teachers. At the time in which the story is set, children learn individually at home under the supervision of a robotic teacher. Although the girl is at first sceptical about the idea of being lectured by an adult human, by the end of the story she daydreams about having fun in a school of the past in the company of other students and a human teacher. In this story, the notion of robotics in education is received with a mix of scepticism and a sense of nostalgia for traditional education. However, reading Asimov's story in 2020, after being made aware of the well-documented benefits of using robots in the classroom to increase children's engagement and facilitate group learning, we cannot help but find it ironic that today's robots seem to offer one of the most promising solutions to the isolation described in the story.

Another popular representation of robotics in education is offered by Mark Lester's (1990) dystopic movie "Class of 1999". The film features a school in a violent neighbourhood troubled by student riots and gangs of young criminals. To help the scholastic institution control their students, teachers are secretly replaced with new models of humanoid robots, who very soon start showing a questionable inclination for repressive methods in disciplining the unruly youngsters. Also, this dystopic scenario seems quite ironic today when robot-children interaction is a reality we have become familiar with. While there is definitively some truth to the idea that robots can become tools of surveillance[1] and deterrence, and that they can—in principle—be used to prevent undisciplined or incorrect behaviour in the classroom environment, the sociable and inoffensive appearance of today's robots contrasts sharply with the dreadful authoritarian look depicted in the movie.

If the representations of robots offered by science fiction have not always been proved realistic by the following historical developments, we must remark that scientific communication can be confusing too. On the one hand, we are being presented with videos of the real acrobatic skills of Boston Dynamics' Atlas robots, while at the same time videos of a computer-generated Atlas robot circulate that are visually indistinguishable from the original (Bartneck and Keijsers, 2020). Moreover, we are confronted with pseudo-robots like Titan that appear to have amazing abilities. Titan is, however, just a guy in a suit. This embarrassing uncertainty does not only depend on the deceptive power that hyper-realistic computer graphics and advanced video have reached nowadays but also depend on the potential vagueness associated with the definition of robots and their powers. The speed of technological development leaves many of us uncertain about what is currently possible and what is not.

Desirable capabilities like sophisticated language processing, complex object recognition, and rich adaptive manipulation of environment have not been achieved yet, and roboticists debate whether and when they will ever be able to achieve them. On the other hand, during the past ten years, through the fast additional development of machine learning and big data, we witnessed enormous advances in computers' ability to recognize patterns, predict trajectories, and extract implicit regularities from huge unorganized data sets which brought, among other things, very powerful models of natural language (e.g., GPT-3). This fast, exciting progress fuelled hope in the ability to create agents that could intelligently operate at least in well-circumscribed domains of activity, but left us with a bitter frustration due to our incapability to reproduce general intelligence, transferring an AI system from one domain of practical application to another. Our current perception of robots is characterized by an irreducible tension between fulfilled and frustrated expectations so that the hope in technological progress at times is replaced by the cynicism deriving from the apparently eternal repetition of the same mistakes; for example, every year ambitious research programmes are shut down due to the lack of concrete positive outcomes (Ackerman, 2018), while other—even more expensive—projects are sponsored every day in the hope of finding the next great idea in AI.

That said, it must also be noted that the difficulty of distinguishing facts from fiction seems inherent to the very notion of robots, whose essence is halfway between reality and the users' perception. The identity of humanoid robots is never exhausted by their physical presence because it always involves also a representation of human possibilities as well. That is why the design of social robots reflects not only our immanent condition and our material needs but also our desires, fears, aspirations for the future, and values. In this sense, robots always are not only technological artefacts but also, to some extent, creatures of imagination and hope. This implies that the conceptual contribution to robotics offered by fiction and artistic representation should never be underestimated or dismissed as mere deception, even when it risks being inaccurate and potentially misleading: it is true that science fiction can often confound the boundaries between realistic and fantastic expectations, but it also plays an important, productive role. Countless times science fiction has helped roboticists develop the vision that they needed to conceive innovative technologies, inspiring their efforts to design more sophisticated social robots. Also, science fiction can help innovative educators prepare the general public for a future in which successful HRI will be considered the norm: fantastic narratives can help adults, no less than children, to familiarize with the idea of confidently working with robots and learning from them, thus creating a culture of inclusiveness and acceptance that prepares both teachers and students to embrace artificial agents as their co-workers and companions.

1.4   Outline of the Book

Our book aspires to shed light on what can be done with today's robots in schools and other educational environments. Although this book is rich in theoretical notions and seeks justification in existing doctrines, our approach is a pragmatic one. We aim to provide a helpful set of orientative notions, examples and future readings, methodological indications, and concrete suggestions to effectively apply autonomous technologies in classrooms so as to facilitate, support, and augment the work of current and future teachers and instructors.

In Chapter 2, we will present the main theories of learning and education, the educational settings that best illustrate them, and how robots fit in them.

In Chapter 3, we will consider the basis of human cognition, introducing the mechanisms and processes that are relevant to learning and to optimizing teaching practices, including those that involve robots.

We will deal with the very definition of robot in Chapter 4, where we will offer an overview of the technological systems that support robotics.

Chapter 5 and Chapter 6 aim to introduce robots in education, examining two distinct roles that robotics can play in a learning environment: Chapter 5 will focus on robots as tools, instrumental to facilitate and augment the learning process; while Chapter 6 will focus on robots as social agents, serving the learning process in humanoid roles such as teaching assistants or mentors.

Introducing robots in the educational environments presents, of course, certain requirements, including the acquisition of technology, the training of personnel, and the preparation of settings and curricula. Chapter 7 summarizes these requirements.

It is in Chapter 8 that we will offer a systematic review of the applications of robotics in education, including a large number of case studies and descriptive analyses in relation to various subjects and skills.

The effectiveness of robots in education strongly depends on the perception of the users and the attitudes of teachers and students towards robots. We address this in Chapter 9.

Chapter 10 addresses the ethical concerns that accompany the introduction of robots in education, providing a theoretical background to understand the moral dilemmas related to the use of robots in the school environment.

Finally, Chapter 11 discusses the specific research methodologies that need to be adopted to study HRI in the educational industry and the effectiveness of learning practices mediated by robots.

Note

1. The "Hello Barbie" doll from Mattel was equipped with a microphone and communicated through the Internet with Mattel's servers. Mattel was listening in on what went on in the children's room at all times. While this probably gave them great marketing insights, it caused a considerable outcry from parents concerned about their privacy.

2 Theories of Learning

Tell me and I will forget, show me and I may remember; involve me and I will understand.

Xun Kuang in Xunzi

What is covered in this chapter:

- An overview of influential theories in formal education;
- How educational theories and robotics meet in the learning setting;
- Models of learning.

This chapter aims to provide the general theoretical background of robotics in education. The purpose is to introduce some foundational notions in learning theory and pedagogy. These notions are necessary to understand the role of educational scienes within human-robot interaction (HRI).

In the first part of the chapter, we summarize the three main theories of learning developed during the 20th century: behaviourism, constructivism, and cognitivism.

The second part of the chapter describes the most common educational settings implemented in the classroom environment, emphasizing their implicit link with the three learning theories: the teaching setting, the tutoring setting, the project-based learning (PBL) setting, and the cooperative learning (CL) setting.

In the third and last part of this chapter, we briefly address the role that robots may play in each of these educational settings, and we advance some considerations on the educational value offered by robots in the light of the three theories of learning.

2.1   Learning Theories

Preschool learning practices are importantly influenced by pedagogical paradigms and explicitly draw on theories of early education. In today's early childhood classrooms, educators like to draw on the work of Vygotsky (1962) and Rogoff (1998) which stress the importance of the development of children in a social environment. It is here that young children learn through their interactions and collaborations, something which now seems rather straightforward. Another influential psychologist was Jean Piaget. Working in the early 20th century, he built a number of theories of learning largely by observing the development of his own children. According to Piaget's theoretical stage approach, knowledge is not *transmitted*, but is *built* through interaction with the physical world. Children begin the discovery of the world through manipulation, a fundamental step according to Piaget (1927, 1928), which allows the formation and development of enactive knowledge, that is, embodied know-how rooted in perception and action. For an educator, recognizing the cognitive stages of a child is essential in order to offer appropriate interventions.

On many subjects, Piaget and Vygotsky never quite agreed. They did, however, agree on the importance of letting the individual construct his/her knowledge through interacting with the physical world.

2.1.1   Behaviourism

Proposed in the early 20th century, behaviourism is the approach to psychology that methodologically suggests to focus only on the observable aspects of behaviour. This approach rejected the role of introspection and downplayed (and in the extreme case rejected) the role of internal (mental) states. This emphasis on observable behaviour was borne out of the application of the scientific method's reliance on empirical data: given that internal thought could not be directly observed, experimental data is necessarily based only on directly observable and quantifiable behaviours.

In terms of education, behaviourism understands learning as the acquisition of new behavioural patterns based on environmental conditions. Acquiring knowledge essentially means mastering large repertoires of fine-grained and sophisticated behaviours in response to fine-grained environmental stimuli. The teacher would promote behaviouristic learning by identifying proper cues for a desired response; arranging practice situations in which prompts are paired with the target stimuli; and making sure that the contextual conditions are set to have learners deliver the desired response in the presence of the target stimuli (Ertmer and Newby, 1993a).

Like Watson, B.F. Skinner was not interested in the unobservable workings of the mind, but in the observable behaviour that is lawful, predicted and controlled, with psychology being the science of behaviour (Delprato and Midgley, 1992; Skinner, 1965). He thus conceptualized behaviour as a disposition to act controlled by reinforcement and punishment, notions known as *operant conditioning*. One example of the impact of the Skinnerian approach to measuring and analysing behaviour on education, though, is precision teaching. This is considered a successful student-centred method to measure learning in various domains (e.g., reading; Hughes et al., 2007). However, the fact that Skinner views humans in a rather deterministic, mechanistic way has contributed to criticism of his ideas.

2.1.2 *Cognitivism*

In response to the criticalities of the behaviourist approach to learning, cognitivism offers an alternative view where mental processes are central for the acquisition of knowledge. This idea goes back to the Gestalt school (Kohler et al., 1973), according to which the mind, as opposed to an empty, passive container, constitutes itself by interacting with the external world, so that what we perceive is influenced by internal mental factors. According to this approach, learning results from the interaction between internal processes, including one's own needs, motivation, and expectations, and the context in which learning occurs.

The cognitive approach to learning thus emphasizes promoting internal processes, such as the student's motivation, to enhance information encode, storage, organization, and retrieval (Ertmer and Newby, 1993b). The means to deliver knowledge include a set of strategies ranging from illustrative examples, demonstrations, explanations, etc. The student, on the other hand, can actively work on knowledge acquisition by adopting strategies that range from a variety of memorization, categorization, and retrieval methods.

Despite their wide use in educational practice, both cognitivism and behaviourism are often blamed for reducing learning to a mechanistic mono-directional process that is ultimately determined by the stimuli provided as input to the learner and, in the specific case of cognitivism, the elaboration done subconsciously by the learner's cognitive systems. Either way, the learner as a person does not deliberately participate in the process of reception and interpretation of the information. Constructivism distinguishes itself from these views because it understands learning as a two-way process that involves negotiation and an active role for the learner, an agent necessarily engaged in deliberate interaction with the sources of input they rely on.

2.1.3   Constructivism

There are two strands of constructivism. The first strand, influenced by Vygotsky (1962, 1978), is called social constructivism, and emphasizes the social and collaborative dimension of learning and the fact that old frameworks and new experiences belong first of all to groups, and only secondarily to individuals. The second strand, promoted by Piaget, is characterized by cognitive stages of development, and emphasizes the individual dimension of learning and the fact that new experiences are elaborated by the individual as (s)he moves through consecutive stages of cognitive development. This second strand is also associated with the cognitive approach, as it provides its foundation—which is why Piaget is often credited for inspiring both the cognitive and the constructivist approaches.

The constructivist approach to education is primarily based on the Piagetian view of learning (Piaget, 1929). In this context, the two fundamental mechanisms of *accommodation* and *assimilation* are explicitly taken advantage of in the learning process. Assimilation occurs when the learner integrates new information within his/her existing knowledge structure. Thus, for example, a child learning about subtraction may relate this to his/her existing knowledge of addition. Accommodation, on the other hand, requires existing knowledge to be adapted or changed according to new information. It relates to the extension of the knowledge structure to incorporate a new means or method of thinking: as such it is typically more difficult from the perspective of the learner. One example might be a student learning computer programming for the first time (using control structure, recursion, etc.) who has previously only written prose. Assimilation would be used if this same student would learn another programming language: (s)he would be able to use the knowledge of some of the common programming principles, even if the syntax differs. Having the teacher understand this process is thus of benefit, as (s)he would be in a better position to understand the relative ease or difficulty of the learner employing these respective mechanisms.

Within a socio-constructivist approach to learning, Vygotsky put a special accent on the importance of the social environment. He argued that a more knowledgeable other will be able to offer substantial help in scaffolding the child's potential/unexpressed competencies to develop further. A peer, a caregiver, or a teacher has the potential to help the child stepping forward in a specific developmental period known as the Zone of Proximal Development (ZPD), that is, where the unexpressed potentialities of the child/learner can be taken to a more advanced level of knowledge. While maintaining that, new post-Piagetian evidence has shown that a peer is often a better partner for learning, because a peer has conceptual knowledge and language which is better aligned to that of the learner. This observation has great impact on the opportunity to have learners work together, scaffolding and co-constructing knowledge.

In the constructivist approach, therefore, the role of the teacher or the learning partner is, according to Vygotsky, to play a scaffolding role to facilitate the learning process by exploiting the student's ability to, according to Piaget, assimilate and eventually accommodate new learning material. An outline of the three main theories of learning and their application in educational practice is offered in Table 2.1.

Table 2.1 Learning theories

	Behaviourism	Cognitivism	Constructivism
Key psychological assumption(s)	Studies direct correlations between stimuli and responses. The internal processes of the mind (black box) are inaccessible or methodologically opaque.	It studies the mind processes. The mind is a set of covert informational processes situated between perceptual input and behavioural output.	The mind is a system that actively engages in the interpretation of information, using previous knowledge to generate information about present and future experiences.
Learning process	Learning occurs through associations between stimulus and response. Acquisition of knowledge is increasingly sophisticated leading to new types of behaviours.	Learning is an internal processing of information that leads to understanding and knowledge retention by means of cognitive strategies, i.e. formation and storage of mental representations.	Learning means updating one's interpretative models, i.e. acquiring methods to elaborate the meaning of new experiences based on the meaning of past experiences.
Nature of the learning process	New behaviours or changes in behaviours are acquired through associations between stimuli and responses. Associations are direct input-output correspondences established through repetition or reinforcement mechanisms.	The learning process is in interaction with environmental circumstances seen as objectively founded and quantifiable. Learning occurs through intellectual processes. Mental processes interact with environmental factors thus affecting learning.	Learning is a process that, whether individual or collaborative, builds up from past knowledge and through an active effort of creative synthesis. As the learning process does not follow a linear trajectory, the learning outcomes are largely unpredictable and hence difficult to consistently be framed within a predefined template.
Role of the learner in the learning process	Learning is a passive process, based on exposure to environmental stimulation. Individual initiative and creativity play little role in it.	The role of the learners is active, because they have to seek information and solve puzzles, but it is entirely intellectual. The embodied component of information processing does not play an active role in it.	Social-constructivism: the learner participates in a social and collaborative process. Stage of cognitive development: the learner elaborates new experiences moving through consecutive stages of cognitive development through assimilation and accommodation.
Activities and tasks on which the learning process is based	Case studies; research projects; problem-based learning; brainstorming; collaborative learning; discovery learning; simulations.	Categorization and chunking of information; association between conceptual contents; definition of logical structures; problem solving; imagery; active strategies of memorization.	Role-play; joint work; social interaction; rote work and drill; incentives to practice and learning; active participation; verbal reinforcement (encouragements as rewards); establishing rules.

Seymour Papert and LEGO Mindstorms

Seymour Papert was a South African mathematician and computer scientist working most of his life in the United States. Building on the work of Jean Piaget, whom he spent several years working with in Geneva, he spearheaded the constructionist movement[1] in education and specifically promoted the use of programming in schools. Together with Wally Feurzeig and Cynthia Solomon, Papert developed the Logo programming language. Logo was an educational programming language and was best known for its "turtle graphics", in which a programmed command moved a pen, the so-called turtle, over the screen to draw lines (see Figure 2.1). The language was conceived to teach concepts of algorithmic thinking and programming. Papert argued that Logo supported "body-syntonic reasoning", helping students to understand, predict, and reason about the turtle's motion by imagining what they would do if they were the turtle. The Logo programming language is still popular in education and many online Logo coding environments exist, for example turtleacademy.com.

Logo, and the pedagogical concepts behind it, had a huge influence on the use of robots in education. In his 1980 book *Mindstorms: Children, Computers, and Powerful Ideas*, Papert maintained that computers should not be seen as an extension of pen and paper in education, and argued against "the computer being used to program the child". Instead, computers should be actively programmed by students, and invite them to construct solutions to challenges through algorithmic thinking. Through this, "the child programs the computer and, in doing so, (s)he acquires a sense of mastery over a piece of the most modern and powerful technology and establishes an intimate contact with some of the deepest ideas from science, mathematics, and the art of intellectual model building". Papert started a collaboration with TLG and his ideas served as the inspiration for the LEGO Mindstorms educational robot kit, which was named after his book. In 1989, TLG endowed a chair at MIT where Papert became the first Lego Professor of Learning Research. The constructionist approach to robotics is still the dominant approach to robots in education, with millions of robot kits, including Lego Mindstorms kits, being used in schools across the world to help children and students learn about science, technology, engineering, art, and mathematics (STEAM).

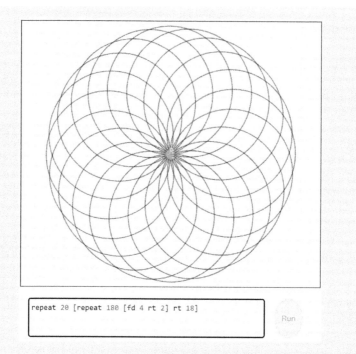

```
repeat 20 [repeat 180 [fd 4 rt 2] rt 18]
```
Run

Figure 2.1 A turtle drawing a pattern using the Logo programming language. The turtle will take a step forward and rotate two steps right, this is repeated 180 times, drawing a circle. After that it rotates 18 steps to the right and repeats the previous instructions 20 times. Logo was a popular first programming language for many budding programmers

Source: Turtle Academy

2.2   Social Learning

A prominent example of a social constructivist theory is Albert Bandura's learning theory (Bandura, 1978), also dubbed "model learning". Bandura illustrated his principles of learning by observation and imitation in the classic "Bobo doll experiments" (Bandura et al., 1963a), in which children observed aggressive behaviours towards an inflated "Bobo" doll, such as punching it in the face, tossing it in the air, sitting on the doll, or being verbally aggressive towards it. Children either engaged in direct observation of such actions, or saw a brief video in which the model acted aggressively towards Bobo, or they watched a cartoon film including an aggressive cat act towards the doll. Findings of the 1963 research study showed that it did not matter which model they saw. In all three cases, the children imitated the model's aggression towards the Bobo doll and displayed twice as much hitting, kicking, and tossing of the doll and used the same verbally abusive comments as the model (vicarious learning). Thus, direct observation and film-mediated aggression not only elicited but also shaped human responses. In the same year, the authors also highlighted the role of reinforcement of a model's behaviour (vicarious reinforcement). If the model was rewarded with candy, children would imitate bad behaviour more than if the model was scolded (Bandura et al., 1963b). This showed that children not only learn from direct reward or punishment, but they can also learn from watching somebody else being rewarded or punished.

The notion of model learning can inform research HRI in that the robot can serve as a model that facilitates desired behaviours in people, for example, in cases where the robot is deployed as a coach to facilitate physical exercise. For instance, robots have been used to demonstrate and encourage patients to keep up with a cardiovascular exercise regime (Casas et al., 2018). The robot is used as a model, with the goal to reinforce positive health-related behaviours. The same principle also applies to the idea of a robot that displays behaviours either conforming or not to ethical and moral principles, as extensively argued in Chapter 10.

2.3   Tutoring

Tutoring is the provision of learning assistance or tutelage to one or more individuals. It can happen in a formal setting (e.g., classroom) or in an informal setting (e.g., home). The key here is that the learning material and the pace of teaching is individualized and that there is a lot of attention for tutor-tutee rapport (Wood and Wood, 1996). Tutoring was hailed as one of the most effective ways of teaching by educational psychologist Benjamin Bloom's research, in which he found that children receiving tutoring have a significant performance advantage over their peers who received traditional teaching in a classroom (Bloom, 1984). This has become known as *Bloom's 2 sigma* and has been used to make a case for more individualized education.

The case for tutoring still firmly stands, as supported in more recent reviews. VanLehn (2011) found that tutoring confers an important benefit over class-based teaching, perhaps justifying why across the world millions of parents shell out huge fees for private tutoring to supplement their children's school education.

Robots are also starting to be introduced into the educational environment as tutors (Belpaeme et al., 2018a; Vogt et al., 2019). Using the social NAO robot, for example, the European research project L2TOR ('el tutor') aimed to support teaching preschool children aged five years a second language (L2), and in particular English as L2 to native speakers of Dutch, German, and Turkish, and Dutch as L2 to immigrant children speaking Turkish as a native language. Inspired by the way human tutors typically interact with children, the robot was programmed to interact with children in one-to-one tutoring sessions and to use both verbal and nonverbal communication, sometimes also adaptively responding to children's actions and providing appropriate feedback. Of course, this project is not exhaustive as, at the moment, social robots are not yet technically able to manage relationships in a totally autonomous way. However, this project represents a significant example of how a set of guidelines can be developed to help design future tutoring robots for large-scale educational use.

2.4   Cooperative Learning

Over the past decades, instructional practices have been highly influenced by cooperative and collaborative learning, which suggest that effective learning takes place in groups with each member seeking to maximize their own and their peers' learning outcomes (Johnson et al., 2014), going beyond an individualistic endeavour. The terms cooperative and collaborative learning often conflate, but contain slightly different concepts. Both forms of learning imply that two or more learners work together to reach common goals. The main difference is that in collaboration, learners do the work together, while in cooperation, learners split the task and work on their sub-task and finally assemble the results into a common output (Dillenbourg, 1999). Cooperative learning (CL) in particular has shown to be effective in one-on-one peer interactions, among larger groups, and with students of various age ranges engaging in learning about a variety of topics (Johnson et al., 2007; Johnson and Johnson, 2009; Slavin, 1996). In formal CL settings, students work together for the duration of a single class or even across a longitudinal time frame in order to reach a joint achievement (Johnson et al., 2007). The mutual goal should be highlighted by the teacher as well as the reward that will be obtained by all group members based on the individual expertise and the role assumed by each group member. That way, all group members realize their crucial individual impact on the overall group performance. Cooperative learning has a rich history and has been empirically studied and validated in a vast amount of empirical studies (Johnson et al., 2007, 2014; Johnson and Johnson, 2009).

Elements of successful cooperation are rooted in social independence theory as proposed by Deutsch (1949, 1962), a psychologist who studied conflict and cooperation within groups. Importantly, group membership per se does not lead to improved learning outcomes—basic conditions must be fulfilled. The five core factors that enhance the success of group work in educational contexts are social interdependence, individual accountability, direct face-to-face interaction, appropriate use of social skills, and group processing (Johnson et al., 2007; Johnson and Johnson, 2009). These five beneficial components of CL will be reviewed briefly. Social interdependence rests on the idea that an individual's efforts and success are dependent on the performance and success of the other learners in a group. The efficacy of positive interdependence has been documented in a wide array of studies (for a review, see Johnson et al., 2007). For instance, learners may be dependent on each other in terms of outcomes, for example, goals and rewards, or with regards to resources, where goal interdependence fosters greater productivity than resource interdependence (Johnson et al., 1991). Knowing that an individual's efforts feed back into the success of the group creates a sense of responsibility and individual accountability. Individual accountability is high when a learner's outcome is assessed and reported back to the group, which also increases perceived interdependence in groups (Archer-Kath et al., 1994). It has furthermore been shown that face-to-face interaction is beneficial for cooperative learning outcomes. That is, the learning context enables direct contact in order to facilitate that learners exchange their knowledge, provide assistance or feed back in close physical proximity. A key element of efficient cooperative efforts is the social skills that each group member brings into the group learning setting. According to Johnson et al. (1998), such social skills serve as job performance skills including aspects such as instructorship, decision-making, trust-building, communication, and conflict management. Finally, group processing comprises the reflection of mutual actions, and the decisions about which activities should be changed or maintained for future learning (Johnson and Johnson, 2009). Johnson et al. (2014) have emphasized that contemporary instructional practices should ideally be informed and guided by validated theory. Here, the vast amount of research findings on

CL comes in handy, in that this evidence can not only be used as a basis for human-human educational practice, but also inform robot-assisted teaching. Clearly, robotics has a strong impact. This was exactly the goal of the experimental research programme realized by Reich-Stiebert (2019). It empirically investigated the effects of the implementation of the aforementioned core elements of cooperative learning when learning with a robot. That is, she translated educational theorizing on successful instruction to the field of HRI. Specifically, within a dyadic HRI context, cooperative learning was used as a strategy to reach the mutual goal of learning the Robot Interaction Language (ROILA (Mubin et al., 2012, 2013a)) with the NAO robot. Students were provided learning materials for ROILA; however, the robot was used as the main tool for fostering objective and subjective learning outcomes. In turn, students had received index cards in order to teach the robot ROILA vocabulary, realizing a mutual collaborative learning experience. Outcomes, learning performance, intrinsic motivation, self-efficacy, and mood during the learning process were measured, along with ratings of the robotic learning partner. Taken together, however, Reich-Stiebert's (Reich-Stiebert, 2019) attempt to empirically test and validate CL theory within the context of HRI documented that the implementation of positive interdependence, social support, and group processing in HRI did not render significant outcomes.

2.5   Project-based Learning

PBL views the student as an active learner who solves real-life problems in a collaborative effort within a project context. To be successful, a project has to focus on a clearly defined issue that needs to be resolved and can be tackled by coming up with a tangible product, with the end product, rather than the process itself being central. To produce a concrete artefact, learners have to go through all phases of production of the desired end product, and collaboration and sharing of resources is essential. That is why PBL also qualifies as a form of collaborative learning (Aksela and Haatainen, 2019). Kokotsaki et al. (2016) have also pointed out that learning occurs in context, with the learner controlling the learning process and the opportunity to yield various outcomes dependent on the project method (i.e., various types of representations, see Aksela and Haatainen (2019)). This approach has been successfully used in STEM education (Science, Technology, Engineering, Maths) (Aksela and Haatainen, 2019) and has been studied cross-culturally in preschool, primary school, secondary school, and higher education contexts. In contrast, problem-based learning focuses primarily on the learning process, and on studying a problem that has been formulated and for which the learner's knowledge is insufficient. PBL, on the other hand, emphasizes the project's end product.

2.6　Educational Robots

Research in HRI has shown that children and adults often treat robots as social agents (Belpaeme et al., 2013; Duffy, 2003; Fink, 2012). Based on this, there is a glut of research showing that interactive robots are able to influence, persuade, and convince. Through their physical and social presence, they grab people's attention and can, when using the right behavioural cues, induce compliance (Bartneck et al., 2020b; Di Dio et al., 2020b). These are all elements which are key to education and as such the educational theories which have been developed to explain and support how people transfer knowledge and skills to others might also be relevant to how robots can be used to tutor and teach.

Consider an imaginary scenario: a personal robot is presented to you as a learning buddy, a peer who joins you on your learning journey and who is just marginally ahead of you. It challenges and cajoles you to keep up, it uses praise and gentle prodding to whet your appetite for more learning. It rewards you if you get things right and scolds you if you get things wrong, just like a friend might. Together you and the robot solve maths problems, working through problems which become increasingly harder. Sometimes the robot makes a mistake. This not only gives you the opportunity to correct the robot and shine while doing so, but also makes the robot appear like an intentional agent (Short et al., 2010). Of course, the robot's actions are carefully chosen not only to help you on your learning journey but also to build your confidence and make you a resilient learner. This hypothetical example is a blend between cooperative learning, tutoring, and socio-constructivist learning, with a smattering of John Dewey; however, no theory exists which can advise robot builders on how to program the AI of these robots. As such, researchers have been taking very pragmatic approaches, learning through trial and error regarding what the most effective teaching approaches are. More on this in Chapter 6.

Questions for you to think about:

- How do the three main learning theories—behaviourism, cognitivism, and constructivism—fit a future in which robots are used in education?

- Since robots are well suited to repetition, would a behaviourist robot application be effective in the classroom?
- How can robots revolutionize existing models of learning in the classroom?

Future reading:

- David Didau and Nick Rose. *What Every Teacher Needs to Know about... Psychology*.   John Catt Educational Limited, Melton, Woodbridge, 2016.
- Gary Thomas. *Education: A Very Short Introduction*.   Oxford University Press, Oxford, 2013.
- Mark Haselgrove. *Learning: A Very Short Introduction*.   Oxford University Press, Oxford, 2016.
- Denis Phillips and Jonas F Soltis. *Perspectives on Learning*. Teachers College Press, New York, 2015.

Note

1. Note the distinction between *constructivism* and *constructionism*: they are related but put forward different ideas.

3   The Interactive Mind

It is a curious fact that people are never so trivial as when they take themselves seriously.

Oscar Wilde

What is covered in this chapter:

- Cognitive processes relevant to HRI in the learning context;
- Processes and mechanisms underpinning human social competencies;
- Demographic factors to be accounted for in HRI.

In order to coherently design and successfully implement robots in education, we need to look at the key cognitive, social, and emotional features that characterize human learners and, secondarily, teachers. In other words, exactly like educational robotics are informed by educational theories, educational theories must be informed by psychological models of cognition and behaviour. In order to develop this idea, this chapter aims to briefly introduce a number of fundamental notions of cognitive and social psychology: the purpose is to highlight the key human features that are relevant to optimize learning and teaching practices, including those that involve robots.

The notions introduced in this chapter offer an overview of the human features involved in learning and teaching processes. These notions are presented drawing on empirical data and models generated by different branches of psychology (social, developmental, and cognitive psychology) and cognitive science.

Social psychology is the discipline that measures how much and in what ways human behaviours, emotions, and thoughts are affected by environmental factors and interactions with other agents (McDougall, 2015), including both natural (human adults, children, and non-human animals) and artificial ones (robots and virtual agents).

Developmental psychology describes how the biological, social, emotional, and cognitive dynamics that characterize an individual evolve through the different stages of personal maturation and ageing (Butterworth, 2014).

Cognitive psychology studies mental faculties (such as memory, control, perception, or decision making) at the level of the underlying informational processes and systems (Reisberg, 2013).

Cognitive science then is the interdisciplinary study that complements cognitive psychology with the tools and methods provided by research in neuroscience, AI, and robotics: the key idea of cognitive science is that synthesising a mental function with the help of a computer or robot is useful to empirically understand the equivalent mental function in a human, exactly like analysing a mental function in a human is useful to effectively construct the same function by computational means (Gallagher and Schmicking, 2010).

Applying the above notions to the study of educational robotics allows us to effectively integrate the scientific knowledge on learning processes in the human mind with the technological knowledge necessary to build educational robots. Recognizing the social context in which teaching occurs, the specific developmental stage of the learner, as well as the distinctive cognitive capabilities and limitations of the general human users is required to design applications in educational robotics tailored to the specifics of human learning.

3.1   Cognitive Underpinnings of Human Learning

Imagine you are sitting in class and the teacher at the front of the class room is explaining Pythagoras' theorem. You are listening to what the teacher says, and trying to understand the diagrams and equations on the screen. Your friend giggles, which briefly distracts you, but you turn your attention back to the lesson. You are trying to remember what square roots and squares were, thinking back to a previous exercise. You know you should be taking notes, your pen hovers over the paper and you try to be engaged (or, at least, to appear engaged).

This simple example highlights a number of demands on our cognitive systems in an educational context: trying to listen and watch the teacher requires *attention*, recalling previous experience requires *memory* (both episodic in terms of remembering the last class, and procedural in terms of how to do things), and trying to ignore distraction requires *executive function*.

The way that we as humans make decisions and the way we reason are an expression of our cognitive faculties. Despite the huge number of cognitive systems and processes that can be considered, however, our intention in this section is to identify the aspects that are core to our understanding of the learning context (see Chapter 2) and subsequently—insofar as learning is a social process—in the socially interactive context (3.2). Following the simple example above, we identify three of these core components: attention (such as paying attention; Section 3.1.1), memory (taking advantage of your existing knowledge; Section 3.1.2), and executive function (such as trying to ignore distractions; Section 3.1.3).

3.1.1   Attention

Attention can be defined as an individual's ability to focus only on the most relevant information at a given point in time, while excluding extraneous, potentially interfering information. The role of attention as a cognitive mechanism is essential in maintaining the ability to remain task-focused: in this sense it is centrally related to the notion of Working Memory (WM) (see Section 3.1.2 below) in that cognitive task demands must be managed in accord with limited attentional resources, which in turn depends on WM capacity (D'Esposito, 2007). Memory and attention work in harmony with one another: limited attention means that only task-relevant information is drawn from memory—which in turn can alter the focus of attention (see the following section for more details).

Attention span also has implications for the activities an individual is engaging in. Even though further research is needed to substantiate this claim, students in higher education settings such as a lecture are believed to process information best within a 10–15 minute time window (e.g., Bradbury (2016) and Wilson and Korn (2007)). One particularly important behavioural manifestation of attention is the use of gaze. While gaze may also be used as a social cue to guide interaction between humans (see Section 3.2.5), the limited visual capabilities of the human eye naturally constrain the focus of visual attention—we can only look at one thing at a time, therefore we need to focus our attention on only one task if we want to maximize our chances of completing it successfully.

3.1.2   Memory

Memory is a core cognitive competence, and is involved in all aspects of human thought, from understanding what you see and hear to how you act in the world. The processes of human memory have, in the broadest terms, been characterized as consisting of three processes: encoding, storage, and retrieval. *Encoding* refers to the transformation of perceived information into a form that can be stored and manipulated in memory. *Retrieval* refers to the process of finding the relevant stored information and accessing it. A close coupling between encoding and retrieval has been noted: according to the encoding specificity principle (Tulving and Thomson, 1973), retrieval is facilitated when the retrieval context matches the encoding context. The *storage* component has received particular research attention in terms of its structure and organization. A number of different functions/types have been identified, with the primary distinction being made between *sensory*, *short-term*, and *long-term* memory. Originally proposed by Atkinson and Shiffrin (1968), this basic multi-store model has been subsequently refined and restructured (see Figure 3.1).

Long-Term Memory (LTM) generally refers to information, knowledge, and skills that are in principle permanently stored to be used at any time—albeit with the capacity to be changed over time. A standard distinction is made between *explicit* memory—containing knowledge of a type that is consciously accessible, such as facts and events—and *implicit* memory—containing knowledge that is not typically consciously accessible, such as skills and actions. Consciously accessible information—explicit memory—encompasses the facts and knowledge that we have and that we may remember from past learning for example (semantic information), and memory of previously experienced events, which would be a collection of information specifically related to a particular episode (episodic memory). Implicit memory, by contrast, is typically gained subconsciously over a period of time. The main category of this type of memory is termed *procedural*; this includes motor skills such as writing.

The Short-Term Memory (STM) component of memory was initially proposed as a passive system that temporarily stored information that was relevant to the current task. Incorporating information from sensory memory (very short time-scales, on the order of less than a second) and long-term explicit memory, STM has subsequently been understood to

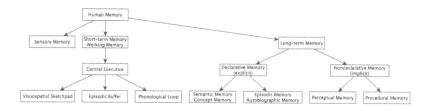

Figure 3.1 Overall organization of human memory

play a more active role. The currently widely accepted model (Baddeley, 1992) allows for the temporary storage and manipulation (under the control of a "central executive") of information specifically in visual (visuospatial sketchpad) and speech (phonological loop) forms, with additional information from explicit prior experience also being taken into account (the episodic buffer). One important characteristic of the WM is that it is limited in capacity, meaning that only a relatively small amount of information can be held at any one time.

Both STM and LTM interact flexibly as nicely illustrated by the phenomenon of "chunking". This is a process by which information with similar characteristics (e.g., based on prior experience) may be grouped together and the chunk is then treated to a certain extent as a separate entity in its own right. This has an impact on the issue of capacity. While the classic "7 ± 2" item capacity limit (Miller, 1956) is still widely referred to this day, the evidence for it is not as straightforward (Shiffrin and Nosofsky, 1994). Indeed, research grounded in neuroscience, for example, Fuster (1997); Wood et al. (2012), has emphasized the tight integration and interaction of LTM and STM systems both at the functional and the underlying neural levels, highlighting the complex interactions that take place between different memory systems in support of cognition. It could be argued that memory thus acts as a substrate for cognition.

The human capability in remembering and recalling information is clearly of importance in the context of education: no learning would be possible without attention and memory functions, as illustrated by cases where those are impaired (e.g., in individuals with Alzheimer's disease). By understanding the distinctive features of our memory systems and likewise, their interplay, we are able to gain some preliminary insight into how information processing can potentially be facilitated, for example, by presenting information in a way that attracts attention, facilitating storage in our LTM, rather than only being accessible in STM, and by taking into account the limitations of human memory so as not to overload the learners. Finally, while older theories of memory organization may have led to an emphasis on repetition as a means of consolidating information in LTM, more recent perspectives emphasize the complex interactions between the different memory systems. Ideally, this could lead to a more nuanced view of the structure of the information presented to the learner and the adequate teaching method used to facilitate learning.

3.1.3 Executive Function

Besides WM, which entails our ability to keep information in mind and to mentally play with it (e.g. when doing maths in your mind), inhibition and cognitive flexibility constitute the core executive functions (Diamond, 2013). Inhibitory control of attention, for instance, helps us exert control over our attentional resources, enabling us to selectively attend to focal information while ignoring distractions. Otherwise, we would be prone to follow our impulses only, being "creatures of habit" as described by Diamond (2013, p. 136). In terms of reactions, research has also shown that children are likely to provide quick, prepotent responses when urged to complete a task and that these responses are often incorrect. However, by shielding a stimulus from their view and thereby reducing the need for inhibitory control, the same children come to a correct answer in the context of the very same task. This is illustrated within the classic Piagetian paradigm using two beakers in which the same amounts of liquid have to be poured by a child, with one beaker being tall and slim and the other being short and wide. Typically, this leads to the erroneous conclusion that the tall beaker encompasses more liquid than the wide one when this phenomenon is studied in children. Research by social constructivists (Friedenberg, 1966) has shown, however, that children aged four to five do not fall victim to this error when they pour the liquid in one of the beakers while the other is hidden from view. The remaining core executive function that we have not yet addressed in this chapter, cognitive flexibility, reflects the interplay of processes related to WM and inhibition. It entails changing one's perspective, which is only possible when an "old" perspective is abandoned and a novel one is retrieved from the WM. Cognitive flexibility is described by Diamond (2013) as the opposite of rigidity and is essential in successful T&L scenarios, as not only do the students need to flexibly adapt to the changing demands of a learning situation, but likewise, the teacher needs to demonstrate cognitive flexibility by not merely blaming a student for providing a wrong response, for example, in the context of the earlier Piagetian example. Rather, by changing instructional practice (e.g., by hiding the second beaker from the child's view), the correct response of the child can be facilitated and elicited. This way, the perspective changes from viewing the child as inherently unable to recognize the task to instead the task being solved by the child.

3.2   Cognitive Underpinnings of Social Interaction

Social cognition is the set of cognitive and emotional skills that allow social agents to recognize each other *as social agents*, make sense of each other's goals and intentions, and understand each other's mental states like beliefs and desires (Gallagher, 2008). It is also the set of interpersonal processes that allows multiple agents to meaningfully communicate, coordinate their behaviours towards a common goal, and share an experience or a motivation to act. In this subsection, we therefore introduce the notions of empathy, imitation, Theory of Mind (ToM), and anthropomorphism, illustrating why these notions are crucial to make education effective and human-robot interaction successful.

3.2.1   Empathy

When we experience empathy, we put ourselves in the place of the "other", that is a sentient being or agent we can somehow relate to. Humans' fundamental capacity to detect and properly attune to the intentions and emotions perceived in the other's behaviour is integral to our social cognition. During the earliest developmental stages of life, social cognition primarily relies on embodied interactive processes and direct sensorimotor engagement (Meltzoff and Decety, 2003). Direct perception of other's intentional and affective states is cognitively simple, as testified by the early appearance in ontogeny and phylogeny, before the emergence of language and complex meta-representational skills (De Jaegher, 2009). Even the most sophisticated forms of intersubjective attunement—which may involve cognitively demanding processes like meta-representation, inductive inference, and language—ultimately stem from and build upon a more basic, embodied capacity to perceptually recognize the goals, intentions, and affects that motivate the behaviour of others (De Jaegher et al., 2010).

The earliest social capacities are associated with imitation. Meltzoff (2002) noticed how newborn babies imitate the facial expressions—such as tongue protrusion and mouth opening—of adults. This is rather special, as it means that the infant has the ability to link perception of others to its own motor actions. Trevarthen (1979) noticed that newborns only interact with one object or one person at a time, calling this "primary intersubjectivity". This allows a direct "second-person" understanding of the other (Gallese, 2013), based on a direct and reciprocally exclusive engagement with them (as opposed to a "third-person" understanding, which is characteristic of the so called "secondary intersubjecvity", which includes more complex social relations mediated by joint attention and coordinated practices focused on an external object).

Imitation is fundamental to the internal experience which we call "empathy", a psychological notion etymologically related to the German "Einfühlung" (experiencing through another's body or experiencing the other through one's own body). Empathy is often described as the capacity to "put oneself in the other's shoes", or experience the world from another's perspective (Zahavi, 2012). According to some philosophers, it is absolutely basic and built into our very perceptual capabilities (Zahavi, 2010), as every subjective experience of the world implicitly gestures at the possibility of a whole horizon of hypothetical experiences perceived by other subjects through different points of view.

Empathy has been defined as an analogical process because it presupposes that one's own past experiences can be used as a model to approach the experience lived by others. Hence higher similarities between subjects would associate to stronger empathic predispositions and better capabilities of mutual understanding. At the same time, empathy is to be intended as a "lived analogy" ("une analogie vécue", as Ricoeur and Jarczyk (1991) called it), that does not draw on rational inferences but on perceived similarities between one's embodied experience and the other's (i.e., the way the world subjectively appears as a function of having a certain body, which allows only certain possibilities of action, and specific qualitative experiences). Psychological research on empathy has highlighted different varieties and levels of this phenomenon, distinguishing among them on the basis of the kind of experience shared with the target and the complexity of the interpersonal attunement (Decety, 2015). Hence, we distinguish between a cognitive empathy (which allows perspective taking and requires one to intellectually simulate the contents of the other's beliefs and intentions) and an affective empathy (which is mostly based on simulating the other's sensorial and emotional experience, and requires a shared background of past experiences). Cognitive scientists have modelled empathy as a sort of "embodied simulation", that is, a largely automatic process that relies on one's own previous experiences to make sense of the experience lived by others (Gallese, 2008).

Empathy is key for human relationships, because it provides a background of shared experiences and competences to regulate social interactions and human communication (Feshbach, 1978). Through this background, empathy allows the comprehension of others' feelings and emotions and the synchronous response to their actions. According to Hoffman (1984), empathy initially manifests itself at the affective level. During the first year of life, children display primary circular reactions and motor mimicry by internally imitating the emotions they are witnessing (e.g., by crying when another infant is crying), but their emotional response is involuntary and undifferentiated (global empathy) (Hoffman, 1984). Later, this ability develops into a fully-fledged, selective imitative ability.

Empathy plays a crucial role in learning and teaching practices as it is one of the key components of the relationship between teacher and learner and a precondition for their reciprocal attunement: the teacher relies on empathy to transmit motivation and purpose to the learner, the learner to communicate his/her needs and struggles to the teacher. That is why empathy has been researched and reflected upon in several HRI studies due to its importance in deriving a more seamless interaction. For example, in the context of educational settings, Obaid et al. (2018) presented research on utilizing a robotic tutor with empathic qualities. Their work was part of the European Project EMOTE[1] that specifically focused on researching empathy-based learning with robotic tutors.

3.2.2 *Imitation*

As empathy is a fundamental mechanism of reciprocal understanding and coordination, it is also the key to developing imitation. Through imitation, babies start mapping equivalences between self and other, which provide an elementary mechanism to scaffold the early development of "social cognition" (Meltzoff and Moore, 1977), that is the cognitive processes we enact to coordinate with others and understand their goals and intentions. The cross-modal match between acts seen in others and the acts done by the self, which enables the possibility of feeling the other's actions in my body and my actions in his/her's, leads to the analogical presentation of the other as a "like me" entity: I understand the other's intentions because I would act like them if I was in their situation and, reciprocally, the other can understand my intentions insofar as my actions match what s/he would do in the same situation (Meltzoff and Brooks, 2001).

I know what the other is doing or may feel because the observed actions, and related feeling, are mapped in the repertoire of motor responses I can familiarly produce. The physiological mechanism by which this match is feasible is subserved by a specific class of visuo-motor neurons called *mirror neurons* (Rizzolatti et al., 1996). Through the activation of these neurons in prefrontal and parietal brain areas, and thanks to their connection to deep structures involved in emotion processing, like the insula (Di Cesare et al., 2016), action observation is automatically translated in the immediate perception of the other's action goal, which already includes an embodied, pre-reflective understanding of the circumstances that motivate that action and the emotions and feelings associated with it. This type of understanding, which is mediated by attendance to the visible aspects of the other's behaviour (i.e., facial expression, body posture, movement dynamics), can be defined as pre-reflective, as it does not require explicit awareness or the conceptual representation necessary to verbally report on one's own actions. As mirror neurons represent a key mechanism for interpersonal attunement and social coordination, roboticists interested in reproducing empathy and imitation have developed biologically inspired models of mirror neurons function based on a robot's ability to model an observed agent's sensorimotor abilities into its own action repertoire (Metta et al., 2006).

Even before mastering the use of language and concepts, humans already have an embodied knowledge of the other's behaviour. When you see your mate smiling, laughing, crying, disappointed, you immediately know his/her feeling and how it feels to be them in that situation. This type of knowledge is not a product of mental reflection or an inference on the hidden mental state of others, but the effect of an automatic, bodily response to emotions and goals that we see overtly expressed in the other's body and that are wired in us as they immediately find a correspondence in our bodily experience. Its social importance is evidenced from newborns' very first attempts to imitate facial expressions (Meltzoff and Moore, 1977). Importantly, not only can imitation be defined very precocious if not even innate, as some would argue but also, and importantly, as goal-directed and purposeful. Newborns engage in imitative behaviours very early, which, with growth, become more and more abstract: it is not just a behaviour-to-behaviour imitation, but it becomes a behaviour that "matches"(Meltzoff and Decety, 2003). This is when infants start making certain movements and monitor if the caregiver does the same in the same way. Understanding attention (the other looking at something without acting on it, an attitude that discloses a distal relationship) appears to evolve after the first year of life. So, it is not just a "gaze following" in a purely imitative sense (imitation of gross head movement): it is more an "attention following", keeping track of the other's focus and interest, see (Shepherd and Cappuccio, 2011) and (Cappuccio and Shepherd, 2013)). "... even making sense of others' visual perception could benefit from experience of oneself as a looker/perceiver" (Meltzoff and Brooks, 2001, p. 190). When this ability is acquired, the sense of agency begins to emerge.

Finally, another building block adds up to social interaction, that is intention understanding. *Pointing, joint attention, attribution of agency* and, *pretend play* are all markers of intention understanding. Imitation is so inherent to the process of learning and so basic in nature that it has a strong impact on interactions with robots as well, particularly in clinical and educational settings.

To illustrate, it was shown in a research study in which computational modelling and a robot implementation were used to explore the functional value of action imitation (Boucenna et al., 2016). Having adults, typically developing children, and children with Autism Spectrum Disorder (ASD) engage in a mutual imitation task with a robot, it was shown that a learning architecture was able to learn from an interaction that involved mutual imitation. Interestingly, mutual imitation enabled the robot to recognize the interaction partner in a subsequent encounter. Moreover, the robot was able to distinguish the social signature of the interaction partners (i.e., a typically developing child, a child with ASD, and an adult). These experiments, using robots as tools for modelling human cognitive development, substantially show how person recognition may occur through imitative experience and intercorporeal mapping—as described earlier in this section—plus statistical learning.

3.2.3 Theory of Mind

Turning our attention back to the evolution of empathy, during the second year of life, children experience egocentric empathy (Hoffman, 1984). During this phase, children offer help when they see, for example, another child crying. The kind of help they offer is motivated by what they would find comforting themselves and, in this sense, the empathy displayed is egocentric. The child still regards the other in a "like-me" fashion, reflecting immaturity with regard to the ability to differentiate another individual's mental states from their own.

At the age of three, role-taking skills emerge and reflect the child's cognitive skill to differentiate between the self and others, and children start becoming aware that other people's feelings can differ from their own. Related to this, children's responses to distress might become more appropriate to the other person's needs. The development of a ToM marks this maturation period (Marchetti et al., 2019). ToM is a cognitive competence studied for over 40 years as a human function that enables individuals to think of others' mental states, such as thoughts, intentions, motivations, desires, and emotions underlying behaviour (Wimmer and Perner, 1983). Through the attribution of states of mind, humans can predict and adequately respond to others' thoughts and actions given a specific context, culture and person's identity. Previous research has by now demonstrated the significance of ToM for the development of social competences: through ToM an individual can understand one's own and other people's mental states (intentions, emotions, desires, beliefs), allowing one to predict and interpret one's own and others' behaviours on the basis of such meta-representations (Perner and Wimmer, 1985; Premack and Woodruff, 1978). Children develop this ability in early years of life, around four to six years of age. This development is not sudden, but passes from a phase of understanding the concrete world to a phase of mental representation also thanks to the development of processes and behaviours recognized as the precursors of ToM (Marchetti et al., 2019).

These include joint attention and referential communication. Over development, ToM becomes increasingly complex. For example, first-order ToM entails a recursive thinking, which implies the meta-representation or the representation of a mental representation of a low complexity level, of the kind "I think that you think…". Children exhibit this competence with the emergence of "false beliefs", the understanding that others do not necessarily know the same things. Second-order ToM further implies a meta-representation of greater complexity, of the kind "I think that you think that he thinks…". Children aged seven and older have typically matured this competence, although it can also emerge at an earlier age. What is important to understand about ToM is that children, regardless of culture, come to explicitly understand that people's actions are determined by what they think, and not just by reality itself (Wellman, 2018; Wellman et al., 2001).

What role does ToM play in education? As substantially argued by Wellman (2018), an eminent scholar in the field of ToM, the development of ToM has wide-ranging, significant impacts on education. These include effects of ToM skills on children's friendships and popularity, their engagement in lying and deception, game-playing skills, strategies for persuading or arguing with others, and transition to school. Furthermore, cognitive skills and actions are affected by children's achievement of ToM insights. The areas in which ToM has shown to play a significant role in education can be summarized as follows:

- Learning strategies and memory
- Academic performance
- Academic motivation
- Reading comprehension and math ability
- Sensitivity to teacher feedback

For example, longitudinal studies (Lecce et al., 2011, 2014) have shown that early ToM competence at five and a half years of age predicts later academic performance at the age of ten, operationalized in terms of children's reading and maths abilities, as well as overall school achievements. Moreover, sensitivity to teacher feedback at ten years of age was shown to be affected by enhanced ToM understanding at the age of five years. Reasonably, being able to show responsiveness to teacher feedback has a significant impact on school achievement.

The importance of ToM in HRI is evident when thinking about a future in which robots can act in educational environments autonomously. Evidence suggests that children who have developed a ToM ability consider the robot as a simple tool, programmed for specific uses (Di Dio et al., 2018, 2020a). However, let us imagine a robot with a ToM.

Equipping the robot with ToM skills would not only allow it to interact correctly given a specific context but also to be recognized and therefore treated by humans as an intentional and educationally effective and trusted partner. In this rather optimistic future scenario, the study of ToM mechanisms, alongside its precursors in childhood (e.g., joint attention, role-playing skills, eye-gaze, etc.), would allow the implementation of cognitive neural networks in robots that resemble human ToM. The first steps in this direction have already been taken within *Developmental Robotics* (Manzi et al., 2020a; Vinanzi et al., 2019) and *Developmental Cybernetics* (Itakura, 2008; Itakura et al., 2008; Moriguchi et al., 2011; Wang et al., 2020) .

3.2.4   Anthropomorphism

Humans have a natural tendency to attribute human-like traits and characteristics to both living things (e.g., animals) and nonhuman entities (Eyssel and Hegel, 2012). For instance, recall those times that you have spoken to your computer or car in anger, or where you have watched a child play with a doll as though it were a real baby, reflecting automatic processes (Zlotowski et al., 2018).

Already Piaget (1929) suggested that children younger than six years of age tend to attribute consciousness to objects—namely the capability to feel and perceive—and that children consider "alive" also those things that are deemed inanimate by adults. This phenomenon is called animism.

Similarly, pareidolia, which is the interpretation of a perceived stimulus as being something meaningful to the observer, is related to anthropomorphism. For example, seeing a face in the clouds or in the arrangement of just a few dots. Experimental evidence has suggested that this effect is due to automatic processing in the visual system that intervene earlier than the attribution of more complex mental features like animacy and agency. It can thus be readily taken advantage of by robot designers, as the design of even minimalistic synthetic faces results in anthropomorphic attributions.

A more complex anthropomorphistic effect is the explicit attribution of agency to inanimate objects, even those that are not necessarily complex in appearance, on the basis of their observable behaviour. This is, the treatment of (or interaction with) these objects in a manner that suggests that it has some degree of autonomy in preparing and initiating action. One of the clearest examples of this are the classic animations of Heider and Simmel (1944), which demonstrate how the movement of simple shapes readily leads to the interpretation of these shapes as agents exhibiting emotions (fear, aggression, etc.). Applying this idea to robots,

Asselborn et al. (2017) demonstrated that a small humanoid robot enabled with small idle motions resulted in higher ratings of friendliness and human-likeness.

Duffy (2003) and Epley et al. (2007) provide an overview of the principles involved in the elicitation of anthropomorphic inferences. Specifically, in their psychological framework of anthropomorphism, Epley et al. (2007) propose that anthropomorphism depends on three core cognitive and motivational determinants:

- Elicited agent knowledge: the accessibility and applicability of anthropocentric knowledge
- Effectance motivation: the motivation to explain and understand the behaviour of other agents
- Sociality motivation: the desire for social contact and affiliation

Social robotics research has highlighted that anthropomorphism correlates with higher levels of likeability and perceived intelligence of robots, which, in turn, predicts more resilient trust and robust interest. When a non-human entity, however, becomes hyper-realistic in appearance, the effect can elicit eerie and disturbing feelings in the human perceiver. This is often referred to as the "uncanny valley" effect (Carpenter et al., 2006; Mori et al., 1970; Zlotowski et al., 2013, 2015). It has, however, been argued that the curve describing the relationship between the human-likeness of the robot and the likeability of the robot resembles more a cliff than a valley (Bartneck et al., 2007a).

At the same time, human-like features and functions in nonhuman entities or human-like behaviours in animals facilitate empathetic responses. Which essentially human cues have a beneficial impact in the context of humans' interaction with robots? In the remainder of the chapter, we focus on the role of social cues that facilitate human-human interaction and communication. As such, these social signals can likewise contribute to successful interactions between humans and robots in educational contexts.

3.2.5   Non-verbal Social Cues

Nonverbal social cues include facial expression of emotions, eye gaze, gestures, body posture, and proxemics—the distance and angle at which we stand to others. The relevance of these social signals becomes particularly evident when you encounter a person who does not display or correctly observe the proper use of some or even all of these competencies. Imagine a teacher who delivers a lecture without making eye contact. Would you listen to him/her for the duration of a lesson? Imagine, this teacher provides you with positive feedback, where the verbal message does not match the nonverbal expression. Would you trust that feedback? These scenarios illustrate the core role of nonverbal social cues for effective interaction between humans.

3.2.5.1   Facial expression of emotions

One of the most widely studied nonverbal social cues is emotion display. The internal emotional state of an individual is often, but not always, displayed through facial expressions and specifically in dynamic activation of facial muscles. Recognition of another person's internal emotional state by looking at the face is an automatic process, possibly relying on our ability for imitation and our ToM.

One of most popular views on human emotions, originated from the work of Ekman (1975), is that there are six universal facial expressions and therefore six universally recognized emotions: happiness, sadness, surprise, anger, disgust, and fear. This is not accurate, as there are more expressions recognized across all cultures. Ekman believed there to be 15 basic emotions, including pride in achievement, relief, satisfaction, sensory pleasure, and shame. The exact number is irrelevant, suffice to say that emotions are often expressed through facial expressions, whether deliberately or not. In order to describe facial expressions, Ekman and Friesen (1978) presented the Facial Action Coding System (FACS), a notation system based on which muscles are active, which is widely used in interactive facial tracking in social psychology and which has inspired not only the analysis of facial expression of emotions but also the developments of emotion synthesis and recognition systems in avatars and robots.

3.2.5.2   Eye gaze

Eye gaze is an essential nonverbal component in successful interactions between humans. Eye gaze facilitates synchronization and alignment of communication, including turn-taking in conversations between humans. Eye gaze also reflects attentional processes, including joint attention. That is, when people look at the same object of interest. Joint attention is key to social interactions at large and learning in particular, because it helps people coordinate their actions.

3.2.5.3   Gestures

Beyond facial expressions as an indicator of an individual's internal state, gestures constitute an important channel of nonverbal communication. In the literature, gestures have been categorized in a variety of taxonomies, such as the work by Efron (1941) and Ekman and Friesen (1969) who defined gestural categories to allow us to understand the human gestural behaviour in social communications. A more commonly used categorization was proposed by McNeill (1985) and McNeill (1992) to define gestural categorization as five types of gestures and each gesture placed into four phases.

3.2.5.4   Proxemics

Interpersonal distance and orientation between individuals has an important function in that it indirectly conveys information about the attitude towards another person and the relationship between individuals. Early work by Park (1924) has informed contemporary theorizing, with Hall's taxonomy of proxemics (Hall, 1966) still being influential today. He proposed four interpersonal zones, the intimate zone being the nearest, followed by the personal zone, the social zone, and the public zone.

3.2.5.5   Body posture

Body posture plays a significant role in nonverbal communication between humans. As such, body posture represents much more than the mere physical position of the body parts. In fact, posture provides "embodied" information about an individual's attitude, emotional state, or interest, etc. An overview on the use of body postures as a means of communication in the classroom has been provided by Caswell and Neill (2003). For example, a teacher with her hands on her hips or with her arms crossed may communicate nonverbally that she may not be happy with a child's behaviour. A teacher leaning towards a child may display particular interest in the child's behaviour.

3.3   Demographics

Typically, a range of individual demographic factors influence how humans carry out any sort of interaction be it with another human or a social robot (Flandorfer, 2012). By taking into account human demographics, we can arrive at a less-biased understanding of the individual's perspective and needs. This is relevant particularly when it comes to developing personalized and "inclusive" systems, ultimately scenarios for educational robots that appeal and address varying needs of diverse users. We will focus on the three core demographic variables in the upcoming section, namely, sex and gender, age, and ethnicity (Fiske, 1998). In fact, a person's gender, age, and ethnicity impacts human cognition, affect, and behaviour, as these social categories are used in impression formation and shape behaviour towards others. Essentially, belonging to a specific social group shapes how we see the world and how others see us. These features are thus essentially relevant, both in everyday life as well as in the research context.

3.3.1   *Sex and Gender*

Taking into account a person's sex and gender, that is, biological versus socially constructed attributes, is important in enriching our understanding of humans in general. Both sex, comprising an individual's biological attributes, and gender, which entails psychological, social, and cultural factors, have an impact on how we think, feel, and act. For instance, stereotypes associated with male or female gender may affect career decisions, leaving us with a lack of female students in engineering and male students in the humanities (Rogers et al., 2006; Screpanti et al., 2018). Related to this, it has been shown that a student's gender elicits gender-specific responses by a teacher, guiding teacher attention and even grading. For example, it has been shown that, particularly in STEM education, female secondary school students receive less encouragement than male students (Lavy and Sand, 2015), with possible impact on females' performance in these disciplines (Backonja et al., 2018). More generally, though, research in any field of scientific inquiry ideally should include gender as a central unit of analysis because ignoring this aspect biases and limits the conclusions that can be drawn from research, which has often focused on studying only men or only women (Tannenbaum et al., 2019).

3.3.2   *Age*

Socio-relational dynamics dramatically change with age. This is greatly due to the development of emotional and cognitive competences which shape the quality of interpersonal relationships. When we see three-years-olds sitting in groups and animatedly speaking, we might be most likely observing a phenomenon that Piaget (1959) referred to as egocentric speech. Children are not actually speaking with each other, but rather they are involved in a personal/private speech, immersed in their own thoughts. In contrast, when older children, teenagers or adults are in a group, you might expect an active exchange going on. Moreover, the quality of the exchanges and group dynamics is influenced by the level of intellectual maturity associated with a given age. Particularly within an educational framework, it is therefore important to take into account both the physical and developmental age in order to address the respective needs and to adapt teaching strategies accordingly.

3.3.3 Ethnicity

Just like with sex or gender, an individual's membership in a specific ethnic group shapes cognition, affect, and behaviour in significant ways. It might be that the social group membership comes along with certain group-specific stereotypes and prejudice related to traits or abilities the person allegedly holds because of his or her social group membership. For example, the literature on stereotype threat has shown that White Americans underperform at sports compared with African Americans when the stereotype about their athletic inability and their group membership is activated (Stone et al., 1999).

3.4 Are you really "Like Me?"

Anthropomorphic agents fit well with the general idea of a socially competent relational partner (DiSalvo et al., 2002; Ishiguro et al., 2003; Wykowska et al., 2016). However, what do we actually know about individuals' perception of robots? As we have learned so far, a social robot should act in a human-interpretable manner to appear as an intentional agent. When interacting with robots, the same cognitive mechanisms we use for interacting with people become active (Cappuccio et al., 2019). We respond to the overt behaviour of the robot, interpreting its motions and sounds, but also conceptualize the robot's mental processes, attributing intentions, beliefs, and emotion to the robot. Furthermore, we may believe the robot to have certain competencies as a social partner, and will often be solicited to interact with the robot as if it could really think, remember, reason, and feel emotions.

Perceiving the robot as a "like-me" entity certainly contributes to facilitate its relational bond with humans. Arguably, this is more likely to happen when human interactants conceptualize the robot as an agent endowed with what we might call a "pseudo-mind" (a cognitive core designed to mimic and progressively approximate the functions of a real mind), rather than perceiving the robot as a simple tool or device. As the attribution and recognition of mental features to an inanimate agent represent complex theoretical issues, researchers are very interested in evaluating and comparing people's ideas and conceptions of the robot's physical and psychological competencies. Not only does this research field deal with people of different ages, socio-cultural backgrounds and intellectual abilities but also with different types of androids and other types of robot agents (e.g., animaloid robots). The diversity between robots is potentially larger than the diversity between people, after all. In general, people are far from thinking that robots equal human abilities on any of the psychological dimensions addressed so far. The robot is commonly not perceived as an autonomous "minded" agent as yet, and it is quite evident, from research studies, that its abilities are determined by predefined algorithms that inform its patterns of movement, speech, and behaviour, with scarce sensitivity to context and only a limited adaptivity. In a study carried out with children aged between three and nine years (Di Dio et al., 2020a), the robot NAO was perceived as less competent than the human on all tested dimensions, either physical or psychological. To children, the robot is a machine pre-programmed to fulfil specific roles in a given context, although younger children do tend to attribute emotions and desires to robots, in line with the animism idea (Piaget, 1959).

We may then see very young children aged between three and five regard the robot as more intentional or able to feel emotions than older children (Di Dio et al., 2019). Of course, cognitive abilities develop with time and a more mature ability to represent the other's mental state in a more objective fashion, based on inferences on the real content of their beliefs, makes older children more resistant to the concept of the robot as an animated agent endowed with its own motivations and beliefs. This phenomenon is linked to the development of cognitive competencies, not least to a Theory of Mind ability that substantially contributes to transcend the merely embodied and perceptual level of social cognition by adding to it inferential and representational abilities that allow reflective awareness about both one's own and the other's mental states.

It is noteworthy that children attribute slightly different mental competencies to robots as a function of their physical features (e.g., Marchetti et al., 2018). By comparing two anthropomorphic robots—NAO and Robovie—it was found that NAO appears more approachable than Robovie, particularly for younger children. This substantiates the common tendency to use, for example, the NAO robot for interactions with younger children, as its inclusion as a social and educational agent may be more effective than a less appealing robot. Nevertheless, older children proved to be more sensitive to the robot's physical performance (action capabilities) than younger ones. This strongly indicates that if we have control over the design of a robot, we need to pay attention to the robot's physical appearance and its features when dealing with different age groups (Manzi et al., 2020a).

Given all the above considerations, the question arises of whether or not (and to what extent) it is desirable that a robot displays complex mental features somehow comparable with (or resembling) the human ones, like those described in this chapter. Our answer is positive, insofar as the goal of roboticists in education is to create and deploy robots that appear as competent, flexible, and responsive social agents. Are we getting any closer to that aim? The answer is: not quite. Researchers from different fields are jointly working towards endowing robots with an artificial mind, or something similar to it. One such an attempt is represented by *Developmental Robotics* (Cangelosi and Schlesinger, 2018). These groundbreaking studies build on the assumption that giving robots the ability to dynamically acquire knowledge from their interactions with the environment is more promising than just programming into them all the factual knowledge needed to successfully interact with the world. To implement this assumption, engineers have taken theories of developmental psychology as a guide to build robots that, like children, progressively acquire from repetitive situated and embodied experiences their sensorimotor, manipulative-interactive, and categorization skills. The vision that ultimately directs this research, originally inspired by the speculation of Alan Turing (1950), is that robots might, at some point in the future, gradually develop a pseudo-mind similar to our own (see, Cappuccio2016-dz).

Questions for you to think about:

- Why is it important to consider human memory when designing applications for HRI?
- How does the uncanny valley relate to the anthropomorphism described in this chapter? How is it applicable to robotic forms and the way they behave?
- How is the ToM associated to academic performance?
- In a one-to-one peer learning scenario with a robot, what are the nonverbal social cues that should be considered? Why?

Future reading:

- Henry M Wellman. Theory of mind: The state of the art. *European Journal of Developmental Psychology*, 15(6):728–755, 2018.
- John White and John Gardner. *The Classroom x-factor: The Power of Body Language and Non-verbal Communication in Teaching*. Routledge, 2013.
- Jakub Zlotowski, Hidenobu Sumioka, Shuichi Nishio, Dylan Glas,

Christoph Bartneck, and Hiroshi Ishiguro. Persistence of the uncanny valley: the influence of repeated interactions and a robot's attitude on its perception. *Frontiers in Psychology*, 6: 883, 2015. ISSN 1664-1078. 10.3389/fpsyg.2015.00883. URL https://www.frontiersin.org/ article/10.3389/fpsyg.2015.00883.

- M. Obaid, E. B. Sandoval, J. Złotowski, E. Moltchanova, C. A. Basedow, and C. Bartneck. Stop! that is close enough. How body postures influence human-robot proximity. In *The 25th IEEE International Symposium on Robot and Human Interactive Communication*, pages 354–361, Aug 2016. 10.1109/RO-MAN.2016.7745155.

Note

1. http://www.emote-project.eu/

4   What Makes a Robot?

[Robots] learn to speak, write, and do arithmetic. They have a phenomenal memory. If one read them the Encyclopedia Britannica they could repeat everything back in order, but they never think up anything original. They'd make fine university professors...

From R.U.R., by Karel Čapek

What is covered in this chapter:

- A technical overview of a robot's hardware and software;
- Input technologies: how can robots "sense" us?
- Output technologies: how can robots interact with us?

Conceptually, we have discussed the emergence of the word robot in our earlier chapters (see Chapter 1). From a technical perspective, a robot is similar to an embodied (i.e., existing in the real world rather than virtual) version of a computer or an interface, capable of carrying out tasks in the real world. In this way, the robots-as-tools identified later (Chapter 5) conforms to this basic definition. A social robot, as an extension, is a robot that is intended to interact and communicate with humans. Social robots are prevalent in many areas such as healthcare, entertainment including gaming, domestic settings, and education (see Chapter 8). To be able to interact with humans in an environment, the robot requires specific input and output mechanisms, respectively, called sensors and actuators. They allow the robot to receive input from the user or the environment and generate appropriate output or feedback. In this chapter, we consider the practical aspects involved in the types of robot we have seen so far in the book. This includes details on the input and

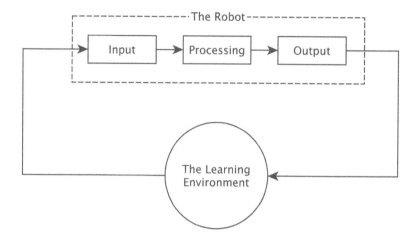

Figure 4.1 The robot in the context of an educational scenario. Four aspects are identified: (1) the robot itself; (2) the sensory modalities that the robot possesses; (3) the output modalities; and (4) the processing that the robot can achieve (e.g., understanding, and decision making).

output technologies and processing software and will give the reader a better understanding of the complexities of bringing robots into the classroom.

In the most general terms, we can distinguish between four main aspects of robots (Figure 4.1)[1]. First is the robot itself, the form it can take and its characteristics. Second are the inputs that the robot has access to, that is, what information can the robot detect about its surroundings. Third are the outputs, or the ways in which the robot can influence the world around it. Fourth, and finally, are the processing aspects of the robot, that is, the way that the robot can process information, both in terms of software and its support for hardware. These four points represent the structure of the remainder of this chapter.

4.1   The Robot

4.1.1   *Types of Robots and Their Control*

As shown elsewhere in this book, there are lots of different types of robots that have been used in terms of education (e.g., see Chapter 1). In terms of appearance and for the purposes of the present discussion, we can distinguish between three main types of robots that have been used in education: the (typically small) wheeled robot, the zoomorphic robot (i.e., one that has the characteristics of an animal—or one that can have animal characteristics attributed to it), and the humanoid robot (i.e., human shaped). There are, of course, overlaps between these categories, for example the humanoid robot Pepper that has wheels, but they are broad distinctions that highlight some of the issues involved in making an informed choice given a particular application.

In practical terms, for example, it is more reasonable to choose a wheeled robot if the focus of the task/activity involves movement—whether this is learning how to program a desktop robot to follow a line, or develop a social robot that can approach people in a classroom (Chew et al., 2010). If the application demands the use of human-recognizable gestures, on the other hand, then a humanoid robot would have some clear advantages. In addition to these practical considerations, there are a range of more theoretically justified reasons that would motivate the choice of one particular type of robot over another. Recall the propensity for humans to attribute agency to inanimate objects (Section 3.2.4): the attribution of particular robot competencies would be influenced by the features that can be seen. For instance, if the robot has eyes, then the expectation may reasonably arise that it can "see". It does not matter whether these eyes are actually cameras or not.

The discussion above has been primarily focused on the visual appearance of the robot. In terms of behaviour, one aspect that is of particular interest is the degree to which the robot, of any given appearance, can operate autonomously. Beer et al. (2014), for example, characterized ten levels of robot autonomy, from the human completely tele-operating the robot to full autonomy where no human intervention is required for the completion of a given task by the robot. Clearly, the choice of what level of autonomy to employ comes with a series of consequences. On the one hand, low levels of autonomy result in a lower development requirement for the robot, but also in a higher human involvement in the task (by requiring tele-operation, for example). However, while full autonomy reduces this load on the human, there are vastly increased requirements with respect to the robot system itself. Therefore, the choice of the appropriate autonomy level should be informed by the characteristics of the task, and perhaps even the practical constraints involved, as discussed in Chapter 7.

For educational robots, there are significant requirements in terms of the robot sensors (inputs), effectors (outputs), and processing. For the application of robots as tools, for example, the learner has to use the information from the sensors and needs to control the motors (see Chapter 5). For the use of robots as social agents, by contrast (see Chapter 6), the robot needs to detect aspects of the interacting human's behaviour, and respond appropriately (whether the decision-making in this context is made by a human or autonomously). The sections that follow in this chapter outline some of the technologies involved in each of these steps.

4.1.2   *Core Robot Hardware*

Another main aspect of robots is the hardware infrastructure required to actually make a robot do something. We will briefly consider three parts. Firstly, all robots that we consider in this work are based on electronics and therefore need power. Secondly, as noted above, as embodied computers, robots need some form of control in the form of micro-controllers/micro-processors to manage the inputs and outputs. Thirdly, in practical terms it is unlikely that the robots used in any of the contexts we discuss operate completely independently. They may need to be connected physically or wirelessly to another computer in order to be programmed, or they need to interact with other computers over a network while running. In this case, the notion of communication is important (at the level of electronics rather than humans).

Educational robots could be powered by connected cables running to external power supplies, but in most cases this is cumbersome, impractical, and maybe unsafe (trailing wire trip hazards, etc.). Therefore, these robots are typically intended to run on battery power. Battery technology has improved rapidly over the years, with lithium-ion batteries being the current standard for mobile devices in general given their high energy density (i.e., they can hold more power in a smaller space than previous technologies), and their relative safety in the process—although recommended charging processes should be adhered to in order to prevent dangerous consequences. There are nevertheless limits to battery life for any given robot. Even though modern mobile phones may lead us to expect extremely long consecutive periods of time during which a robot could be operational, in reality the battery life of robots is significantly shorter. A major contributing factor to this is that electric motors (used to move wheels, joints, etc.) consume significantly more power than the control electronics. This problem (battery discharge due to motor use) becomes more pronounced the more motors there are, but also the bigger the motors are (i.e., larger robots need bigger motors to move their heavier load). A partial counterbalance to this is that larger robots typically have more space for more batteries, but this does not necessarily compensate for the problem.

The second consideration is that of the control of the physical robot itself. Micro-controllers (sometimes more generically known as microchips) are generally used to access information from sensors and control motors. They do not generally perform complex processing: this would be achieved either by more powerful microprocessors, or by sending the information to another computer that is not on the robot. Indeed, for computationally intensive processes, such as image processing (see Section 4.2.2), information (such as camera images) is often sent over a network connection to a more powerful remote computer for processing, with only the result sent back (or processed further). Even in this case, there is still a requirement for the robot to have some processing power itself, as the motors will not activate themselves, and the sensors will not return any information unless it is explicitly handled.

The final part we will consider here is the necessity for communications, in the sense of electronics. Computers, and by extension robots, are now rarely stand-alone devices. They are typically connected in networks, or at the least connected to a range of peripheral devices that add significantly to their functionality. For example, a keyboard, mouse, and screen make a desktop computer usable, and a connection to a network (local area and/or the wider internet) extends the functionality substantially. In the same way, a robot needs to be able to communicate. Within the robot itself, there is a need to connect together the sensors, motors, and micro-controllers described above. Outside of the robot, there are further connections required. For example, in the case of learning how to program using programmable robots, it is typically necessary to physically connect the robot to another computer with a USB cable. During the actual operation of a robot where physically connected cables would not be suitable, for instance when using social robots[2], then connection to a wireless network (e.g., Wi-Fi) may be necessary.

4.2 Input Technologies

Robots can have a variety of sensors to collect information about themselves, their environment, and the humans therein.

4.2.1 *Speech Recognition*

Speech is one of the most natural and easiest forms of communication for humans. Communicating with a machine by speaking to it in one's native language is intuitive and requires little to no learning (Westall et al., 1998). Therefore, most social robots provide the facility and ability to users to engage and interact with them using speech or dialogue. If a robot is intended to teach a second language, regardless of its role, then it seems obvious to communicate with the student through speech.

In most instances, robots are equipped with an inbuilt, single microphone or an array of microphones that detect speech as analogue input.

Speech is first processed acoustically, trying to match the input with internally stored sound patterns, which are then forwarded to higher levels such as morphology, grammar, and semantics. Thereafter, a dialogue manager determines the robot's appropriate verbal response using methods from natural language processing.

Speech interaction in the field of robotics is not without challenges: speech recognition can be affected by general aspects of sound transmission (ambient sound, distortions, and motor noises from the robot itself). It can be complicated by phonological aspects of language variation (local vs. standard accent), or it can even be influenced by higher levels of language processing, such as ambiguity and vagueness (Mubin et al., 2014). This is even more of a dilemma in child-robot interaction, when pitch and inconsistent developmental changes in the child can make speech recognition especially difficult (Kennedy et al., 2017c)[3].

Several strategies have been developed to overcome these problems in order to improve the recognition accuracy. One approach is to constrain the language itself by limiting vocabularies and grammar (Mubin et al., 2012). Another strategy is to constrain the interaction context. A robot would then only be able to converse about specific topics. Some robots use an intermediary interaction medium, such as the touch screen similar to Pepper's chest screen (see Figure 1.3 on page 9). A last resort is to use a human operator in the background to recognize what was said. This is called the Wizard-Of-Oz (WoZ) approach and is described in more detail in Chapter 11.

In addition to these speech recognition problems, speech synthesis, that is, the way the robot speaks, is often inferior to the results we are used to, for example, when using our smartphones. There are a number of technical issues in achieving this, such as the generation of appropriate prosody given the text to be spoken (Dutoit, 1997). Since such processing is computationally expensive however, it is typically processed on a separate more powerful computer than the robot—without such a connection (see Section 4.1) it becomes difficult to achieve. MaryTTS, for example, a commonly used open-source text-to-speech engine that has commonly been applied to a range of robots (Schröder and Trouvain, 2003), is able to use a range of different languages and is generally used on a different computer than the robot.

4.2.2   Computer Vision

Computer vision technologies have been around for a number of decades, relying mostly on image processing algorithms. In the past decade, with the advent of digital camera technologies and improved processing power, computer vision has become one of the essential input sources in robots. It gives them a perceptual power that is not unlike that of a biological eye. Standard digital cameras can detect red, green, and blue light. Specialized cameras can detect infrared light to provide a thermal image. This makes it easier for a robot to distinguish between an object and a human. To achieve a sense of depth, robots can be equipped with two cameras similar to how humans require two eyes to sense depth. Recently, specialized depth cameras have been developed that can achieve a similar perception with only one camera.

Depending on the type of captured imagery, algorithms enable robots to recognize objects, understand facial expression, track the gaze of a human, and create thermal maps of the environment. These maps in turn allow the robot to avoid obstacles and to plan its movement path.

The work presented by Davies (2017) outlines what computer vision technologies and algorithms can achieve. When considering the use of computer vision technologies, it is important to assess the factors that might compromise accuracy. The lighting in the environment, for example, can dramatically change how well the robot performs. A cluttered background can also make it more difficult for robots to detect specific targets. This becomes even more difficult if a part of the object of interest is occluded by other obstacles. This is especially difficult if the goal is to track a specific person in a group of people.

Computer vision systems can be used to capture relevant aspects of a student, such as his/her affective state. For this purpose, it can be useful to combine the information gathered from the cameras with other sensor information, such as skin conductivity (Obaid et al., 2018). This enables the robot to plan an appropriate emphatic strategy to optimize the student's learning experience. Another example is that computer vision tracking technologies can enable a user to control the robot using body motions, such as using depth camera tracking to navigate a robot in an environment using body gestures (Obaid et al., 2014, 2016a).

4.2.3   *Proximity Sensors*

Robots operating in the real world in a changing environment are likely to encounter numerous obstacles and objects of interest. Whereas the depth cameras mentioned in Section 4.2.2 are able to detect the distance between the robot and the obstacles to some degree, it is also possible to use dedicated proximity sensors. These sensors are usually much cheaper and require far less processing power.

Two common types are sonar sensors and infrared sensors. Both work on the principle of emitting sound/light and measuring the time it takes for them to be reflected from the obstacle ahead. The longer the signal travels the further the object is located from the robot. This allows the robot to avoid walls or, for example, to detect a human standing in front of it (Csapo et al., 2012; Han et al., 2012). If a human is detected, the robot might then decide to engage in an interaction. Popular robots, such as NAO and Pepper, both have sonar sensors and they have been used in educational settings to, for example, wake up from a sleep state in case a human approaches the robot or to activate safety features (Tanaka et al., 2015).

4.2.4   Touch Sensors

Equipping a robot with touch sensors allows the robot to detect collision with obstacles, but it can also be used to detect a human touching the robot on purpose. While these sensors can be very affordable, they record events that might need to be avoided to start with. A robot, for example, should avoid driving into obstacles or humans. Detecting that it happened is useful information, but ideally the robot would have used proximity sensors to change its path beforehand. Touch sensors mounted on different parts of the robot can be used to detect different events. (An interested reader might consult Seminara et al. (2019) for a review of haptic sensory perception in robots.)

4.2.5   Physiological Sensors

Physiological sensors record bodily processes. The great advantage is that these processes are often involuntary. Participants in studies cannot mask them or provide socially acceptable responses. A simple example of a physiological sensor is a skin conductivity sensor. It measures how well the skin conducts electricity. This is highly dependent on the amount of sweat the skin produces which in turn relates to stress. Similar inferences can be made with recordings of heart rate, heart rate variability, respiration rate, and body temperature. Even brain activity can be measured through electromyography.

One challenge associated with physiological sensors is that the bodily processes can be very complex. The skin conductivity of a person might increase not because the person is stressed, but because he/she is exercising. Distinguishing between relevant signal and unrelated noise is one of the main difficulties. Furthermore, these processes are often not binary but continuous. A handshake, for example, can evoke different responses depending on the pressure exerted. The same applies to finger presses as reported in (Chincheng et al., 2019).

Another clear challenge is that physiological sensors often need to be attached to the person. These sensors then need to communicate their readings to the robot. This poses a considerable technical challenge, which makes these sensors mainly suitable for controlled lab experiments.

The information collected can, however, be very useful to adapt the robot's behaviour to the student. For example, if the learning task is too difficult then the student might become stressed, which could be sensed through a skin conductivity sensor. The robot could then offer an easier task or provide additional support. Obaid et al. (2018) used a Q-sensor[4] to measure skin conductance and systematically determined the arousal level of the students. The arousal level was used by the robot to adapt its emphatic strategies in interacting with the student.

4.3 Output Technologies

The robot needs to be able to act in the world. This can be as simple as driving around but it can also include many other activities.

4.3.1 Motor Movements and Mobility

The importance of movement and mobility for robots in educational settings is well documented (Causo et al., 2016). Robots use different types of motors to move on their wheels and to set their body parts into motion. Almost all motors are powered through electricity and need to be regulated using a micro-controller. This allows the robot to move around, pick up objects, or to animate its body gestures and face. For example, in the work presented by Obaid et al. (2017) they have utilized gestural movements in an instructional scenario to implicitly measure the level of the user's engagement with a robot. Moreover, robots can use their capability of motion as a form of body language to communicate with humans. A robot could, for example, move its head in the direction of a student to signal that it is paying attention to him/her. The robot could also use its arm and fingers to direct the attention of the student to the learning content.

4.3.2 Haptic Feedback

A distinguishing feature of a robot in comparison to a screen-based character is its embodiment. The robot can touch the user and it can be touched by the human in return. This physical interaction is unique and allows a robot to teach students motor skills and even be involved in rehabilitation, as described in Chapter 8.

For a successful physical interaction, the robot needs to be able to detect touch as described above, but it also needs to be able to regulate its force and acceleration. This can be used to guide the user along a certain trajectory or to utilize a form of vibration as communication modality.

The robot could, for example, take the hand of the student and guide the student's movement. If the student deviates from the intended path then the robot needs to increase its force to bring the student back onto the path. The further away the student moves from the intended path, the stronger the robot should apply force to counteract this movement. This form of physical feedback is often referred to as force feedback.

4.3.3   Audio

Robots often have speakers or buzzers to create auditory signals. This can be useful in communicating with the student, in particular if the robot is using speech. The robot can play back pre-recorded sounds, including pre-recorded speech. A robot can also use its computing power to generate a synthetic voice. This allows the robot to "speak" any required text. Besides generating the content of an utterance, the robot can also apply supra-segmental phonological principles, such as stress or intonation, to modulate its speech to give implicit signals, that is, information about its internal state. The robot could speak louder if it wants to attract the attention of the student or change its pitch and speech tempo to simulate an emotional expression (James et al., 2018). Changing these parameters of the robot's voice is relatively simple and gives the robot the opportunity to adapt its voice to the requirements of the classroom and even to individual students (Edwards et al., 2018).

4.3.4   Eyes

As described in Section 3.2.5, eye gaze can play a vital role in the process of human-human interaction. A robot that has eyes will raise the expectations in the user that it has full vision capabilities. The robot's gaze thereby communicates what the robot is paying attention to. The eyes can also be used to express emotions in combination with bodily movements, for example, a robot that is looking down could be perceived as being sad.

The work by Admoni and Scassellati (2017) summarized several studies in the area of human-robot interaction that shed light on different aspects of gaze, such as mutual gaze, joint attention, gaze aversion, and deictic gaze.

Andrist et al. (2014) investigated how people react to a robot that is able to avert its gaze. They showed this influenced how the robot was perceived in terms of being thoughtful, intentional, and conversationally capable.

Several robots have eyes that emit light through the integration of LED lights which can change colour. Eyes are sensors and integrating lights into them reverses their purpose. Unlike most biological life forms, the NAO and Pepper robots are examples of such a reversed metaphor where the eyes are used as torches. Not to mention that the eyes in these robots are not the location of their cameras—they are located in other areas of the face. The engineers for these two robots used the same approach for the robots' ears. They are speakers and not microphones. These robots use microphone arrays around the head.

Nevertheless, the engineers of the robots built these features in an attempt to allow the robots to express particular emotional states (Ahmad et al., 2016; Häring et al., 2011). Also, the shape of the eye has been used as a medium to convey emotional expressions (Greczek et al., 2011). While the exact relationship between colour and emotions remains to some degree ambiguous, the colours of the eyes have been used to teach children about the concept of colour (Alkhalifah et al., 2015).

Eye gaze can also be analysed by the robot. Alnajjar et al. (2019b) propose a system dubbed "Attention in Class" that assesses the students' attention levels in a classroom set-up. They equipped a Pepper robot with the capability to autonomously assess the attention levels of students and report on a scale ranging from 0 (no attention) to 10 (full attention). The robot permanently scans the audience and logs the degree of attention of individual students. Figure 4.2 shows an example of the system's application measuring the attention of eight students in a classroom environment.

While such an application does not in principle require the presence of a robot (for example this would be achievable with a set of cameras), there are a number of benefits that may result from using a physical robot in the environment. For example, the social facilitation effect, building on the notions of anthropomorphism and the attribution of agency (Section 3.2.4), leads to a change in behaviour when being observed, which has also been investigated for robots (Riether et al., 2012). In addition, since groups of social robots have the capacity to persuade people (potentially with children, though not with adults (Brandstetter et al., 2014; Vollmer et al., 2018)), these effects combined could be used to improve class-based attention.

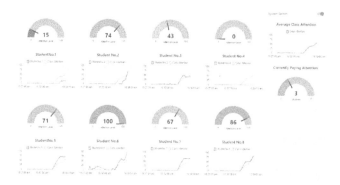

Figure 4.2 The attention app dashboard illustrates the attention level of each student in the classroom

4.4   Processing Software

A robot is a computer interface that processes data input depending on the intended task. The core part in handling any input data is run by software algorithms that are customized for specific robotic platforms. In this section, we demonstrate some of the tools used to process the data input and output outlined in Section 4.2.

4.4.1   *Development Tools*

Most robots used in education require some form of programming. While general purpose Integrated Development Environments (IDEs) exist, robot
manufacturers often offer either extensions to existing IDEs or their very own IDEs. For example, LEGO Mindstorms comes with its own visual programming environment that is based on LabView, but there are also plugins for the popular Eclipse[5] and Visual Code IDEs[6].

Another example is Choregraphe, which is a visual programming environment that can be used to program the Softbank Robotics robots NAO and Pepper (see Figure 5.4 on page 77). Choregraphe also has access to the integrated programming language Python to program more advanced features, and, on top of that the robots can be programmed using Python without using the Choregraphe platform.[7]. Such dedicated IDEs can be used to create interaction scenarios and to animate the robot. These tools are typically easy to use and well suited to the quick creation of robot behaviours.

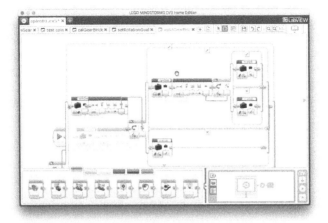

Figure 4.3 The visual programming environment for LEGO Mindstorms

The advanced user will find many software systems and frameworks that are provided as a form of open source and/or in the cloud Application Program Interfaces (APIs) in conjunction with Software Development Kits (SDKs) to eventually make programming robots easier. For example, a popular API for computer vision algorithms is OpenCV[8], which is an open-source set of libraries that allows developers to process captured imagery from cameras to extract information about the location of a human face, and to recognize a human face, its emotional expressions, and the body gestures of the student.

4.4.2 Robot Software Middleware

In this chapter, we have seen a range of functions, processes, and algorithms referenced. A key question is how to put these together and make them operate as part of a single robot system. The main way of doing this is the use of *middleware*, which is effectively a communications infrastructure (in the computer science sense) that allows this.

Taking the example of LEGO Mindstorms or similar modular educational systems, attaching sensor or motor modules to an existing robot is a simple matter of physically plugging them in. In order for the controller to recognize and use them, however, there is underlying software (not typically directly accessible to the user) that allows these modules to communicate. All the technical complexity of this task is hidden from the user and just works. Middleware such as this is, however, specific to particular robot platforms: if a new type of robot were to be used then the controller would have to be rewritten from the beginning.

When dealing with robots which require the integration of a large number of both hardware components (such as sensors) and software components (such as machine vision, or planning), such as required with social robots in particular, there is a particular need for middleware. Furthermore, if the middleware is widely used across different robots and computer systems, then it becomes possible to reuse components (such as emotion recognition from faces) instead of having to rewrite them. This is where the open-source Robot Operating System (ROS)[9] has become an increasingly important part of the robotics community over recent years. As a middleware system for robotics, it is increasingly prevalent in both academic research and industrial robotics. With increasing prevalence comes an increasing number of components that can be relatively straightforwardly re-used for new robot control systems. So, for example, algorithms for navigation, people detection, object recognition, limb control, etc., are all available for re-use.

4.4.3   Speech Processing

To be able to recognize speech, manage the flow of the conversation, and to synthesize speech, robots require specialized software. These can run on the robot's computer or can connect to online services through APIs. An example for a local speech software system is Sphinx from the Carnegie Mellon University. It has been integrated, for example, in Jasper[10], a system that turns a Raspberry Pi into a conversational agent.

Most of the major software companies, such as Amazon, Google, and Microsoft, offer APIs to process speech and language. The great advantage of these APIs is that they require very little local processing power. They do not need a full PC which in turn would require considerable space and powerful batteries. A possible disadvantage is that the communication to all those online services requires a persistent and fast internet connection.

It is important to note that the speech processing systems support many languages. It is almost trivial for a robot to converse in a multitude of languages. For example, Softbank-based robots fully support a dozen languages, including English, Arabic, and Chinese.

If the robot is using Google's API, then it can speak in more than 30 languages and it can recognize more than 100.

4.4.4   Limitations

Software development for robots does, however, come with a number of risks, particularly if robots are being used and programmed over extended periods of time. The software eco-system is highly dynamic. Some tools are being abandoned, others evolve, and new products enter the market. A robot that uses several development tools and APIs might be confronted with incompatibilities.

For example, if a product ceases to be made or sold, then it is likely that the software tools provided with this product would also eventually cease to be supported. Naturally, a similar case may occur with open-source software if the development team no longer supports/maintains their code base. In this case, however, there is a higher likelihood of some-one else being able to take over, since everything is accessible which is in the nature of the open source philosophy. A similar problem arises if a particular robotic product and associated software is updated but no longer compatible with the previous iteration[11]. This can be particularly problematic if significant resources have been assigned to an older ver-sion, from which the company, and indeed possibly the community, has moved on.

4.4.5 Localization and Mapping

Particularly for mobile robots, an important problem to handle is know-ing where it is and where it is going. This is generally known as *local-ization* (where am I?) and *mapping* (where are other things/places?). This leads us to consider two aspects of the problem. The first one is more low level: if even a small mobile robot is trying to move a certain distance, how does it know when this has been completed? The second aspect is more complicated: for a larger robot moving around between rooms, for example, there is a necessity to know where the rooms are, and where the robot is within this map.

The first problem is particularly relevant to the small mobile robot kits (e.g., LEGO Mindstorms) that are used in education. In these cases, the tasks set for the learners typically involve movement, such as making the robot move one metre forwards in a straight line. The question then is, what information is necessary to know (for the robot and for the learner) when this has been completed? In terms of sensors, wheel encoders (of various types) may be used to determine how much the respective wheels have turned. Termed *odometry*, this enables an estimate of how far the robot has moved. Based on this, the technique of *dead reckoning* may be used to estimate where the robot is with respect to its starting point based on the distance it has moved.

Beyond odometry and dead reckoning is a more complex issue when the robot has to navigate between locations or perhaps rooms. If a map of the space is available to the robot, then the problem is how to localize the robot within this. A number of approaches may be used, and as noted above (Section 4.4.1) there are a number of available tools that facilitate this. If a map is not available, then the problem is one of having to simultaneously generate a map, and localize within this in a consistent manner: the process of solving this is known as simultaneous localization and mapping (SLAM) (Durrant-Whyte and Bailey, 2006), which is a difficult problem to successfully solve in all situations. However, as before, there is a range of open-source tools available that perform this task.

4.4.6 *Artificial Intelligence*

Artificial Intelligence (AI) is the simulation of human intelligence processed and presented by the robot. This is a huge area that has many different methods and applications. The term AI brings with it many connotations and expectations, driven both by actual technical developments and its portrayal in the media. The media reports with various degrees of accuracy on the actual technical advances and the use of AI in science fiction. There are generally fairly large disparities between fact and fiction and we discuss this field of tension in Chapter 9.

Take the example of "reading". Being able to automatically recognize characters, and hence words, that have been written by people is a difficult task, even for other people: consider for example the poor handwriting of your doctor or lecturer (see Figure 4.4).

In this case, having a robot automatically recognize what characters are written (which it has never seen before) poses a significant technical challenge—this is AI. Being able to achieve this particular task with high performance does not however mean that the robot would subsequently be able to understand what has been written: that would require another set of algorithms trained for another specific task (e.g., characterizing sentences and their grammatical structure, extracting topics/themes from text). This is where one of the typical misunderstandings of AI arises: in real AI systems there is a lack of generalized/generalizable intelligence in the way we would recognize it in humans.

Many of the techniques that have been described earlier in this chapter are essentially examples of specific applications of AI. For example, speech recognition, image recognition, Natural Language Processing, and interpersonal distance prediction all benefit from AI systems to increase the robot's capabilities and seamless interactions. AI algorithms, reinforcement learning, supervised learning, and neural networks rely on modelling data to enable them to predict/process input data coming from these interactive technologies.

Figure 4.4 Handwriting at its best

While there are exciting developments in each of these domains, another area in which current technology may lag behind expectations is the area of learning. The typical AI (or *machine learning*) approach is to gather relevant data on the task to be learned, and then train the AI system using this. After it is trained, the system is used, but then not typically changed further: the "learning" part is independent of the application part. This is known as *offline learning*. The type of learning that we typically consider as humans is rather *online learning*, where learning happens during the performance of the task. This type of learning is used on occasion in AI, but is far less prevalent for a number of reasons. This includes interference, where aspects of the task that are learned later reduce performance in tasks learned earlier.

For these reasons (the necessity for high levels of computation to process these complex algorithms) and related reasons, one method that is commonly used in robotics is to move the "intelligence" (as described above) off the robot itself and have it run on external devices, or in "the cloud" (see Section 4.1.2 for an overview of robot communications). For example, IBM Watson[12] performs a range of complex tasks that can then be applied in robotics, such as handling verbal requests and retrieving the appropriate information.

Characterizing and understanding the capabilities and limitations of AI in the context of educational robotics is important, as it can be used to ground expectations of what the robots can actually achieve in the learning context, for both the educators and the learners. For example, for a robot to make ethical judgements (see Section 10.2, page 160), there is an assumption that the robot is adequately able to characterize the current situation to a sufficient extent, be able to accurately interpret this, and also infer the consequences of any potential actions. As we have seen above, this would involve the application of a range of complex AI systems that do not currently fully exist. In another example, we have seen that AI technologies have been increasingly applied to educational robots (Section 5.7, page 88), with this likely to increase. The issue remains, however, of how to piece together the different functionalities. For instance, if the robot can perceive an angry face, then a reactive behavioural response can be easily programmed (e.g., recoil). However, if more complex responses are required/desired, then there is a requirement for far more substantial programming, including logic, reasoning, etc. This quickly runs into the problem of a current lack of *general intelligence* as noted above.

Questions for you to think about:

- What sensors does a robot have that humans do not (and vice versa) and how does this change the way in which they interact?
- What is the better form of moving: walking or rolling? In what situations does this apply?
- Can a robot *really* think and feel?

Future reading:

- Bruno Siciliano and Oussama Khatib. *Springer Handbook of Robotics*. Springer, 2016. ISBN 978-3-540-23957-4.

- Maja J. Mataric. *The Robotics Primer*. MIT Press, Cambridge, MA, 2007. ISBN 9780262633543. URL http://www.worldcat.org/oclc/604083625.
- Christopher M. Bishop. *Pattern Recognition and Machine Learning*. Springer, 2006. ISBN 0387310738.

Notes

1. We are not taking any particular theoretical position about the nature of embodiment and/or cognition—the single flow from input to output is merely a practical convenience for the purposes of explanation.
2. A physical connection could be unsuitable for practical reasons, as the robot may move, but also for other reasons. For instance, if a social robot is plugged in, even if only to recharge, this may give some observers the incorrect impression that the robot is remotely controlled.
3. When NAO and Pepper robots are using their English language packages, for example, they need to be addressed in American rather than in British English. This requirement might lead to problems in those contexts where a postvocalic "r" is pronounced: hear, here, hair, etc.
4. http://qsensor-support.affectiva.com
5. http://www.bartneck.de/2017/06/04/tutorial-on-how-to-install-and-run-java-on-lego-mindstorms-ev3-using-eclipse-on-mac-os-x/
6. https://marketplace.visualstudio.com/items?itemName=lego-education.ev3-micropython
7. Since 2019 Softbank Robotics has been delivering all new Pepper robots with Android as their new developmental environment, and have left their NAO robots with a newer version of Choregraphe.
8. https://opencv.org
9. https://www.ros.org/
10. http://jasperproject.github.io
11. There are currently two NAO versions: NAO V6 and the older NAO V5. Both can be run using Choregraphe, however, in two versions, which are incompatible with each other.
12. https://www.ibm.com/watson

5 The Robot as a Tool

True happiness comes from the joy of deeds well done, the zest of creating things new

Antoine De Saint-Expury, *Cioccolato Baci Ferrero*

What is covered in this chapter:

- Working *on* robots as tools;
- Computing skills: what you need to know;
- How robots fit in the educational environment: effective integration;
- Challenges we are faced with.

Since the 1970s, robots have been used as part of a constructionist approach to education. In this, learners build and program robots to form an understanding of the world and technical concepts through active experience. The robots are thus tools and the learners work on them to achieve the learning outcomes. The very first educational robots were built upon the success of the Logo programming language. In Logo, a cursor, dubbed the turtle, was programmed to move on the screen and in doing so drew lines (see also p. 21). Turtle robots were also programmed using Logo and drew lines on a sheet of paper using a pen. Since the 1980s, a range of robot turtles were produced and sold and were adopted in school curricula to teach children programming and related skills (see Figure 5.1).

Robots as an education tool have been around for almost 50 years. This chapter looks at how robots are adopted by educators, how they fit into curricula, and the successful and less successful outcomes of the robotic revolution in schools.

Figure 5.1   The Valiant turtle robot, a popular Logo-based educational robot in the 1980s

Source: Valiant Technology Ltd

5.1   Why Are Robots Used in Education?

As the use of robots as educational tools grew out of the first forays into teaching computer programming, robots were used as an extension to programming on the computer with the goal to make the output of programs tangible and manipulative. However, soon the potential of robots as a substrate for teaching or elucidating a wide range of topics became clear. Now, robots are traditionally seen as a way to engage, enthuse, or teach learners about the four STEM subjects. In recent years art has been drawn in, as aspects of the design, form or the behaviour of the robot require more than just engineering. As such, robots are now considered as being an ideal tool to support STEAM education (see Figure 5.2).

Educational robots are being used across the spectrum of formal education. Starting in preschool, from the age of three or four, with simple robots that can be programmed to execute a sequence of movements (Roussou and Rangoussi, 2019), all the way up to university education, where more complex robot kits are used to teach and practise advanced concepts in engineering. Robots also have a firm place outside formal education, with extra-curricular activities and hobby clubs centring their activities around the building and programming of robots (Ribeiro and Lopes, 2020).

Robots are used to teach, illustrate, or reinforce a wide range of subjects. In most settings, however, robots are being used to teach robotics (engineering) itself. Jung and Won (2018) note that for the majority of applications of robots as educational tools, the intent of robot sessions is to teach about robots, and although learning gains in related STEAM subjects are welcome, they are not the focus of educational robots. Such STEAM subjects include computational or algorithmic thinking, mathematics concepts, or physics.

It is worth noting that robots are increasingly being used to spice up teaching about subjects not considered to belong to STEAM. For example, robots have been used to teach literacy in early years (McDonald and Howell, 2012) or computer literacy and media competence in secondary and higher education (Zeaiter and Heinsch, 2019).

Robots are being offered in education for several reasons. The first reason finds its origins in educational theory. Specifically, in constructionism from Papert and constructivism from Piaget (see Chapter 2). Robots are used to invite learners to design, build, and program, and in doing so to change their views, knowledge, and skills on everything flowing from the activity of doing so. This is a firm *learning by doing* approach, as far removed from traditional teaching as possible. Not just doing by engaging in exercises, but by actively and preferably tackling a problem in a group, coming to a solution through several iterations, learning as you go along.

The second reason for embracing robots in education is that robots are assumed to appeal to a wide range of ages and backgrounds. Robots are touted as the perfect marriage between enjoyment and learning (Ahmad et al., 2019; Vogan et al., 2020), and to a large extent this is indeed confirmed with many studies stressing the motivational aspects of robots as educational tools (Anwar et al., 2019).

Robots are also promoted as a means to widen participation, increasing diversity, and drawing a wider audience to STEM subjects in secondary school and university. For instance, we know that STEM subjects have a very pronounced gender imbalance[1]. There is a dearth of evidence on how successful these initiatives really are, but it is interesting to note that children at a young age do not seem to show a gender imbalance in aptitude. Sullivan and Bers (2013) found that boys and girls had equally successful learning experiences when programming robots in kindergarten.

Jung and Won (2018) argue that given the masculine image of STEM professions and misconceptions about the achievement gap between girls and boys, gender, and its effects on STEM warrants discussion in a much wider context and is perhaps a social construct rather than a biologically determined matter. While there are high expectations for the widening

Figure 5.2   In the WeGoSTEM initiative thousands of preschool children build an art robot. The robot is made up of a small computer board, two motors and linked bars holding a pen. The children program the robot using a visual programming language (www.wegostem.be)

participation potential of robot education, the discussion and specific evidence base for learner's race, culture, ethnicity, languages, socio-economic background, and prior experience are currently lacking.

5.2   Computational Thinking

The use of robots as a tool in education has its origin in computer programming education and developments there tend to feed into how robots are programmed. Computer programming education focuses mainly on the teaching of computational thinking: the systemic division and solving of problems through a number of steps and processes which could be carried out by a computer. Key concepts include decomposition, abstraction, and pattern recognition, data, and algorithmic processes (using sequencing, iteration, symbolic representation, and logical operations). Computational thinking has been on the radar since the 1970s, but received renewed attention after Jeannette Wing drew attention to it in a short but influential position paper in 2006. She pointed out how computational thinking is a universally applicable skill, not only relevant to programming, and that it should be central to school curricula.

Some programming languages, such as Logo, were developed to address computer education. Other languages, such as Java or Python, while being general purpose programming languages, have been adopted across secondary and university education to teach computational thinking and, following on from that, programming. Perhaps noteworthy is that teaching computational thinking does not necessarily require programming: the *CS Unplugged* initiative uses engaging games and puzzles that use cards, string, crayons, and lots of running around to teach concepts of computer science.

An interesting development is the adoption of visual programming ("drag and drop") methods in education, which popularized computer programming for younger learners. While visual programming as a concept is old, the use of visual programming in education broke through due to two developments: the use of visual programming for the LEGO Mindstorms robot kits and the increasing popularity of the Scratch visual programming environment.

Scratch, since its first release in 2003, quickly gained popularity as a free visual programming environment in which children combine code blocks to draw and move elements on a canvas (see Figure 5.3). The Scratch visual style influenced the Blockly visual programming language[2], which has been built to allow connections to different pieces of software, including software running on robots. Blockly is, among others, used in code.orghttps://code.org/ and their Hour of Code [3] initiative, where learners are taught algorithmic thinking and computer science principles using visual programming. The Minecraft extension, called Minecraft for Education, uses Blockly to introduce students to concepts in computer science and elementary artificial intelligence.

5.3 Hardware

The creation and modification of robotic hardware adds a new dimension to the learning experience of the students. Aspects of mechanical engineering, such as motors, actuators, gear ratios, and levers can be included into the curriculum as well as ambient intelligence in the form of sensors and internet of things. There are several hardware systems available that offer building blocks that can be combined to create custom robots. LEGO Mindstorms is arguably the most popular example of such a hardware system (Kubilinskiene et al., 2017), but it is by far not the only one.

5.3.1 Ready-to-Run

If the focus of the curriculum is on computer science then robots that do not require any assembly are a good choice. This way the students do not

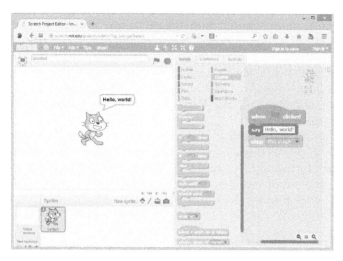

Figure 5.3   The Scratch visual programming environment allows children to program interactive animation by snapping code blocks together

Source: MIT

need to waste any time on the hardware and all students have exactly the same standardized hardware right from the start.

The well-established NAO robot from Softbank Robotics is a good example of such a ready-to-run robot. It requires no assembly and offers a visual programming environment called Choregraphe (see Figure 5.4). Underlying the visual programming environment, the Python programming language is used to control the robot. Choregraphe includes a virtual version of various versions of Softbank's robots, however, it only allows a restricted simulation of the robot's interactions with other objects/people in the world. It is therefore possible to test the stand-alone behaviour, in particular animations, of the robot, but it is not possible to test how the robot would react to its environment or speech elicitation. The NAO robot has a powerful processor that is able to perform advanced human-interaction skills, such as face identification, face recognition, and voice recognition. The robot can do these tasks without having to resort to internet-based services. It also comes with a large number of useful sensors such as cameras, microphones, and distance sensors.

While NAO and its bigger sibling Pepper are excellent platforms, they come with a considerable price tag as pointed out in Chapter 7 (p.115), notwithstanding their fragility. Not many schools in the developed world would under normal financial circumstances be able to afford equipping

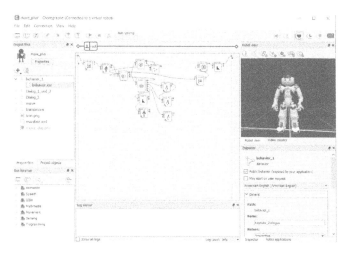

Figure 5.4 Softbank Robotics's Choregraphe Integrated Development Environment

whole classrooms with them (see Chapter 8). For learning how to program, less complex robots and thereby more affordable ones are typically a better option.

Several major educational robotics providers, such as VEX and Make-Bot, offer a full range of products ranging from ready-to-run options to custom hardware. A popular form factor is a little puck-shaped wheeled robot that has an array of sensors around its outer shell. Vex is offering its 123 platform[4], while the famous Khepera puck robot is still available, now in its fourth generation[5]. In terms of educational application, each of these are essentially ready to use. Below we provide a narrow glimpse of the wide range of robots that are available and that can be classed as "ready-to-run".

5.3.1.1 Sony Aibo

Sony with its Aibo robot was arguably one of the first commercially successful zoomorphic robots and during its first production period (1999–2013) it also featured a programming environment called R-CODE. The RoboCup competition included a dedicated Aibo league for many years. In 2018, Sony entered a second production period by releasing its ERS-1000 (see Figure 1.4). In 2019, Sony made new programming tools available. They offer a visual programming platform similar to Blockly for beginners[6] and a developer program for experienced programmers.

5.3.1.2 MakeBot

MakeBot is promoting its mTiny robot that is shaped like a little cat[7]. Giving a robot a zoomorphic shape is intended to make the robot more recognizable, which is particularly appropriate given that this robot is targeted at younger children. Along with external tools, programming this robot relies on basic devices rather than making use of separate computers, keyboards, and mice, which is more appropriate for this intended user group.

5.3.1.3 Ozobot

Ozobot is marketing its Ozobot Bit platform[8] (see Figure 5.5) that can be programmed using Blockly, but also through a colour system that does not require any computer. Aimed at older learners than the MakeBot, for example, there is more of an emphasis on a group educational context. Common with many other robots of this type is that it is a small wheeled robot intended to operate primarily on desks/tables.

Figure 5.5   Ozobot Evo Robot

Source: Ozobot by Evollve, Inc. (www.ozobot.com)

5.3.2 *Construction Kits*

Consistent with the constructionist application of robots to supporting learners in the development of their computational thinking (for example), the construction (or at least modification) of the robot itself prior to the programming may be an essential part of the activity. In this case, it is desirable to make use of robotics products that facilitate this construction process. Below, we provide a brief overview of some of the currently available products. One point to note is that these "kits" are typically not inter-compatible: that is, if parts are not designed specifically for the particular kit you have, then they would not work when used together.

5.3.2.1 LEGO Mindstorms

In Chapter 1, we introduced the history of LEGO Mindstorms. Here, we would like to point out that since the introduction of the latest Mindstorms iteration in 2013, called EV3, little progress has been made by TLG. Instead of creating a more powerful programmable brick that would enable more natural human-robot interaction, for example by using speech recognition or computer vision, TLG released even simpler programmable bricks, such as Spike and WeDo. Several companies are offering more powerful extensions for the Mindstorms platform. Mindsensors, for example, is offering a variety of sensors and actuators, but one of the more advanced products is the Vision Subsystem that enables a Mindstorms brick to use computer vision (see Section 4.2).

5.3.2.2 PiStorms and BrickPi

Both PiStorms and BrickPi offer extensions to the popular Raspberry Pi computer that makes it compatible with the LEGO Mindstorms platform. For this purpose a so called "Shield" is added to the Raspberry Pi that includes the connectors to the LEGO Mindstorms sensors and motors (Figure 5.6). The Raspberry Pi maintains its extendability through its other ports. USB devices, such as microphones, can still be used and also the Raspberry Pi camera module can still be connected. The combination of the processing power of the affordable Raspberry Pi computer with the convenience of the LEGO building system makes this an ideal tool for an advanced robotic learning curriculum.

5.3.2.3 Tinkerbots and Thymio

Both Tinkerbots and Thymio are offering integrated robotic bricks that are compatible with the LEGO system. Neither is able to take advantage of Mindstorms' sensors or actuators. While Tinkerbots has its own modular system of sensors and actuators that can be combined in different ways to create a variety of robots, the Thymio robot (see Figure 5.7) is more similar to the puck robots discussed above.

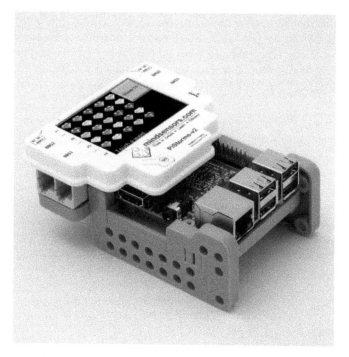

Figure 5.6   The PiStorms shield attached to a Raspberry Pi
        Source: www.mindsensors.com

Figure 5.7   Thymio Robot, made by "the Mobsya Association"
        Source: www.thymio.org

5.3.2.4   SBrick

LEGO is offering electrical components that can be used to build a robot that are not part of the Mindstorms system. The Power Functions product line, for example, features several motors. SBrick is a micro-controller that can be programmed using the Scratch environment described above. It then communicates with a computer using Bluetooth.

5.3.2.5   VEX IQ

Vex Robotics is offering a building system that contains many structural elements such as beams, axles, gears, and wheels. They can be combined with sensors, actuators, and the programmable bricks. None of the elements are compatible with the LEGO system though.

5.3.2.6   REV Robotics (FIRST Global Set)

Rev Robotics is also offering a building system in a manner similar to the LEGO and Vex systems, though incompatible with either. It is, however, currently part of the First League competition as described below (Section 5.5). It therefore is the basis for many robotic projects around the world.

5.3.2.7   Makeblock mBot

Makeblock is offering a building system called mBot, which includes a programmable brick and a metal-based construction kit that allows the students to build a variety of robots.

5.3.3   TurtleBot

The TurtleBot is aimed at higher education and goes through a number of iterations. The first TurtleBot was a modified version of a Roomba vacuum cleaner, made available by iRobot. The latest TurtleBot is sold by the Korean company Robotis. Unique about the latest version is its open nature: all parts, from the plastic to the electronics, and all software are open source and can be replicated with the help of a 3D printer and advanced electronics manufacturing. The computational core, a Raspberry Pi, is one of the most affordable and popular single-board PCs. The TurtleBot runs the ROS and is used to teach university students advanced concepts in the programming and control of mobile robots (see Figure 5.8).

5.3.4   Custom Hardware

The arrival of affordable 3D printers has enabled students to create their own robotic components. This can be used to extend existing systems, such as the LEGO System, with parts that are not commercially available (see Figure 5.9). But it can also be used to create completely new and/or customized robots. These robots and their parts can be freely shared online to enable others to benefit from the designs. Dedicated online sharing websites, such as Thingiverse[9], and GrabCAD[10] are popular forums for exchanging 3D data, including plans for robots or parts of robots.

This culture of "open source hardware" empowers students by not having to start from scratch. A good example of such an open source hardware project is the inMoov robot[11]. The life-sized humanoid robot can be printed with a conventional 3D printer (see Figure 5.10). Only the electrical parts need to be ordered separately. A number of these robots have consequently been built with variations in colour, for example, and in some of the smaller parts, as desired by the makers.

Robots require a micro-controller as described in Chapter 4 to process sensory data and to control all of the robots' movements. The inMoov robot, for example, uses the popular Arduino controller which is available in different versions[12]. Also the Raspberry Pi (in its various versions) is often used in robotic projects (Alnajjar et al., 2021).

Figure 5.8   A TurtleBot 3 robot with modified hardware. The robot interacts with people and serves snacks during meetings. The robot is programmed over a six-week period by masters in engineering students

Figure 5.9 A 3D-printed LEGO brick

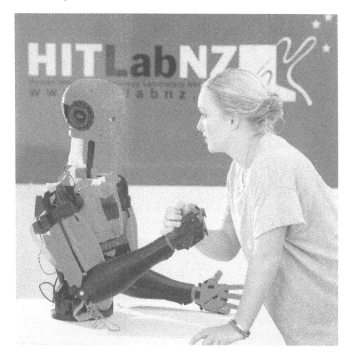

Figure 5.10 The open source hardware robot InMoov

5.4 Software

In addition to the hardware of the robot—those aspects you can see, feel, and manipulate, for example—there is software that is required to do the programming. The software is important as this is the part that the learners will interact with (both after construction of the robot body itself, but also if it is ready-to-run) given the typical programming tasks assigned to them. In this section, we take a look at the aspects of the software that are accessible to the learner (for the aspects of software that allow the robots to operate, see Chapter 4).

5.4.1   Programming

Almost all robots require some level of programming and often learning how to program is the main educational goal. Robots and robotic platforms offer a huge variety of development tools ranging from visual programming, such as Scratch, to higher level programming languages such as Java. If desired, students can also dive into the lower levels of software systems and program the robot using programming languages that are closer to the hardware such as C or even Assembly.

Good robotic platforms offer a variety of software options. The LEGO Mindstorms robotic platform, for example, can be programmed using visual programming language based on National Instruments' LabView, with Java using LeJos[13] and even C[14]. NAO robots use the virtual programming environment Choregraphe with the underlying programming language Python. NAO robots can also be programmed in various languages with the assistance of the NAOQI API.

5.4.2   Simulation Environments

Building, testing, and optimizing a robot's software and hardware is time consuming and several tools have been developed to speed up the process. One approach is to create a complete simulation of the robot that then operates in a virtual environment. The simulation often includes important aspects of our world, such as gravity and collision detection. The robot's sensors are able to detect the virtual world's walls just as they would detect a real wall.

Testing and optimizing programs can be greatly improved since even systematic testing is possible. For teaching a robot how to maintain balance it might, for example, be necessary to try out a range of different parameters. In a virtual environment, a series of simulations for each parameter can be scripted and played through automatically and the results recorded. A similar activity with a real robot would require lengthy changing of parameters, downloading the software into the robot, running the robot in the environment, and recording the results. Moreover, a

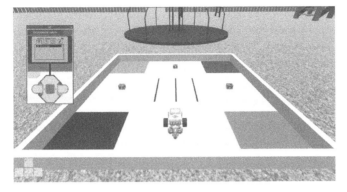

Figure 5.11   A LEGO Mindstorms robot is simulated in the Virtual Robotics Toolkit

Source: Virtual Robotics Toolkit, a software from Cogmation Robotics Inc., Winnipeg, MB, Canada

simulation does not necessarily need to run in real time: time can be sped up allowing the simulation to run faster and produce results sooner.

There are simulation environments available that can simulate different robots. CoppeliaSim[15] and Webots[16] are aimed at higher education and allow various simulated models of robots to be programmed using text coding. The latter has a library of robots that include NAO, Mindstorms, and many others. For the LEGO Mindstorms platform, the dedicated Virtual Robotics Toolkit (see Figure 5.11) is available[17] that not only simulates the Mindstorms robot but can also import the enormous library of LEGO parts that can be used with the Mindstorms. Custom-made LEGO models can be built with established digital LEGO building tools such as LEGO Digital Designer[18] and LDraw[19]. These models can then be imported and their function simulated with the Virtual Robotics Toolkit.

5.5   Robotic Competitions

A popular tool to promote robotics, and indeed wider engagement in STEM, is competitions. In these events students compete against each other, often in teams, to accomplish a set of tasks. Many competitions are local, in individual schools, or regions, but there are also international competitions in which the learners can participate. The First League and Robocup are two main examples of such robotic competitions.

One discipline in these competitions is based on a robot platform that all participants would use, such as Aibo, NAO, or Pepper. All teams use the exact same robotic hardware and their task is to program the best behaviour to accomplish a task. This leads to a focus on the programming aspect rather than the robot hardware itself.

Another, more open, competition is to give each team the same set of components, such as REV Robotics's FIRST Global Set or LEGO Mindstorms. Here, the students have to build a robot and program its behaviour, thus fully incorporating the constructionist perspective (Section 2.1.3, p.18).

Finally, there are competitions in which only certain limiting factors are defined, such as the maximum dimensions of the robot. Within these constraints, the teams are allowed to build their own custom robot.

Robotic competitions are not limited to students. The Defence Advanced Research Projects Agency (DARPA) organizes Grant Challenges in which, for example, autonomous vehicles have to drive by themselves to a destination. The difficulties of these tasks exceed that of what could be expected of a school team, but nevertheless provide a significant motivation for novel development (albeit in the research domain).

5.6   Challenges

While the use of robots as an educational tool has been enthusiastically embraced by educators across the world, there are still some challenges. We discuss here the main challenges and possible solutions.

5.6.1   *A Lack of Teacher Confidence*

While many schools will invest in the purchase of robots, the initial enthusiasm sometimes wanes and the robots remain locked away in a cupboard without being used or without their full potential as an educational tool being realized[20]. Teachers' lack of enthusiasm for robots can often be traced back to their lack of confidence in using robots, which is probably due to their lack of technical affinity as shown in prior work (Reich-Stiebert and Eyssel, 2016), or to a lack of buy-in or mistrust of technology. In many schools, the use of robots is not part of the core curriculum and the effort involved in setting up a session with robots often is seen to outweigh the benefits of using robots. In schools with successful and sustained robot education, the sessions are often carried out by a single, dedicated teacher or a parent who goes well beyond the call of duty in organizing and offering the robot programming sessions (la Velle and Georgeson, 2017).

Teachers receive no formal training in the use of robots as educational tools. And, while there is continued professional development available for teachers, most teachers never receive the training required to become confident in the use of digital media, let alone in offering robot sessions or sessions with robots. As a teacher typically has a career spanning 40 years, a reluctance to engage with robots as education tools is likely to persist. A teacher graduating now (2020) without receiving training will still be active in 2060. This is likely to change as more teacher training programmes offer robotics courses to their students. Most are still on a voluntary and non-assessed basis, but some teacher training includes robot education as part of the curriculum[21]. Another important fact is that all teachers entering the profession now are part of a digital world. This can only benefit the use of robots in education and, subsequently, the benefits that this may bring.

5.6.2 Robots in the Curriculum

While computational thinking is by now rolled out across all primary and secondary school curricula, the use of robots is not necessarily part of that. The European Union has through its initiative encouraged member states to implement computational thinking and computer science in compulsory education. Grassroots initiatives such as the EU Code week, in which thousands of activities are organized throughout Europe to bring children into contact with coding, are supported by the European Commission and industry partners. The United States launched the "Computer Science for All" initiative encouraging computational thinking and computer science to become core to the curriculum starting with primary education.

Robots, however, are largely missing from these recommendations and it is entirely up to schools, local authorities or countries to decide whether or not they wish to invest in robots. Given the initial outlay for robots being quite substantial, schools often look towards alternative ways of teaching computational thinking and programming, as this often does not require any additional investment.

5.6.3 Effectiveness of Robots in Education

Robots have been used in schools for decades for reasons discussed earlier. They are not only advertised as supporting the constructionist learning of STEM subjects, but also are seen as offering an opportunity for widening participation, as a way to address the shortage in a technically skilled workforce, or in addressing the digital literacy of learners.

But despite the many years of practice and hundreds of reports on the use of robots in education, there is little information available on their effectiveness and impact. Recently, Pedersen et al. (2020) set up a review to help schools decide on which robotics products to invest in. They looked at 29 educational robotics products and collated 301 studies looking at their outcomes. They concluded that there were not enough studies to compare the effect of the products and more research is therefore needed. Measuring the impact of robot education is feasible in the short term—testing whether children have acquired certain concepts through the constructionist learning with robots—but effects over the long term are difficult to measure as they are impossible to separate from the other influences on learning outcomes and attitudes.

5.7   Outlook

After 50 years of using robots in formal and informal learning, it is clear that robots (as a tool in education) are here to stay. It is difficult to say what the future holds for robots in education, but we can be fairly confident that some core concepts will remain and that new developments will trickle through to education.

The mobile robot, whether as a ready-to-run device or construction kit, will likely remain the mainstay of robot education, with exercises such as building and programming a line follower being a key component in any course. But new forms of robots are entering the classroom. Social robots are a different family of robots that are not built to move around like mobile robots, but instead are aimed at interacting with people using the same social signals used in human-to-human interaction. These robots might have eyes, a head, a mouth, and a body, and programming these robots will require very different components. Elements such as moving forward, moving backwards, or rotating are not relevant here. Instead skills such as gesturing, understanding language, speaking, detecting people, or recognizing people become relevant. These robots open new possibilities and are bound to draw in new audiences (see Figure 5.12).

An important development in the field is the renewed interest in AI. Through the increase in computer power and the availability of large data sets, AI can now do things which were up until recently impossible. Speech recognition, object and face recognition, translation, or speech production have all been lifted to new levels in the recent AI revolution. Through the use of cloud computing, these technologies have also become

Figure 5.12 The Opsoro (Open Platform for Social Robots) robot kit: a social robot aimed at teaching STEM by building social interaction

available to everyone with an internet connection. A rather standard computer connected to the internet can now send camera images or audio recordings to servers in the cloud, and moments later state-of-the-art AI will report on who and what can be seen in the image, and what was heard or said in the audio recording. This means that robots can still be cheap and battery powered, as the high-powered computation is done in the cloud. This opens up new possibilities for robots, possibilities which involve AI. Imagine a robot now recognizing you and reacting to your emotional expressions, coming towards you when you smile, comforting you when you frown, and cowering in fear when you look angry. Already LEGO Mindstorms robots are connected to Amazon Alexa, the interactive voice assistant of Amazon, NAO robots can be linked to chatbots, and the blending of educational robots with cloud services is only expected to increase. This issue has already been explored further in Chapter 4 (p.51).

In recent years robots have been explored as taking an active part in education (interacting socially *with* learners), with the robot taking over tasks of teaching staff as tutors and assistants. All of this is discussed in the next chapter.

Questions for you to think about:

• Why and how do you think robots can support the Arts within STEAM education?

- What are the main components to consider when adapting a robot in an educational context?
- From your own personal experience, how did working with robots at school help your learning?

Future reading:

- Peter J Denning and Matti Tedre. *Computational Thinking*. MIT Press Ltd, Cambridge, Massachusetts, 2019.
- David P Miller and Illah Nourbakhsh. Robotics for education. In Bruno Siciliano and Oussama Khatib, editors, *Springer Handbook of Robotics*, pages 2115–2134. Springer International Publishing, Cham, 2016. ISBN 978-3-319-32552-1. 10.1007/978-3-319-32552-1_79. URL https://doi.org/10.1007/10.1007/978-3-319-32552-1_79.

Notes

1. Data in Europe shows that computer science degrees at university level struggle with gender balance. In Belgium only 7.0% of (computer science) students are female, Germany has 20.6% female students, with Bulgaria having the highest number at 29.8% (Europe, 2020).
2. https://developers.google.com/blockly
3. Open source and a wide range of computer science and programming based tutorials are provided, such as one-hour tutorial sessions known as the Hour of Code.
4. https://www.vexrobotics.com/vex123
5. http://www.k-team.com/khepera-iv
6. https://visual-programming.aibo.com/us/
7. https://www.makeblock.com/mtiny
8. https://ozobot.com/educate
9. https://www.thingiverse.com
10. https://grabcad.com
11. http://inmoov.fr
12. https://www.arduino.cc
13. https://lejos.sourceforge.io
14. https://www.ev3dev.org/docs/tutorials/getting-started-with-c/
15. http://www.coppeliarobotics.com
16. https://cyberbotics.com
17. https://www.virtualroboticstoolkit.com/
18. https://www.lego.com/en-us/ldd
19. https://www.ldraw.org

20. Similar tendencies to not or wrongly use classroom technologies can be identified in the context of Interactive Whiteboards.
21. One operational example is the 6 ECTS module RoboTeach offered to student teachers at Marburg University, Germany (see Chapter 8).

6 The Robot as a Social Agent

...robots show great promise when teaching restricted topics, with effect sizes on cognitive outcomes almost matching those of human tutoring

Belpaeme et al., 2018a

What is covered in this chapter:

- Working *with* robots as social agents;
- The definition of social robots;
- Roles social robots can take up in education;
- The promise and excitement of social robots in education.

6.1 What Makes a Social Robot?

Robots that are available for use in educational contexts range from robotic kits, such as the LEGO Mindstorms (as mentioned in Chapter 5), to robots with a head, arms, and legs—the so-called humanoids—to even androids and geminoids—robots that are virtually indistinguishable from people. However, what features and functions does a robot need to have to be a *social robot*? A social robot broadly speaking needs two elements: its embodiment on various dimensions (Ferrari and Eyssel, 2016) and its ability to interact with humans on an emotional and cognitive level (Breazeal, 2005; Vogan et al., 2020). Embodiment as a concept is multi-faceted—here, we simply mean the robot's physical presence. This gives you the feeling of co-presence and co-location with the robot in a physical space. This is different to a virtual agent that offers interaction capabilities only through digitally mediated environments, such as a computer screen, augmented reality, or virtual reality (Obaid et al., 2011).

Equally important is the behaviour which makes us perceive a robot as a social agent. The ability for a robotic agent to interact on a social level with a human user is based on an exchange of information that is exhibited by the verbal and/or non-verbal social cues. That means, in human-robot interaction, the ability of the robot to display social cues, such as verbal and nonverbal interaction abilities, for example speech, the display of emotion through gestures, or the signalling of attention through eye gaze. These have been shown to contribute positively to the perception of the robot as an interaction partner, the interaction quality, and associated outcomes of the joint interaction between the human and robot. For further details on the human social aspects and the robotic technologies that support them you can refer to Chapters 3 and 4, respectively.

The robot does not necessarily need to be humanoid. Simple robots can also be social. A box on wheels (such as electronic kits like Boebot or Thymio) that responds to your presence, reads the emotion in your voice and responds appropriately can also be considered as a social robot. Much like some animals—think of dogs, cats, and horses—can interpret human signals and respond in a contingent manner, so can robots. However, a human-like appearance and the behaviour of a robot may require less effort for human users to interpret (Manzi et al., 2020b).

6.2   Roles of Social Robots in Education

While social skills most certainly are part and parcel of education, there remains the question of how a social robot could be incorporated into an educational application. People, be it children or adults, learn in different situations in which they take on different roles: for example, one could learn by working through a problem with a colleague or friend as a co-learner just as one could learn by being instructed by another. Or one could also learn by teaching a peer or manipulating a tool or artefact.

These different roles may be appropriate in different situations or even dependent on the material/topic to be learned. In the same way, social robots may take on a variety of different roles in the educational context, each of which builds on the social competencies described above. Mubin et al. (2013c) made one of the first attempts to delineate the primary roles of a robot in the classroom and identified three roles: tutor, tool, and peer.

In this section, we provide a summary of these and many more roles, explore their requirements and features, and provide examples of how these social robot roles have been applied in research and commercial settings. Many of the roles make an appearance in the context of child education; hence, the lion's share of research has focused on these. At the same time, there are a growing number of projects aiming at integrating robots into higher education.

6.2.1 The Robot as a Tutor

The most common role of a robot is as a tutor. In a survey of recent robots in education studies, 48% of robots were used as a tutor (Belpaeme et al. 2018a; see also Reich-Stiebert and Eyssel 2016). In this role the robot typically has a one-to-one interaction with the learner (Serholt et al., 2014) and occasionally has a one-to-few interaction (Mubin et al., 2019a). The robot as a tutor is perhaps the most pragmatic, most promising yet most challenging use of a social robot in education. The robot can offer individual attention in a manner that can augment the work of a teacher in a typical classroom set-up. It can help children who fall behind, or can challenge children who are ahead, without disrupting the usual classroom activities. It has infinite patience and the learner can practise subjects as long as the robot remains available. Furthermore, the robot is often seen as non-judgemental by the learner, thereby removing the anxiety often associated with answering questions with a human tutor or teacher.

A tutor robot adapts its responses and tutoring style to the learner and this personalization can go beyond the curriculum. A tutoring robot might have information about your life outside the classroom or about how you felt the last time it met you (Ahmad et al., 2019). It might engage in some friendly conversation, enquiring about how you did in last weekend's football game, or whether you enjoyed swimming with your friends. These behaviours add to the social appearance of the robot and in human teachers such aspects are known to be conducive to a good relationship between the teacher and the student, often resulting in better learning outcomes (Wilson and Locker Jr, 2007; Witt et al., 2004).

With the robot as a tutor, a range of research studies have explored the impact of the robot in terms of learning outcomes, as well as their perceptions of the learning process. The typical arrangement used in these experimental settings is a single robot tutor supporting a single child (although there are examples of tutor robots guiding a small group of people), where the learner receives targeted support in addition to their regular taught activities. These interactions can take place in a classroom with other children and teacher(s) present or in more quiet spaces outside of the classroom.

There are a number of variations in robot tutoring that have been explored using controlled studies in university laboratories and field trials (for example in schools or hospitals). Just like good human teachers are known to use more verbal and non-verbal expressivity, a similar effect has been demonstrated in robot tutors. For example, Kennedy et al. (2017a) demonstrated that children recalled more of a story told to them by a robot if it employed non-verbal behaviours used by human teachers compared with if it did not. The concept of personalization has been similarly shown to have a positive impact on the perception of the tutor robot. Gordon et al. (2016), for example, demonstrated an increase in valence of learners interacting with a personalized robot tutor, and subsequent learning outcomes. Leyzberg et al. (2018) showed that when the robot personalized the lessons to the level of the learner this led to improved learning outcomes. Important to note is that there are some limitations and concerns related to the use of robot tutors. The three most important ones are privacy concerns, the challenges with classroom discipline, and technical shortcomings. Serholt (2018), for example, analysed interactions of a social robot tutor with children in a school over a period of three-and-a-half months. It was found that breakdowns in the interactions occurred, often caused by a misunderstanding of context and content on the part of the robot. Designing a good robot tutor is particularly challenging: a number of studies have shown that simply adding human-like behaviours to the robot does not necessarily lead to improved learning outcomes for the learners (Kennedy et al., 2015), as the social behaviour of the robot can sit in the way of the tutoring task of the robot. Social behaviour should be used sparingly and appropriately (Kennedy et al., 2017b) and only when it supports the educational role of the robot. For example, gestures and speech can be effective social cues, but when used at the wrong time they can be utterly distracting. The same applies to the personalization of social behaviour. One study found that the personalization of verbal encouragement led to worse task performance than having a robot show a wide range of encouragement (Gao et al., 2018). These examples, and others besides, demonstrate that despite the promise of social tutor robots, there remains a range of practical and principled issues that limit, at the moment at least, the more extensive deployment of such devices.

Language learning, and specifically second language (L2) tutoring, has been identified as a particularly promising application of robot tutoring (Belpaeme et al., 2018b). A child's first language is acquired through interacting with parents, siblings, and peers, but quite often a L2 is learned in a formal school setting and the process of learning is radically different. No longer is the language learnt through interaction, but instead through the rote learning of vocabulary lists and grammatical rules. This stark contrast in mode of learning is to a large extent due to resource limitations. The teacher is not in a position to interact in the target language with individual children in the classroom and instead resorts to class-based teaching. In addition, the teacher might not be confident enough to speak the target language or does not master all aspects of the target language. For example, native English speaking teachers will often struggle with French pronunciation and make "un, deux, trois" into a mangled "uhn, doh, twah".

This is where a robot tutor can make a contribution. The robot can support the child in learning a L2 language through not just offering tutoring, but through offering genuine interaction in the target language. Not only can the robot offer language lessons, but the robot is likely to have a better accent than the teacher and it allows for practice to be repeated as often as needed (Chang et al., 2010). Moreover, the learner might experience less foreign language anxiety: we all have felt the pang of anxiety when we were asked to speak or read out loud in a language which is not our own but this fear tends to disappear in front of a robot. Not only because the robot is the only one overhearing your strangled pronunciation but also because robots are generally considered to be non-judgemental. The robot does not care if your "Quel âge as-tu?" sounds like "kell arge ass too". It will correct you with infinite patience and no judgement.

The L2TOR project studied how robots could support L2 tutoring for young children (Vogt et al., 2019). In 2018, a team of international researchers tried to see if a social robot could teach French to Dutch preschool children. The *critical age hypothesis* in developmental linguistics suggests that learning a language is best done as young as possible, certainly before hitting puberty, as beyond that age the ability to learn a language with native proficiency is lost. For this reason the researchers focused on children aged five. Younger than that and the children not only struggle with the structure of the tuition, but often are also intimidated by the robot.

The robot, a Softbank Robotics NAO humanoid, sat next to children on the floor, and together the child and robot could operate a tablet screen on which pictures and animations were shown (see Figure 6.1)[1]. To counter the limited ability of the robot to understand children's speech (Kennedy et al., 2017c), the tablet also served as an input device. To give their responses to questions, the children were asked to tap the correct response on the screen. The robot taught the children a series of 34 English words, embedded in short sentences. These words were nouns, such as giraffe, monkey, boy, but also counting and spatial words, prepositions and action verbs, such as one, two, three, behind, or jumping.

Figure 6.1 A social robot supporting a five-year-old during the learning of a second language

The children took a pretest, followed by seven lessons and finished with a post-test and a delayed post-test. Children came from preschools in The Netherlands, and were assigned to one of four groups. A group who learned using a tablet but without a robot, a group who learned with a robot, a group who learned with a robot which used gestures to support the meaning of words (e.g., words like *monkey* or *behind* were acted out by the robot), and a group who received no instruction at all (the control group). The study investigated the effectiveness of a social robot for teaching children new words, looked at the added benefit of a robot's iconic gestures on word learning and retention, and asked if children learn more from a robot than from a tablet alone. The team could show that children are able to acquire and retain English language taught by a robot tutor to a similar extent as when they are taught by a tablet application, but found no beneficial effect of the robot using gestures.

6.2.2   The Robot as a Peer

Social robots have also been applied in education as companions or peers. In this case, the robot would typically take on the role of a co-learner with the person, though generally this has been used with children. In this context, the child and the social robot would explore or work through a task together, incorporating some degree of interactivity such as collaboration, competition and/or turn-taking that builds on the general social behaviours of the robot. Collaborative peer learning has been proposed to come with both motivational and cognitive benefits in terms of both encouraging discovery and learning of basic concepts (Damon, 1984), with further benefits in the acquisition and practice of transferable skills such as improved communication and cooperation (Topping, 2005). Indeed, this approach of using the social robot as a companion/peer is consistent with the tenets of constructivist learning theories, since there is a better alignment of the conceptual structures and language between the learners (see Section 2.1). In fact, there are initial experimental results which suggest that a peer robot, as opposed to a tutor robot, may bring advantages in terms of length of engagement in an activity (a tangram game), with consequent improvements in task performance (Zaga et al., 2015).

In terms of applications, the typical set-up in the context of a social robot as a learning peer is similar to that used when the social robot is applied as a tutor: that is, typically one-to-one interactions between a robot and a single child. There are consequently a range of similar considerations for the robot peer learner: the impact of personalization and interactive behaviours are of particular relevance.

One important element when considering peer robots is the concept of relative social standing or status (Obaid et al., 2016b). In contrast to a tutor whose role is relatively superior in terms of status (having more knowledge/skill in the particular learning domain), a peer would ideally be of the same social status as the learner. This is facilitated by physical size for instance: in the context of mediated interactions, the height of the robot had an impact on the expression of dominance in an interaction (Rae et al., 2013), where if the interaction partner was taller, then dominance was lower. Studies have shown that a taller robot can maintain control over a classroom and children consider a smaller robot more friendly (Bae and Han, 2017a,b). This suggests, though does not definitively prove, that a peer robot should not at least be excessively higher/taller than the learner (Reich-Stiebert et al., 2019). In accordance with this consideration, the robots used are typically smaller—indeed, the NAO small humanoid robot is a standard robot used (Figure 6.2).

Having peer social robots in a classroom to extend the existing support provided by teachers and teaching assistants is one application of great potential. The aim would be that the robot could provide targeted support to individual learners who are perhaps behind or ahead of their classmates, leaving the teaching staff with more time for the other pupils. Given the high cost and/or low availability of additional human teaching support, the use of social robots is promising. Particularly in the case of learners who may be struggling, the potential benefits of interacting with a peer (such as improved communication, cooperation and confidence) provide a good justification for the social robot peer role. However, in the more general case of extending existing teaching structures, the presence of a peer learner in the form of a robot provides a complementary approach to the teacher's role.

In one study, this effect was characterized. Baxter et al. (2017) explored the impact of personalization of a social robot peer on learning outcomes in a UK-based study that put two robots with associated touchscreens into two classrooms for a continuous period of two weeks. Using the same tasks, one robot personalized its actions according to the behaviour and performance of the interacting children, while the other robot maintained consistent non-personalized behaviour throughout. Over this time, the robots operated autonomously and without technical oversight. There was no roboticist present watching what happened, only the usual teaching staff and the children were involved.

In this study, personalization encompassed three different aspects, related both to the *adaptation* of the robot behaviour dependent on the learner's behaviour, and to increasing the *personable* aspects of the robot behaviour. In terms of adaptation, the robot would both align its behaviour with that of the child (including movement, speed, and accuracy) and the performance of the child (i.e., modifying the content of the learning activity according to how well the child was doing). In terms of personable verbal expressivity, this included using the child's name and more informal feedback utterances.

A total of 59 children aged seven to eight took part in the study. They were in two separate classes in the same school—they were independent groups with similar characteristics in the same educational context, and thus ideal in terms of rigorous experimental methodology. There were two learning topics for the children: mathematics (times tables), which they had some familiarity with (but not yet mastery) as part of their existing curriculum, and history, with which they had no prior experience in their curriculum (verified by a pre-study knowledge test). The activity took the form of a two-category sorting task, where both participants (the robot and the child) could drag images around on a touchscreen: as a joint activity, there is the possibility to collaborate on the task.

The results of the study indicated that interaction with the personalized robot peer led to improved learning outcomes in the novel (history) task compared with the non-personalized robot, while this was not as clear in the familiar task (maths). While the children's opinion of the personalized robot was slightly better than the non-personalized robot, this difference was not significant (statistically).

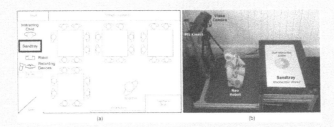

Figure 6.2 (a) The robot was placed in a working classroom, with other children and the teacher, with no roboticists present; (b) the robot and touch-screen that the children used to complete the learning tasks together

6.2.3   *The Robot as a Novice*

In a reversal of roles, a robot can also be used as a student. Here, the robot is presented as a less-knowledgeable peer and the intended learners are invited to teach the robot. This takes the "learning by teaching" approach beyond just learners teaching each other and introduces the robot as the one being taught. This approach builds on two key elements. One is that explaining something to others is perhaps the best way of building a deeper understanding of a skill or subject. The other is that a less-knowledgeable learner, in this case a robot, can boost the confidence of weaker learners. If there is someone who is less able than you and you are asked to help out, and especially if that someone is a robot, then for many children it is a confidence booster. In educational theory this is sometimes known as the *protégé effect*, and the learning outcomes of students teaching others is well-documented (Chase et al., 2009).

The Swiss CoWriter project studied how children could improve their handwriting through teaching a less able robot. The project is interesting not only because it presents the robot as a novice, but also because it uses the robot to teach fine motor skills (Figure 6.3).

The researchers looked at how a robot could be used to improve handwriting. Handwriting is still an important skill and poor handwriting is known to be correlated with poor academic performance later in life. As such, early intervention has been suggested as a possible way to help children. Here the *learning by teaching* approach is used. However, as children with the poorest handwriting skills do not have anyone else to teach handwriting to, a robot was brought in and presented as having even poorer handwriting. The robot, a NAO humanoid, "writes" on a tablet by moving its finger over a tablet upon which poorly formed letters appear, after which the young learner is invited to correct the robot's writing (Hood et al., 2015). Case studies show that teaching the robot forces the children to reflect on their own handwriting and that they become notably better at drawing consistent shapes in a repeated manner (Lemaignan et al., 2016).

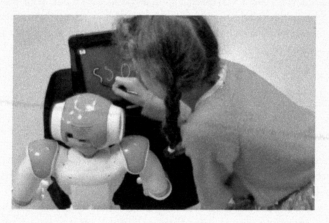

Figure 6.3   Improving handwriting skills by teaching a robot fine motor skills

6.2.4   The Robot as a Classroom Assistant

As pointed out in the introductory chapter to this book, T&L are changing dramatically. Knowledge delivery and knowledge acquisition in many areas are now digital and self-guided and the necessity for people to deliver knowledge in class is increasingly being questioned. Thus, the necessity for personal knowledge delivery by humans or robots may reduce somewhat over time. However, such T&L scenarios of digital integration still involve in-class phases. Such "flipped classroom" scenarios have been advertised for quite some time (e.g., Baker, 2000; Lage et al., 2000) and have increasingly become standard in 21st century T&L. The teacher's role becomes that of a guide who assists the students in performing predefined tasks such as research tasks, question answering, topic-specific competence training, and construction tasks. In such in-class scenarios, the human guide has to apply two central competencies: content-related competencies and technical competencies.

Content-related competencies, that is, flexible question-answering or support during projects, cannot yet be supported by robots. Their ability to understand context, understand natural language, and respond appropriately is currently insufficiently advanced (see Section 4.2.1). On the other hand, they can assist with the closed tasks. For example, the robot can orchestrate a multiple choice quiz or report on live-voting outcomes.

The role of the robot as an assistant can simply be to spice up a lecture, but can also be more instrumental to the subject. For example, Alemi et al. (2014) used a robot to teach English to Iranian secondary school students. While the lessons were taught by the teacher, some of the elements were delegated to the robot. In this context, the robot can be presented as more skilled than the teacher: in L2 learning the robot does not necessarily have a foreign accent and could be used to demonstrate the correct pronunciation of words and sentences.

In a joint project between Marburg University in Germany and the Chinese University of Hong Kong, a so called "Classroom Application Packages" (CAP) was developed which bundles several classroom activities into a complex robot application for Pepper robots, letting the robot autonomously take over many administrative, technical, and content-related tasks (Figure 6.4). The principles of developing and using such CAPs, as well as the technical requirements, are described in Section 8.1.6.

Figure 6.4 Pepper as a classroom assistant

6.2.5   *The Robot as an Examiner*

Assuming that in modern T&L scenarios many exams are electronic exams, where the computer takes full control over delivery of the examination process, a new potential role for robots as examiners emerges. On the one hand, robots could serve as individual examiners, evaluating students during a face-to-face examination. On the other hand, they could help prepare students in class for their assessments by using pre-prepared questions. This form of revision would be particularly attractive for groups, even for large class sizes.

Figure 6.5 A sample application where a Pepper robot takes up the role of examiner

Robots can also act as examiners. In this example, the learner is facing the robot. Questions are displayed on a touch screen while the robot reads out the questions and allows the student to go back or repeat questions. At the end of the test the robot generates the result which is instantaneously sent to the overseeing human examiner (Figure 6.5).

As the robot takes up some of the more menial aspects of examination, the human facilitator is given the opportunity to provide individual and personalized assistance in class rather than merely asking questions. As an application of social robotics, this role thus has the potential to provide a useful function in learning environments.

As a complement to the examination process, there are also examples of a robot functioning as an invigilator. In one study (Mubin et al., 2020), it was shown that while a robot can inhibit cheating in an exam setting, it may be unable to control indiscipline or chatty behaviour during a testing scenario given the technology constraints outlined previously (see Chapter 4).

6.2.6   *The Robot as a Mediator*

Learners are all different; they differ in terms of background, linguistic proficiency, intellectual ability, and social ability. In school, they need to deal with peers that they might or might not get along with and are continuously put to the test both socially and intellectually. Therefore, for some, the educational environment may be extremely challenging. These challenges alter the learners' attitudes towards each other, can increase social tension, and ultimately affect the learning process itself. It is often difficult for a teacher to properly and effectively deal with the students' learning as well as with the social issues that may surface in the class. As such, there is potential for a social robot to act as a mediator in social contexts. It could be a robot that can ease tensions between children and students by providing non-judgemental and independent advice while fulfilling a similar social role (as a peer). While research into the robot in the role of a social mediator is still in its early stages, it has been shown that robots can successfully intervene to prevent conflicts from escalating between children.

For all the determinants and characteristics that have been discussed so far in relation to the robot's abilities and features, the robot may have the potential to create a relational space in which children are engaged, feel comfortable and may be lifted to new levels of learning (recall the several learning theories discussed in Chapter 2, including the Vygotskyan idea of scaffolding and the ZPD—Section 2.1.3). When such a relational space is created, we may assume that the robot-child relationship can be extended to include (at least) another person, another peer for example (Marchetti et al., 2019). The robot may mediate relations and collaborative work, thereby facilitating knowledge and competence learning, or helping to resolve conflict (Vrochidou et al., 2018).

However, we are still quite far from reaching this goal because peer conflicts differ in nature and are very much age-dependent. For example, conflicts at preschool age occur quite often but typically are quickly resolved. Children have conflicts over possession of toys, because they perceive others to invade their space, or because they get in the way of their current activity. The majority of these conflicts are resolved with no external intervention. Teenagers, on the other hand, may engage in more subtle conflicts that involve cultural, religious, and political stances and which can linger for months or even years.

Peers have been found to be effective in resolving conflicts and often the teacher will assign the role of a mediator to one or two children in the group. Through the Teaching Students to Be Peacemakers (TSPs) programme, which emphasizes the internalization of learning and repeated practice (Johnson and Johnson, 1995), some studies showed how young children's conflict resolution competencies can be very effective in resolving conflicts in groups of children (Stevahn, 2004; Stevahn et al., 2000). While these studies involve only children, they provide a suggestion of how a social robot may be able to play a useful role as mediator.

In a successful attempt to develop children's interpersonal conflict resolution skills, children aged between three and six years engaged in a 50-minute play session (Shen et al., 2018). Children were asked to play in pairs and the proposed activities were facilitated by a KeepOn robot. KeepOn is a simple, small, yet expressive robot. The use of this simple robot was to allow the children to engage with each other and not draw attention to the robot (Bridgeland et al., 2013). Also small robots tend to not be as intimidating as a taller robot. To implement the interaction between KeepOn and the children, two experimenters teleoperated KeepOn's movements and speech from behind a screen. They followed a specific interaction protocol, which is in line with the WoZ technique (Chapter 2). To facilitate interaction with the child, KeepOn spoke with an androgynous, child-like voice. Finally, to be able to effectively interact with the children, the robot was endowed with a repertoire of behaviours children typically engage in during normal play. KeepOn's play session interaction was sequenced following the Interaction Pattern approach used in previous investigations (Kahn et al., 2008; Kahn et al., 2012).

Figure 6.6 Two children experiencing a conflict over the sharing of toys, with a KeepOn robot acting as a mediator

Source: Shen et al. (2018)

The introduction of KeepOn to the two children was followed by a stage during which the robot learns something about the children (e.g., their favourite colour), and engages them with humour and play, which not only lets children warm towards the robot but also informs them about the robot's capabilities (Figure 6.6). The experimenter then assigns roles to the play partners and the game, made up out of five activities, begins. The robot directs and facilitates the group activity by encouraging play and complimenting the children's achievements. The core conflict mediation intervention was put in place when children came into conflict over object possession. The conflict mediation consisted of three elements: identify the conflict, offer prompts for constructive conflict resolution, and wrap up and move forward from the conflict. As predicted, children were more likely to resolve interpersonal conflicts in the condition in which the robot provided mediation as compared with a condition in which the robot did not provide such support. Children were four times more likely to resolve object possession conflicts in a constructive manner, not only when the robot facilitated and directed the play, but,

more importantly, when it also offered solutions for the conflict resolution. As argued by the authors of the study, it is likely the robot's
effectiveness in helping resolve the conflicts was also due to some
children perceiving the robot as an *authority*, not only when direct-
ing the play, but when offering prompts to conflict resolution. Another message drawn from the study is that it is very important that
a robot mediator is able to capture children's attention *at the onset* of
the conflict. In fact, children who paused longer after the robot conflict intervention were also those who resolved conflicts in a more
constructive way than those who did not. This pause may in fact
represent the moment in which children retrieved previously learnt
behavioural norms about sharing and turn-taking and allowed themselves to regulate their emotions to face the situation in a calmer
state of mind.

6.2.7   The Robot as a Learning Advisor

Robots that are part of digital T&L scenarios can benefit from increased
computing power and the growing availability of data, which in turn allows for the use of machine learning. One of the reasons for the enormous
amount of data is that many learning processes are taking place through
Learning Management Systems (LMSs), such as Moodle or Blackboard.
Via such platforms, learners create data traces that can be used to determine the frequency and intensity with which they access and process
the learning materials. The analysis of that data is referred to as *learning
analytics*.

One option to analyse and feed this data back to students is to use
chatbots. However, whereas the chatbot technology has become an important and operational feature in many areas, true learning analytics using chatbots has shown little promise so far, mainly due to the difficulty
to build chatbots that can have a fluent conversation on open domains.

A recent combination of a natural language interaction and a humanoid robot, such as Pepper, is shown in Figure 6.7. The robot not
only collects and analyses data on learning but also privately reports the
results and potential concerns to the student. The robot generates an individual student model, which it uses to provide students with feedback on
their performance on the online components of the courses they attend.
Furthermore, the robot can make suggestions about how to improve the
learning process. And last but not least, the robot can act as an info-
point about general questions of selected courses (such as office hours,

Figure 6.7 Pepper discussing a student's learning progress

examination dates, grading). The principles of using humanoid robots in the context of learning analytics are explained in Section 8.2.2.

6.2.8   *The Robot as a Telepresence Tool*

Distance-learning formats are currently widely used (see Chapter 1) and represent a special opportunity for learners and teachers to attend and give classes regardless of large geographical distances, medical restrictions, or restrictions imposed by authorities. With a telepresence robot, a remote operator connects over the internet to a robot and interacts with students and/or teachers via audio and video conferencing, and navigates from a distant location. The application of telepresence robots (Kwon, Oh-Hun et al., 2010) opens up new possibilities at this point as they make distance learning more immersive—allowing interaction partners to have a more embodied experience—and they allow the remote robot operator to move within the distant environment. A robot can be a dedicated telepresence robot, often just consisting of a LCD display or tablet mounted on wheels (such as the iRobi), or it can be a humanoid robot with manipulation capabilities, allowing the remote operator to use the robot arms and hands to manipulate objects near the robot. Thus, a telepresence robot enables the user to virtually attend in a distant location with the ability to see, hear, talk, and move around as if the user were physically present.

About 20 years ago, first attempts were made to include telepresence technologies into educational settings, enabling students to remotely participate in classes. For example, the PEBBLES project helped to connect hospitalized children to their classroom (Weiss et al., 2001). To maintain the connection, two robots, one placed in the classroom and one in the hospital, acted together via real-time audio and video, while the child operated them using a hand-held controller. More recently, mobile telepresence robots—such as the Beam (Suitable Technologies), GoBe (GoBe Robots), or Double (Double Robotics) telepresence robots—have been introduced in educational settings, making it possible to move around the classroom and achieve greater mobility. For instance, mobile telepresence robots were used to teach students a foreign language by a native speaker from a remote location (Tanaka et al., 2014) or have been applied in university courses to enable students from different locations to study together (Fitter et al., 2020).

The great benefit of telepresence robots, as opposed to other distance learning technologies, is that learners can have access to expertise often unavailable at their location or due to personal circumstances, while at the same time experiencing the effects of increased social presence and independence in the remote environment (Kristoffersson et al., 2013). In fact, research findings on the use and effectiveness of telepresence robots highlight their contribution to minimizing physical separation and isolation, and increasing feelings of presence, self-awareness, and social connectedness to others in the distant learning environment (Bell et al., 2016; Fitter et al., 2020; Newhart et al., 2016).

It should be noted, however, that there are considerations that have to be kept in mind. Issues of privacy are a critical topic for telepresence robots, and by extension all social robots, as they can record and store personal data (Newhart and Olson, 2017; Sharkey, 2016). In addition, findings suggest that users are hesitant to engage in social interactions using a telepresence robot due to the difficulty of interpreting nonverbal signals through the robot (Khojasteh et al., 2019). Accordingly, the creation of a safe space fulfilling privacy requirements of the current state, country, or organization (Fischer et al., 2019) and the need for facilitating the initiation of conversations (Khojasteh et al., 2019) present some of the challenges for the purposeful use of this technology. Moreover, data or bandwidth requirements related to high audio and video quality to avoid communication breakdowns, manipulation-capable robot arms to increase the users' capability to actively engage in the remote classroom activity, and height-adjustable platforms to allow eye contact with the interaction partner have been suggested to maximize the functionality of telepresence robots (Cha et al., 2017; Zhang et al., 2018).

In an exploratory case study, the potential of telepresence robots to virtually include homebound children in the classroom was evaluated (Newhart et al., 2016). Children from a public school were equipped with a Double telepresence robot (see Figure 6.8) to attend school in their former classrooms in real time. Due to chronic illnesses, these children could no longer attend classes regularly, which led to severe academic interruptions and social isolation from their classmates.

To obtain a comprehensive insight, classroom observations, focus groups, and interviews were conducted with the children, their parents, classmates, teachers, and school administrators—a total of 61 people were interviewed. Findings have shown that the robot was accepted as a regular member of the classroom and the presence of the robot was considered normal after an initial familiarization period. The most striking result was that all participants indicated that the classroom experience was close to normal, with the added benefit of maintained social connections between peers via the robot.

Figure 6.8 Pepper in class supporting university students

6.3 Outlook

While there is considerable excitement around the potential of social robots in education, it is still early days. Technical progress, while impressive, still is insufficient for the robot to operate as a substitute for human effort in education, or indeed even as an autonomous agent in anything but relatively constrained contexts. And while progress in artificial intelligence and social signal processing is impressive, with computers and robots making impressive leaps in speech recognition, emotion detection, decision-making, and other components essential to making autonomous social robots, robots and computers are still not able to handle things that people excel at. Moravec's paradox still holds: anything that seems hard to us is easy for a machine, and vice versa, anything that people find easy is virtually unattainable by machines. We can build robots which play better chess than anyone on the planet, but we cannot yet build a robot which understands sentences as well as a two-year-old.

Despite the considerable technical hurdles, social robots do have a meaningful contribution to make to education. When the learning task is sufficiently restricted, the teacher available at close hand and the reliance on open social interaction is constrained, social robots put into a wide range of roles have been shown to result in high engagement and enjoyment levels and, under certain circumstances, reliable improvements in learning outcomes. The point here is not that the use of social robots results in *better* learning outcomes than with expert human teachers/tutors, but that given these outcomes, there is plenty of promise in the application of social robots to augment and extend existing and future educational practices.

Furthermore, robots are not often considered as substitutes for a teacher. This on the one hand is due to the undesirability of such a scenario. Replacing teachers by robots is generally frowned upon. On the other hand, teachers have skills that go well beyond what a robot can offer. A robot can teach a narrow subject, take over technical tasks and evaluate the learners' understanding, but it is blind to anything that happens beyond that. The robot cannot read the subtle nonverbal cues of the students, does not know about the tension on the playground, or is unaware of parents splitting up. Teachers do know these things and can instantly and emphatically respond, but robots will, for the time being, fall very much short of what a teacher can offer.

Perceiving the emotional state of the student remains difficult for any robot. Nevertheless, a considerable effort has been made to enable robots to at least utilize expression that could be interpreted as emotions. Even though this communication channel might remain uni-directional for a while, it is important to note that it is impossible not to communicate. Even if the robot is not programmed to express any specific emotions, the student will perceive the robot to have emotions anyway—a phenomenon known as the "media equation" (Reeves and Nass, 1996).

Questions for you to think about:

- What challenges need to be overcome before a robot can be autonomously applied as a tutor in the classroom?
- A teacher would like to use Pepper to teach mathematics to primary school children. Draft learning scenarios for each of the possible roles that Pepper can take in the classroom in this context: tutor, peer, novice, classroom assistant, examiner, and mediator.
- Consider different domain areas that a robot can be used to "teach" in the classroom. What social cues are integral to each domain area (for example, speech and language)?

Future reading:

- Tony Belpaeme, James Kennedy, Aditi Ramachandran, Brian Scassellati, and Fumihide Tanaka. Social robots for education: A review. *Science Robotics*, 3(21):eaat5954, 2018a.
- Terrence Fong, Illah Nourbakhsh, and Kerstin Dautenhahn. A survey of socially interactive robots. *Robotics and Autonomous Systems*, 42(3-4):143–166, 2003. 10.1016/S0921-8890(02)00372-X. URL https://doi.org/10.1016/S0921-8890(02)00372-X.

Note

1. The connection to the computer via a network cable, as shown in Figure 6.1, is necessary to ensure a stable connection between the robot and a computer for image retrieval and image processing. This is discussed further in Section 4.1.

7 Deployment Requirements

Education costs money but then so does ignorance.

Sir Claus Moser

What is covered in this chapter:

- What robot shall I use? Technical requirements;
- Setting up the appropriate context for effective robot deployment: what issues to consider;
- Programming issues: a developmental team.

Before deploying a robot in an educational setting, an educational institution should consider the following questions: Who are the end users? What is the space that the robots will operate in? What educational functions are the robots going to have? And, how are they going to supplement the teacher's role? Answering these questions will help the institution determine the technical requirements and take the necessary administrative steps to set up the context in which the robots will be deployed, considering educational, administrative, and commercial factors.

Furthermore, the use of robots, in whatever setting, requires a number of parameters to be defined, ranging from logistics, via financial to developmental parameters. This chapter will examine the technical and practical requirements for introducing and maintaining a robotic system in an educational setting.

7.1   Selecting a Robot

As described in the previous chapters, robots are available in a large number of different forms and shapes, which support several input/output modalities. The choice of the robot should revolve around the audience and their needs. It may simply even be a question of how much budget the institution may have. The robot should be selected primarily for its capability to perform a target application; moreover, it should facilitate the users in taking advantage of this application and make the learning experience pleasant.

For example, one important aspect concerning the purchase of the robot Pepper from SoftBank Robotics is that you should consider if you want to buy it or lease it. Pepper has a relatively tall stature (120 cm), which is appropriate to convey a greater sense of authority in adult settings. Figure 7.1 specifies further technical details of this robot.

The robot NAO, in contrast, is only 58 cm in height; therefore, it cannot persuasively present itself to adult users as a collaborator or an assistant (see Figure 7.2).

This does not mean that NAO cannot successfully be used as a tool by adults, but the range of its applications hardly involves roles or functions in which the robot needs to have an authoritative role. Further, Pepper is ideal for multi-user interactions whereas NAO is suitable for one-to-one or desk-based interactions. A robot can be multi-functional as different applications can be programmed into it. For example, the robot can be used for modelling, as an information point and for special topic-related information or it can take over specific tasks in class. Also, as shown in Chapter 6, the robot can provide feedback and tutoring to individual learners. If the educational institution's goal is to utilize robots as a tool or an instrument to augment and practise existing curriculum (say learn programming), robots such as LEGO Mindstorms may be more practical.

7.1.1   *Practical Failures and Errors*

On the whole, and apart from their general input/output restrictions pointed out in Chapter 4, robotic systems can face unpredictable practical problems when in use. For example, the robot's reaction may be impaired through lack of visibility or image distortion. Another example is that the embedded interactive devices (e.g., a tablet) and sensors can get involved in interactive situations that are not accounted for, such as sensors being occluded by unprecedented objects or malfunctioning due to dust. Beyond these simple failures, robots may fail completely due to heavy physical interaction with humans. Even a simple network failure

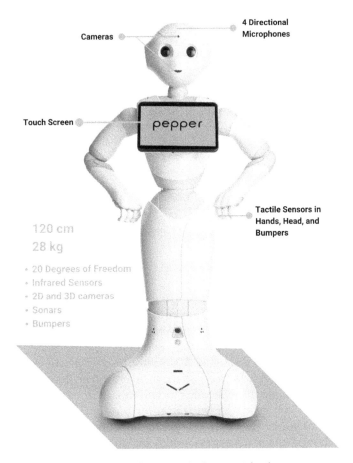

Figure 7.1 The specifications of Pepper, the humanoid robot

Source: SoftBank Robotics

and the inability of the researcher's computer to connect to the robot may mean that the robot is rendered useless.

7.2 Financial Issues

To use a robot in educational settings, you can either purchase a new robot that suits your requirements; customize a robot that you already own; or even build a new one if you require specific functions. Nowadays

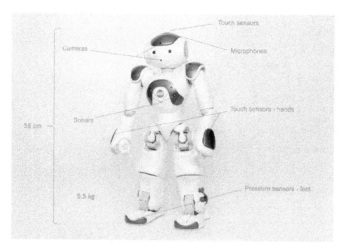

Figure 7.2   The specifications of NAO, the humanoid robot

Source: SoftBank Robotics

3D-printing technology has become a convenient solution to acquiring various kinds of robots with basic functionalities. A robot blueprint can be easily selected and downloaded from an online database to be subsequently printed out with a suitable 3D printer in rigid plastic or other kinds of materials. Designers freely share their prototype designs online and any associated code through wikis or GitHub.

Leasing is also an option for an educational institution or user who does not want to buy or construct a robot: in the future, we will see more and more robot leasing as a business model, making robots affordable to schools with limited budgets for the time frame in which they use it. In the long term, however, this may not be the cheapest option. Many companies or research labs may provide and invoice for consultancy through this model, charging educational institutions a premium to use their robots and their codes.

To purchase a ready-made commercialized humanoid robot costs anywhere between 5,000 € (for a NAO robot) to 16,000 € (for a Pepper robot—educational version). On the other hand, the price of a home-built robot can vary greatly depending on the needs and functionalities combined and starts from 4,000 € (such as the BuSaif robot shown in Figure 7.3). These prices may vary and may depend on other factors such as shipping costs and quarantine requirements.

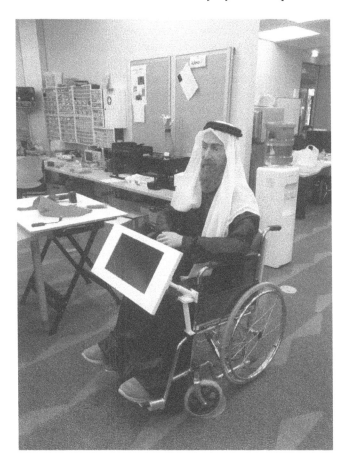

Figure 7.3   The BuSaif humanoid robot (Android-based system developed in UAE University)

7.2.1   Maintenance

Unless you are a professional software or mechatronics engineer, the maintenance of a robot can be a challenge. In order to avoid dealing with malfunctioning robots, it may be convenient to extend the warranty on the robot from the vendor or enlist the assistance of a professional engineer. As it is relatively difficult to find a licenced technician for your robot's maintenance, it is important that the mode of maintenance and the availability of maintenance staff is agreed with the seller during the stipulation of the contract. A manufacturer should always offer initial training to ensure correct robot use and therefore reduce the need for

maintenance, but also provide fast maintenance services and user training to fix technical problems with malfunctioning robots. Previously, Soft-
Bank Robotics, the company manufacturing the famous NAO and Pepper
robots, required robots to be shipped to their head office in Paris, France,
when any repairs were necessary. More recently, it has opened up re-
gional offices which can also provide technical and maintenance services.
This can save crucial time in an already time-critical research project and
guarantee the permanent availability of a sufficient number of robots in
the educational setting.

7.2.2   Insurance

Robots are expensive and can be prone to damage. Legs can break, the
sensors may be impaired, or the robot could lose its ability to move
around, therefore they frequently need to be repaired. Many users of the
NAO robot have commented how its fingers have simply snapped during
packing and unpacking the robot. Any kind of repair will involve additional costs. With technical insurance, these problems can be eased and
repairs can be financed. For example, as a guideline, the annual insurance flat rate for a Pepper robot in Germany is about 200 €. Sometimes,
the insurance of the robot may be included in the assets insurance of the
educational institution which owns the robot.

7.3   The Infrastructure

The infrastructure in which robots are used and maintained heavily depends on its use. For their use as assistants in the classroom, for example,
they need to be transported to their "working" area. It is also useful to
test them in a safe training area before the time of performance. If they
are used as tools, then a possible setting is that they have a permanent location where they are programmed and taken care of. Even the simplest
issue can arise, as to where the robots will be stored overnight if the experiment or research runs for multiple days. The following sections seek
to define and address the central infrastructural parameters for robots.

7.3.1   A Development and Testing Arena

Programmers should have a testing area where the robots can move
around almost freely without any obstacles in the way. The area should
be modelled relatively similar to the real environment to allow for realistic testing scenarios. In addition, this area should be as close as possible

Figure 7.4 The Robotikum makerspace

to the place where the robot is programmed and maintained to avoid excessive movement.

A completely different set of rules can be defined for using robots as tools in specific makerspaces. Here a sufficient number of PCs or laptops should be available for the training groups, free areas for the testing of robot mobility should be created, and simple backgrounds, e.g., white walls for the application of object recognition principles, should be part of the environment. And to protect the robots from damage, the floor must be cleared and ready to be moved on to ensure the robots are not damaged when falling over. An example of such a makerspace is the "Robotikum" as shown in Figure 7.4 and discussed in Chapter 8.

7.3.2 Transport

Currently, robots cannot move freely in unknown territory and, if they can, they are far too slow or can only move short distances. Thus, they cannot move independently to their destination but have to be transported to where they will be used. For example, small robots, such as NAO, can simply be put in a suitcase that would fit on board an aircraft. On the other hand, a Pepper robot is more difficult to move around a building. They can be moved on purpose-made trolleys, but for other locations over

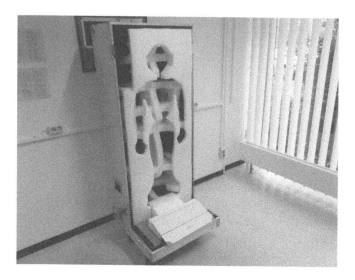

Figure 7.5 A standard transport box for Pepper robots

longer distances they need a purpose-built transportation box. Figures 7.5 and 7.6 exhibit typical transport devices for NAO and Pepper.

As a consequence of these logistical challenges, the regular location of a robot should be easily accessible. For example, a clear exit with a ramp for Pepper robots is necessary to transport the robot from place to place, for example from the development area to the classroom. Special transportation also needs to be arranged for Pepper, as it does not fit in a normal sedan car, rather it is feasible to use accessible taxis and SUVs for this purpose. Such transportation vehicles will also charge for their services.

7.3.3 Preparation for In-Class Use

Preparing a robot for classroom use is another complex logistical enterprise. Apart from the aforementioned transportation issues, where in many institutions staircases, elevators, and narrow corridors have to be taken into account, time may be another problem. To set up a robot so that it can execute applications in time, at least 30 minutes is required. This allows for time to remove the robot from its transport device, put it into a safe but accessible position, boot the robot, connect it to the internet, prepare the desired applications, and have it ready to start on time.

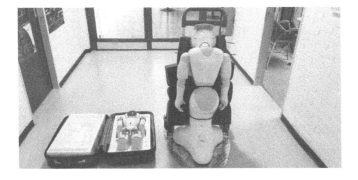

Figure 7.6 Transport devices for NAO and Pepper robots

Additionally, one has to consider audio issues in classes with more than about 30 participants, where it may be hard to understand what the robot says without speech amplification. In such cases, it is common to equip the robot with a wireless microphone, link that to an amplifier and carefully test it before class starts (see Figure 7.7).

Moreover, one has to select a suitable position for the robot: free from visual disturbances, such as bright light and big light bulbs, or audio distractions. Since extended motion is currently not required for classroom applications, and would anyway be too complicated to implement, further actions are not necessary. Robots such as Pepper and Baxter have extensive arm reach and should ideally be more than an arms distance from any obstacles such as furniture or humans.

Finally, the on-board batteries of robots such as NAO (90 minutes) and Pepper (12 hours) enable a limited run-time. So, when working with robots, one has to ensure sufficient power supply and special socket outlets with surge protection from voltage spikes are nearby.

7.3.4 Internet Access

Whereas robots that are used as tools can dispense with internet access in most cases (a big advantage for schools with slow or even no internet access, where Bluetooth can be an alternative) most partnership applications on robots require stable internet access that has a bandwidth of 2.4 hertz or 5 hertz. This is to avoid complications with existing networks and for security and confidentiality reasons. It is recommended not to use standard networks, instead robot applications should have their own dedicated network (Giaretta et al., 2018). On many occasions, due to the extensive security of such networks, robots cannot even connect to them.

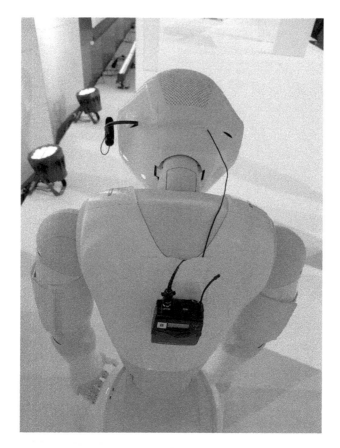

Figure 7.7 Pepper with a wireless microphone

In some institutions, these networks will even be activated only in dedicated areas and, additionally, for a predefined duration. When internet connectivity is not essential, the most robust networked set-up is to use a local router. This bypasses any networking glitches.

7.4   Development/Programming

Programming the robot should not be a big challenge. In the following section, we provide the reader with advice on how to handle robot programming and development.

7.4.1   *The Developmental Team*

Robot development should not rest on the shoulders of one individual. While one or several programmers are required, team members increase the potential of robot applications and thus challenge the programmers. This combination seems best suited to enhance the robot's potential. It combines interdisciplinary and algorithmic thinking.

If there is no alternative, one can purchase programs for NAO and Pepper robots from commercial software developers. However, since these are often not specialized for educational applications, this alternative must be considered the ultimate alternative rather than a standard solution.

Each user-friendly robot should be supported by a community. The aim of the community is to provide technical and practical support for the use of the robot. You do not have to be a professional programmer to handle the robot, however, you need to have basic computer user skills, basic programming, and logistical skills, as well as access to technical support. For example, for the NAO and Pepper robots this community development area is: https://developer.softbankrobotics.com/. SoftBank also provides an online forum where one can receive responses from the community to technical or software-related predicaments—see here: https://community.ald.softbankrobotics.com/en/content/welcome-aldebaran.

7.4.2   *Social Media*

Today, the development and programming of digital applications and scenarios also requires the use of social media. Collaborative tools such as Facebook, Instagram, Twitter, or even YouTube should become integral not only to the development of the robots, but also as platforms for the target audiences. Using these channels, additional explanations can be given, questions can be posed and answered by the communities, and new developments can be advertised. Some of these channels even have licenced their videos as CC BY (Creative Commons Attribution), allowing their download and reuse. An example is the video channel of the German RoboPraX-Project: https://bit.ly/2ON8qLX.

Some YouTube channels are dedicated to robot programming, such as the YouTube channel showcasing how to program NAO and other robots: https://www.youtube.com/user/robotphilip.

In addition to these options, there are first MOOCs on educational robots in general or to support the use of robots as tools (e.g., NAO). The best known example is the online course RoboBase that precedes

NAO makerspaces thus allowing Flipped Classroom formats to be used: https://www.oncampus.de/weiterbildung/moocs/robobase.

7.4.3 Installation

Setting up a newly purchased robot is not as simple as setting up a laptop PC or a smartphone. Even though you do not have to be "fluent" in all areas of web technology, a certain amount of expertise is required. For example, one has to register the robot on the manufacturer's website, connect the robot to the internet to install the desired language packages, download the latest robot apps for the respective model, and make the robot ready for use. This also requires the installation of the development software on one's computer and setting up necessary paths for each library within the computer. One critical issue to keep in mind during installation of robot software, is the operating system that the user owns. Windows and MAC can have drastically different installation requirements. Setting up appropriate paths is an integral step in installation of any robotic software. In Windows, this can easily be done through the environment option in the control panel. In MAC environments, setting up paths requires knowledge of UNIX commands. Also, for example, Pepper cannot work on the latest versions of MAC (such as 10.13) unless System Integrity Protection is turned off. A primer on installing Pepper's SDK on the latest versions of MAC can be found here: https://ai-coordinator.jp/pepper-python-2-7-sdk.

7.4.4 The Developmental Environment

In some cases, such as the NAO and Pepper robots, a standard laptop or desktop PC is needed in order to connect to the robot and ultimately control the robot. Mobile devices such as smartphones or tablet PCs can be utilized to control a robot, like a remote control, but can rarely be used for development purposes. Both NAO and Pepper provide flexibility in terms of how they can be programmed. The visual software Choregraphe can be used to animate Pepper and NAO in both physical and virtual form. The software development environment running in the background of Choregraphe is programmed in Python, so researchers and users can also program these robots externally to Choregraphe in any Python IDE. Recently, this situation has become slightly more complicated since SoftBank Robotics introduced Pepper robot updates programmed in Android/Java in 2019.

For example, Figure 7.8 shows a simple WoZ interface designed in Python to generate responses from Pepper at the click of a button.

Figure 7.8   A sample WoZ interface for Pepper

7.5   Outlook

At first glance, any sum of money invested in using a humanoid robot in class, such as Pepper, hardly pays off. The logistical problems, the developmental effort and the costs are currently overwhelming. But has that not always been the case with modern technology?

Let us recall that 20 years ago hardly anyone could easily move a data projector around let alone finance it. Costs and logistics were almost insurmountable. Today, no one talks about data projectors anymore: they are cheap, omnipresent and easily moved.

The parallel with robots is obvious: not only from an economic point of view, in which the robot could be a good investment in the long run, but also from the perspective of having a robot in a classroom to add innovation and creativity.

But more importantly, robots can also unlock new educational options. And in the case of makerspaces with robots of whatever kind, the investments have already paid off.

Questions for you to think about:

- What trade-offs are prevalent in the choice of a robot for educational scenarios?
- What software implementation methodologies can be employed while creating educational scenarios with humanoid robots?
- Does drag-and-drop software provide sufficient capability and features for creating educational scenarios? What are the pros and cons of the different approaches to programming a robot?
- Should a checklist or protocol be drafted detailing logistical requirements prior to running experiments in educational settings? And who should approve and sign off this protocol?

Future reading:

- Softbank Robotics. Softbank robotics documentation. http://doc.aldebaran.com/2-8/index.html, 2020. Accessed: 2020-02-02.

8 Applications

Quiet now, I am doing the talking!

Elektro, *At the World Fair 1936*

What is covered in this chapter:

- What knowledge and skills can educational and social robots teach?
- How we can use robots to assess learning progress?
- How may learning benefit from robots?

In Chapters 5 and 6, we have introduced two possible ways of understanding the role of robots in education, focusing first on robots as tools, that is, as impersonal instruments to support, facilitate, or augment the process through which disciplinary contents are taught and learned, and then on robots as social agents, in which the function of robots consists of taking on the role of a teaching assistant, tutor, or other anthropomorphic agent. In this chapter, we will take a closer look at just how broad the range of applications in these two domains is. These applications cover domains as different as: language learning (first and second); mathematics; rehabilitation of motor skills; programming and information communication technology (ICT); social skills (therapy intervention for autism and/or dementia); physics and kinematics (e.g., gravity); STEM and STEAM education; mechanical engineering education (building robots); and music. The scope of this review goes beyond the confines of formal educational establishments such as schools and universities to include informal educational practices.

The present chapter is divided into two parts. The first part focuses on *learning* applications (Section 8.1), where we describe how robots of all types can support human learners in acquiring or deepening knowledge or skills. The second part discusses *assessment* applications (Section 8.2). Assessment and performance evaluation represent key components of teaching because they allow teachers to measure and—if necessary—improve the outcomes of the learning process. Assessment is a prerequisite for learning success because it allows teachers to tailor their explanations to what the learner already knows.

Within the main application categories, we define both *knowledge* and *skills* as distinct components of learning. This acknowledges that learning entails more than memorizing facts or knowledge; it also encompasses the ability to generalize and apply knowledge by using skills.

Given that the focus of this chapter is on applications of robotics in educational contexts, the learner, rather than the human educator, is in the spotlight. This is not to downplay the role of human teachers, tutors, or assistants, who play important roles in the applications discussed over the course of this chapter. The implications for this group may be seen over the course of this chapter and will be picked up again (see Section 8.3).

8.1   Learning

8.1.1   *Knowledge*

Robots can be and have been a good support for teaching many knowledge-based subjects, including geography or history. In knowledge-based subjects, learning often requires repetitive practice, with the levels of the exercises increasing in step with the performance of the learner. We will illustrate the benefits of robot-assisted individualized learning by providing examples from science and mathematics.

8.1.1.1   *Robots in Science Education*

The practice of using robots as tools for teaching STEM subjects and computer programming is well established and constitutes one pillar of robots in education. However, thanks to the high mobility and multiple degrees of freedom of more complex robots, we are witnessing robots being used for teaching principles of kinematics and physics beyond simple, linear movements (Alimisis and Boulougaris, 2014; Karim et al., 2015; Mitnik et al., 2009). Namely, students can intuitively learn scientific concepts such as velocity and force by observing how a humanoid robot simulates the skilful movements of the human body (like a robot kicking a ball) using its own actuators (Carpin et al., 2007). The Thymio robot (Riedo et al., 2012), for example, has been showcased as a valuable tool to illustrate concepts of gravity and acceleration. Its compact nature, "batteries included" approach and its compatibility with LEGO bricks provides teachers and parents with a wide range of interactive scenarios.

In another fascinating example, the Cellulo robot (see Figure 8.1) is used - a tabletop robot, half the size of a grapefruit. It has a clever wheel configuration which allows it to move in any direction—something which most robots cannot do—but it can also be moved by the learner. Through an innovative drive design relying on permanent magnets to actuate coated metal balls, the robot can resist or support being moved around, providing haptic feedback to the learner. In addition, the robot carries a camera which can read localization patterns made up of tiny dots almost invisible to the eye and which can be mixed with illustration on ordinary paper. This allows the robot to know exactly where it is on a sheet of paper. Cellulo has been used to support the teaching of science subjects to children. In one application the robot moves over a map mimicking how air moves from areas with high pressure to areas with low pressure. In another striking application, a set of ten robots are used to illustrate how atoms respond when heated, going from being locked in a crystal structure in a solid, to vibrating in a liquid and moving freely in a gaseous state (Özgür et al., 2017).

Figure 8.1 The Cellulo robot can both move on its own and be moved by the learner. When it is being moved it can resist or cooperate and by doing so provides haptic feedback. Here the robot shows how wind moves from high to low pressure areas, acting out wind direction and speed (CHILI Lab EPFL)

8.1.1.2   *Mathematics*

The subject of mathematics ranges from simple numeracy to learning about complex calculus and integrates the use of knowledge and of skill. Robots have been applied to assist in both aspects. Given the relatively fundamental nature of mathematics, this has typically been explored in research with children rather than with adults. For example, Kennedy et al. (2015) made use of a social robot to guide children aged seven to eight years old through an understanding of prime numbers, with a similar case study demonstrating the learning and practice of multiplication in a collaborative robot context (Baxter et al., 2017). Similarly, in a learn-through-play approach, Janssen et al. (2011) show how children can learn aspects of arithmetic when playing related games with a robot, showing a particularly positive effect when the robot's behaviour is adapted to the child's performance (Schadenberg et al., 2017). We also have instances of non-humanoid robots being employed to illustrate mathematical or numeracy principles. One example concerns a toy being used to teach maths through simple programming of its movement (such as linear, scale, rotations; Highfield et al. (2008)). Another example is that of the Turtle-based robot being used to interpret angles and geometry (Mubin et al., 2013c).

8.1.2   *Skills*

8.1.2.1   *Programming*

Learning how to program computers, especially doing so for the first time, requires not only the learning of syntax (i.e., those terms and commands that have specific functionality), but also the learning of the process and logic underlying programs. In the context of learning applications, this is closely linked to the idea of *computational thinking*, which is the ability to consider and decompose problems over multiple levels of abstraction (Wing, 2006). Robots, thus, represent highly useful platforms, as they represent physical devices that can be explicitly controlled, where the outcome can be directly observed in terms of behaviour.

In terms of acting on robots (robots as tools—Chapter 5), there is extensive application in the context of learning how to program. The use of LEGO Mindstorms is particularly widespread—learners, whether they are children or adults, can write code, or construct a program and see how the robot behaves as a consequence. This could be following a line or avoiding hitting objects. As an embodied experience, it is consistent with the constructionist learning paradigm (Section 2.1.3). Indeed, recommendations for the application of this methodology (using Mindstorms as an example) to undergraduate (i.e., university) programming education emphasize these points (e.g., Lawhead et al., 2002), with competition being used to extend this principle and provide additional opportunity for learner motivation (Grandi et al., 2014). As a relatively straightforward set of hardware to deal with, LEGO Mindstorms have also been used extensively with children to introduce concepts of programming (e.g., Chaudhary et al., 2016), with other robot platforms being used in a similar way, such as Dash (e.g., Milne and Ladner, 2018) and Thymio (e.g., Riedo et al., 2013).

There have also been programming applications in the context of social robots. In this case, there is a distinction between the programming *of* a social robot and programming *with* a social robot. In the first case, programming of a social robot, rather than learning how to program robot movement (as is typical with the LEGO Mindstorms for example), there is an emphasis on programming socially interactive behaviours. A number of graphical programming environments are provided with existing popular social robots that facilitate this (e.g., the Choregraphe suite that is provided with the SoftBank Robotics NAO and Pepper robots, see Chapter 7), with a range of other visual programming platforms having been developed to program higher level abstracted social behaviours. For example, Diprose et al. (2017) implemented an abstracted language that facilitates the programming of social behaviours, which has subsequently been extended with a graphical programming environment (Datta et al., 2012).

When programming a social robot, the robot often is more akin to a partner in the learning process. For example, Gordon et al. (2015a) designed an application whereby children would show tokens to a small robot with instructions on, which would "program" its social behaviour. The means of checking the program is interacting (socially) with the robot. Evidence suggests that this results in an engaging experience and a better understanding of computational ideas (Gordon et al., 2015b). In a similar manner, Gorostiza and Salichs (2011) allow learners to use verbal commands to program the robot, again relying on subsequent social interaction with the robot to validate the outcome of the programming process. This grounds the learning of programming in the learners' existing experience of social interactions.

RoboPraX

The idea of using social robots to prepare students for digital challenges as future teachers has recently been extended to secondary school education and teacher training at universities. To illustrate, the German RoboPraX[1] project systematically introduces makerspaces using NAO robots to extend the regular curricula at schools and into teacher training at universities (Zeaiter and Heinsch, 2019). Prior to working in a robot-enhanced makerspace including NAO robots and classroom technologies like interactive whiteboards, students have to work through a preliminary online course called RoboBase. This is offered as a MOOC which can be accessed at any time, thus also introducing the students to self-guided online learning. RoboBase addresses different target groups depending on the age of the learner and the type of robot they have (NAO Version 5 vs. NAO Version 6). The course introduces the learner to humanoid robots, their development environment, and related topics, and introduces the makerspace, the so called "Robotikum". That way, they come prepared before starting in the actual activities in the Robotikum. A flipped classroom scenario in which students are expected to prepare before coming into school is therefore used. As part of the Robotikum, the robots are programmed over a three-day course. The students work towards a final project, which involves the development of a fully operational robot application, including a project description, a flow chart, and a semantic script. The course is concluded by a public presentation on Day 4[2].

8.1.2.2   *Complex Topics*

Robots can also be used to support learning in the context of complex topics. In this, the robot often plays the role of a mediator, inviting learners to reflect on and discuss their views. This is a very different role to the traditional instructor role: the robot does not teach or tutor, but rather observes the learning process, and prods and encourages the learners to explore the topic further and question their actions and outcomes.

The Embodied Perceptive Tutors for Empathy-based Learning (EMOTE) European project explored how a robot, which was presented as an "empathic" agent (Paiva et al., 2017), supported secondary school students. In one example, the students learned about the complex dynamics of energy and sustainability (see Figure 8.2). They did this through building a city in EnerCities, a simulated game in which the players balance the needs of the people, the planet, and the energy suppliers. The robot tutor prompts students to discuss competing needs and helps them make decisions. The students and the robot try new strategies to solve sustainable problems, such as the implementation and creation of new policies for the city (Alves-Oliveira et al., 2016, 2019).

Figure 8.2 Two secondary school students learning to balance energy use and production in a simulated city game. The robot takes the role of a mediator, inviting the students to reflect on the task and question their decisions

Source: Alves-Oliveira et al. (2016)

8.1.2.3 Rehabilitation and Social Skills Development

Robots have been extensively used in application for rehabilitation and the development of social skills, for instance, investigating individuals with mild cognitive impairments or with ASD or special learning needs (Kavale and Mostert, 2004). Robots in this context serve as training partners, monitoring the cognitive and emotional status of the individual (Alnajjar et al., 2019a).

Regarding children with ASD, it has been shown that they may react well to characteristics that are specific to robots (Scassellati et al., 2012; Thill et al., 2012). For example, in one of the earliest examples, Dautenhahn and Werry (2004) employed a small-wheeled mobile robot to encourage a range of social activities in children with autism. Using a simplistic, yet highly expressive robot (KeepOn), Kozima et al. (2009) found that it was sufficient to elicit social interaction with people with autism. Extending the autonomy of the robot, Gomez Esteban et al. (2017) developed a supervised autonomous system that can participate in a therapeutic intervention for children with autism focusing on basic skills such as joint attention, turn-taking, imitation, and emotion recognition. Promising results have been achieved in terms of progressive development of the children's social skills that commensurate with that expected by a human therapist alone (David et al., 2018). Moreover, over the past decade (Wood et al., 2019), vast amounts of research has been conducted with the humanoid robot (Kasper) that is designed to support autistic children. More broadly, we even find examples of robots being used to "nurture" and train humans to be kind to each other (Borenstein and Arkin, 2017).

The Cognitive Mirroring project

Alnajjar et al. (2019b) proposed a system that can help children with ASD to recognize emotions. In their Cognitive Mirroring project, the robot is carrying a small android tablet on its chest on which emotions are displayed, as the robot does not have an expressive face. Children with ASD are invited to recognize and imitate the emotion. The robot assesses the child's attention and engagement through processing camera data, using information on eye contact, joint attention, facial expressions of emotion, vocal responsiveness, and imitation (Figure 8.3).

Figure 8.3   A NAO robot with a screen attached to its chest showing various emotions (Alnajjar et al., 2020)

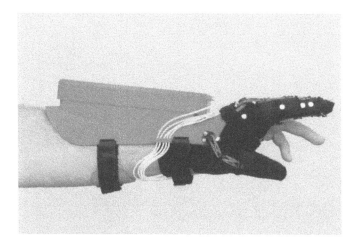

Figure 8.4 A 3D-printed wearable device (Alnajjar, et al., 2021)

Moreover, the ability of robots to repeat movements over and over again without getting tired or bored can be utilized for motor skills development, such as rehabilitation. Robots such as wearable exoskeletons can play an important role in rehabilitation programs for the elderly and post-stroke patients (Okajima et al., 2018). Figure 8.4 shows an example of a wearable robot to illustrate this special robotic application.

Another example is a system that is currently developed at the United Arab Emirates University (UAEU). The "Avatar Robot" set-up (see Figure 8.5) uses a body motion capturing suit to record the movements of a human therapist. In real-time, the therapist's movements are mapped to a co-located robot. During the therapy sessions, the learner is then asked to imitate the movement of the robot. To enhance the interactive dimension of the session, the therapist has the ability to—through the robot—talk to the user via a voice system that converts a human-voice into a robot-like voice.

8.1.2.4 *Behaviour change*

The capacity to change people's behaviour by encouraging and helping them to change habits and perspectives is an area that clearly has the potential to provide real-world impact. However, long-term behaviour change over extended periods of time is difficult to monitor beyond the extent of a given study, and there has consequently been relatively little direct evidence in support of it, at least in the context of robotics. There are, however, a range of attempts involving robots that address this, if

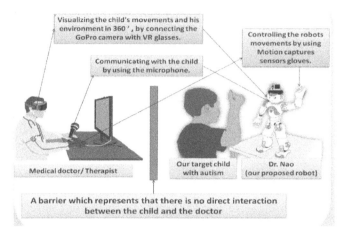

Figure 8.5   An example of a scenario in which the therapist communicates with
the child through the robot (Alahbabi et al., 2017)

not the long-term behaviour change itself, then some of the pre-requisites
such as the learning of relevant concepts. This field of research is known
as *persuasive robotics* (Ham and Spahn (2015).

One particular application of social robots concerned gaining insights
into the mechanisms of long-term behavioural change in children with
diabetes (Blanson-Henkemans et al., 2012), as demonstrated in the EU-
funded ALIZ-E project[3]. One of the core ideas in this case was that robot
and child could form a bond over time (Belpaeme et al., 2013). There
were a number of aspects of learning that were part of this broad effort: a
combination of activities was found to support motivation (Coninx et al.,
2016). One of these aspects was the learning of foundational concepts
related to healthy eating and living, including concepts in terms of diet
(that would help in the control of carbohydrate intake (e.g., Coninx et al.,
2016)) and exercise (related both to increase of physical effort, but also in
terms of embedding other concepts (e.g., Ros et al., 2016)). Robots have
even been used for the purposes of coercing humans to promote energy
conservation (Ham and Midden, 2014).

8.1.3   Robot-Assisted Language Learning

Earlier, we not only discussed how speech is the most natural form
of interaction between man and machine (Section 4.2), but, also, how
a variety of social cues exhibited by a social robot allows for verbal
interaction between a user and a robot (Section 3.2). A social robot
can implement a list of interaction modalities such as facial expressions,

variations in pitch, and voice, possibly lip movement and head movement, all attributes which are integral to human-robot speech interaction, supplementing speech with visual cues.

Given the potential of social robots for verbal and nonverbal interaction, it is a small leap to use social robots for language teaching. This is also known as Robot-Assisted Language Learning (RALL) and is one of the more popular application areas in educational robots (Chang et al., 2010). While the use of social cues by robots might be conducive to language learning, another clear advantage is the robot's ability for repetition (see also Section 3.2). A robot does not get tired or frustrated, no matter how many mistakes a student makes when practising articulations.

Furthermore, in addition to nonverbal cues, a social robot has the capacity to augment verbal dialogue through the use of gestures. These nonverbal cues and gestures not only serve to augment the communicative element of the interaction, but also improve the social engagement with the learner. It is this engagement which is essential for the interaction, and subsequently the learning, to be successful.

Finally, telepresence technology and robots such as iRobiQ (Han, 2012) can also facilitate the integration of a remote teacher in the classroom. In the context of language learning, one can bring in a native speaker of the target language and have them interact with the learner through the robot.

8.1.4   *How Robots Support Language Learning*

Despite some limitations with linguistic interaction, robots, just like other digital technologies, offer great flexibility. Deploying robots to teach French one day and German the next could simply be a matter of loading a new dialog database and software onto the robot. Compare that with finding a new human teacher with a day's notice. Another key advantage of including a robot as a language teacher is the aspect of the complete lack of any biased behaviour or judgement on behalf of the robot. Prior research (Chang et al., 2010) has shown that children have a tendency to feel less shy when interacting with a robot in a foreign language.

The potential of robots for second language (L2) learning is readily recognized in the research community and has already been introduced earlier in detail (see, for example, the L2TOR project on page 96). Typically, game-based elements, playful interactions, collaborative scenarios, and animations are an integral component of such learning scenarios. This encourages the young learner to maintain interest and motivation while learning a L2. Next to learning a L2, social robots have also been used to practise and improve proficiency in a student's first language (Han,

2012). A third rather unique scenario is the case of RALL for the learning of artificial languages—languages designed and created by humans. Two examples which stand out are the Robot Interaction Language (ROILA; e.g., Mubin et al., 2012) and Toki Pona (Saerbeck et al., 2010). Both are artificial languages designed to simplify communication and thereby potentially increase the success of interacting with robots. The languages have specifically been created to minimize misunderstanding in speech recognition and ambiguity in interpretation, which is ever present when using natural language in human-robot interaction. For a comprehensive review of RALL we refer the reader to the survey by Randall (2019).

8.1.5　Challenges of RALL

Despite the promise of RALL, the use of robots also faces a number of challenges. Speech recognition is a key to human-machine interaction and central to language learning. However, in a noisy classroom environment, autonomous speech recognition is less than optimal. Most speech recognition engines have been trained and optimized to recognize adult speech. Children's speech is different in nature, not only in its pitch, but also in the number of disfluencies and lexical errors children make. Kennedy et al. (2017c) showed that state-of-the-art automated speech recognition, while performing near perfect for adult speech, struggled to recognize the speech of five-year-olds. They showed that when children counted to ten, the best speech recognition engine at the moment (Google's cloud-based ASR) only correctly recognized 40% of the numbers. If children were asked to tell a story, the speech recognition barely recognized a single word. Furthermore, in order to adapt the tutoring of the robot it is necessary to determine the learner's language proficiency. Adequate measurement tools have to be identified.

To date, robot language tutoring focuses on the learning of vocabulary or simple linguistic constructs, with linguistic interaction still being firmly beyond our technical abilities. As language is a complex construct—relying heavily on world knowledge, context, and common ground—it is unlikely that robots will ever be able to have a fluent conversation in a first or even second language with a learner. Even if progress is rapid in some technologies, for example in chatbot technologies, the complexity of integrating linguistic interaction on a robot remains a formidable task.

8.1.6　Higher Education

In higher education, that is, education at college or university level, robot applications outside engineering are rare. Even in science fiction, there are hardly any examples of robots acting as educators in higher education settings. However, in digital T&L scenarios, there are new options where robots take over the role of assistants in the in-class phases of inverted classrooms. With highly specialized, and very much technology-focused robot applications, robots cannot only take on a new role but also create considerable benefit for the human educator and the students.

Classroom Application Packages

In a joint project between Marburg University, Germany, and the Chinese University of Hong Kong, so-called Classroom Application Packages (CAPs) were developed. CAPs allow the robot to take over some of the tasks of a human educator. A CAP bundles several classroom activities into one complex robot app, so that the robot takes over the tasks in the classroom for a certain period of time. The tasks and their duration can be modified at run-time through a direct interaction between the robot and the academic guide. For a CAP to be used, a number of prerequisites have to be met. Importantly, the use of a CAP requires a digital T&L scenario with a collaborative, competence-oriented in-class phase where students work on specific tasks to increase their topic-related competencies. Additionally, they are all using their mobile devices for support and the robot takes a position visible and audible to all students. Figure 8.6 displays this set-up.

Figure 8.6 Pepper in class supporting university students

The robot and the students require internet access and access to an e-learning platform to retrieve and act upon the data to be presented to the students[4]. A typical scenario of using a Pepper robot executing a CAP runs through the following steps (where steps 4 and 5 can be iterated):

1 Administrative actions (e.g., announcing the session ID)
2 Welcoming and describing the learning outcomes
3 Checking prerequisite knowledge
4 Defining and presenting a learning task for the students
5 Asking one or more questions to assess the students' learning
6 Summarizing the responses and giving feedback
7 Evaluation of the session

The students not only depend on the robot's verbal announcements, all robot activities are also transferred to the students' phones and can be followed up. Students can choose to work individually or in groups. And since the duration and the sequence of the tasks the robot has to execute can be manipulated by the students or the guide (via communication with the robot), there is always an option to change these central parameters of the tasks on the robot (Figure 8.6). Figure 8.7 shows the robot and a student's smartphone, together with the current coaching time gained by the coach.

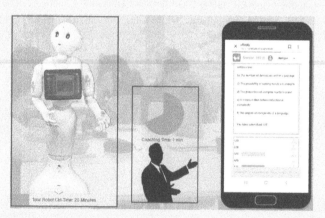

Figure 8.7 Components of a CAP at work

The main advantage of a CAP is that it liberates time for the human educator. Due to the autonomous actions performed by the robot, the educator no longer has to bother about technical aspects, but can instead concentrate on supporting the students.

8.2   Assessment and Feedback

Key to offering a quality educational experience is the robot's access to the learner's state. This comprises information on the learner's progress, and, on the other hand, on the learner's immediate social and emotional state.

8.2.1   Robot as Assessors

Assuming that in modern teaching scenarios many exams are electronic, where the computer takes full control over the examination process, a new role for robots as examiners emerges. On the one hand, robots can serve as individual examiners presenting questions face-to-face to students. On the other hand, they can prepare students for their exams using questions from the previous assessments.

The "Quizmaster" App for Pepper robots developed by Marburg University has realized both roles (Figure 8.8). To start, it allows a user to either choose a pre-existing quiz from the database of the e-learning platform (and make pre-settings) or create a new quiz based on some parameters. The parameters include: question types (multiple choice, input, counting tasks, calculation tasks, listening tasks, selection tasks), number of questions, time per question, and time until warning about the remaining time. Figure 8.8 shows the situation in a class.

The face-to-face exam is a suitable option especially in cases where students have to confirm certificates taken online, for example MOOC degrees, and humans have no capacity for oral examination. Whereas group preparation is an extremely attractive option for in-class scenarios, where students are told in advance that several questions drawn at random from the exam question database will be presented and discussed. In both cases, the human guide is given more freedom for complex in-class activities: enabling him or her to provide individual assistance in class instead of being occupied with oral exams.

8.2.2   Learning Analytics and Feedback

Understanding the performance of learners is important to allow educators to adjust and adapt their delivery to the students. One approach is

Figure 8.8 The Quizmaster App in a class

to use learning analytics to assess the learner's performance. According to Keller et al. (2020), three types of learning analytics can be defined:

- descriptive learning analytics (information about the underlying data)
- predictive learning analytics (projections based on the current data)
- prescriptive learning analytics (forecasts what should be done)

Many institutions see great potential in deploying learning analytics as a part of proactive feedback and predictive analytics. For example, the Student Advisor App for the Pepper robot developed at Marburg University[5] uses learner data to provide personalized feedback to students. The system uses data on class participation, frequency of access to online learning units, test performance, and activity on communication channels to build a profile of the student. In this context, the robot needs access to data such as information about courses (content, people, deadlines) and information about the students (personal data, course-related data). The information is used to perform a natural language dialogue on the student's progress and performance.

The following example illustrates the communication with a Pepper robot (Yuki) and a student (Lisa):

YUKI   Hello Lisa, welcome. You are working excellently in the course "History of English."

Figure 8.9 Pepper identifies a human via a QR code

LISA   Hello Yuki. Thank you for the praise. Do you have anything to complain about?

YUKI   Not much. However, to be on the safe side, you should repeat the second Mastery Test on "Proto-Languages" in order to achieve a higher percentage than the previous 75% which only gave you a "Junior Badge". Do you still have questions?

LISA   When is the final exam?

YUKI   On February 02, 2020 at 10 o'clock.

Registration for such an "office hour" with a robot should ideally be done via face recognition. To avoid recognition errors, the human-robot contact is made via a Quick Response (QR) code that students can download from their learning platform. This QR code identification has shown to be absolutely reliable (see Figure 8.9).

After identification, the robot gains access to the database and starts a dialogue with the student acting on the data. After each conversation, the robot summarizes it and sends it to the student by e-mail. The evaluations carried out in the H.E.A.R.T. project suggest that students prefer humanoid robots in such an "office hour" to non-embodied chatbots. As one student put it: "I can talk about things with the robot that I would not mention in front of my human class instructor".

8.3   Perspectives

Broadly, robots are expected to become cheaper and their abilities to respond to analytical data and the social environment will increase. Consequently, we can expect an increase in educational applications for robots. It is important to note, however, that the human element of education should never disappear. Human teachers have skills and abilities that go well beyond those of robots: their flexibility, empathy, and perceptiveness are unrivalled and concerns about robots replacing teachers are therefore unfounded.

What we do envision, however, is a role for the robot in assisting the teacher. Perhaps classrooms in the digital age will feature a handful of robots to the side of the classroom, ready to provide individual assistance or extra challenges. Perhaps the robot will serve as a vocabulary trainer or provide advice in case of interpersonal problems with peers. Keep in mind, though, that we are still in the early days of educational robotics, having just begun to explore their use and effectiveness in the laboratory context and in the field. Further research on a short-term and longitudinal time scale is needed to inform and reform educational practices.

Questions for you to think about:

- Could robots be slotted into current forms of teaching? Or would radically new teaching practices be preferred to use robots to their full potential?
- What are the main obstacles to the use of robots in education? Are they purely technical, or do we need a change in the attitude of learners, educators and the public?
- Why would it be impossible, and perhaps even undesirable, to completely replace the human element of education?
- Are there any applications in which robots in education should not be applied?

Future reading:

- Tony Belpaeme, James Kennedy, Aditi Ramachandran, Brian Scassellati, and Fumihide Tanaka. Social robots for education: A review. *Science Robotics*, 3(21):eaat5954, 2018a.
- Dimitris Alimisis. Educational robotics: Open questions and new

challenges. *Themes in Science and Technology Education*, 6 (1):63–71, 2013.

- Mohammad Obaid, Ruth Aylett, Wolmet Barendregt, Christina Basedow, Lee J. Corrigan, Lynne Hall, Aidan Jones, Arvid Kappas, Dennis Küster, Ana Paiva, Fotios Papadopoulos, Sofia Serholt, and Ginevra Castellano. Endowing a robotic tutor with empathic qualities: Design and pilot evaluation. *International Journal of Humanoid Robotics*, 15(06): 1850025, 2018. 10.1142/S0219843618500251. URL https://doi.org/10.1142/S0219843618500251.
- Omar Mubin, Catherine J Stevens, Suleman Shahid, Abdullah Al Mahmud, and Jian-Jie Dong. A review of the applicability of robots in education. *Journal of Technology in Education and Learning*, 1(209-0015):13, 2013c. URL http://dx.doi.org/10.2316/Journal.209.2013.1. 209-0015.

Notes

1. https://www.roboprax.de
2. https://www.roboprax.de/en/home
3. http://www.aliz-e.org/
4. Currently, the CAPs under development use the uREPLY platform: https://ureply.mobi/
5. Project H.E.A.R.T. https://www.project-heart.de/research-eng/

9 Attitudes Towards Robots

Robots are interesting because they exist as a real technology that you can really study—you can get a degree in robotics—and they also have all this pop-culture real estate that they take up in people's minds.

Daniel H. Wilson

What is covered in this chapter:

- Attitudes towards robots and what fosters technology acceptance.
- How do researchers measure attitudes towards robots in general?
- What factors impact on people's attitude towards robots?
- Attitudes towards educational robots.

9.1 Attitudes Towards Robots and Technology Acceptance

The term "robot" derives from the Czech word "robota", meaning autonomous work. Thus, in a literal sense, a robot is an automaton which is used to support human users in various deployment areas like industry, health services, within the home, or as part of the educational system. Thus, visionary ideas that once inspired depictions of robots in popular media and science fiction literature have—at least in part—become reality. However, because user attitudes might be informed by robot representations in popular media (Mubin et al., 2019b, 2016; Sandoval et al., 2014), it is important to find out what people actually think and feel about co-working or co-existing with robots.

149

Attitudes are broadly defined as positive or negative evaluations of any kind of object (Ajzen and Fishbein, 1980). Thus, naturally, robots, too can be deemed objects that elicit positive, negative, or even ambivalent evaluations in potential end users.

De Graaf et al. (2017) have adapted the Unified Theory of Technology Acceptance (UTAUT) for human-robot interaction research (Venkatesh and Bala, 2008) in order to understand how attitudes towards robots impact user behaviour. The authors differentiate between utilitarian and hedonic attitudes, which reflect the value attributed to the robot as a "tool" or as a "toy", respectively. Specifically, on the one hand, utilitarian attitudes include trust-related features like perceived usefulness, ease of use, adaptability to the users, and perceived intelligence of the autonomous system. Hedonic attitudes, on the other hand, include the experience of enjoyment and attractiveness of the robot. These aspects are in turn closely related to the robot's perceived sense of realism, sociability, and perceived companionship.

Our willingness to use a robot is also predicted by social norms and behaviour control (Ajzen and Fishbein, 1980). That is, subjective norms influence what others think about robots and their adoption as assistants or companions in their lives. Finally, perceived behavioural control includes factors that may affect or hinder the correct use of robots, such as the availability of necessary epistemic or cognitive resources, e.g., an individual's self-efficacy in the interaction with a robot, that is, his or her subjective ability to interact competently with a robot. Perceived safety of a robot and user anxiety also impact these control beliefs (Kamide et al., 2012; Nomura, 2017; Nomura et al., 2008; Nomura and Kanda, 2003).

9.2   Measuring Attitudes Towards Robots

Clearly, even the most sophisticated and technologically advanced robots would be useless in an industry, in people's homes or in the classroom environment, if potential end users would not be willing to use them. That is, intentions to use such technology, and ultimately the actual effective use of robots in a professional environment such as in educational settings, strongly depend on the attitudes the user brings to the specific context.

To assess such evaluations, researchers in social robotics have proposed a wide range of questionnaires (Eurobarometer, 2012; Nomura et al., 2006a,b). Attitudes towards robots have been studied among various user groups, ranging from children to seniors in various national and cultural settings (e.g., Arras and Cerqui, 2005; Bartneck et al., 2007b; Eurobarometer, 2012; Nomura et al., 2006a). Within Europe, the

Eurobarometer Survey, one prominent example of a large-scale EU-wide survey endeavour, has revealed fairly positive attitudes towards robots in general (Eurobarometer, 2012). These were affected by demographic variables, such as age, gender, or level of education, with males, younger, and more educated people being more in favour of novel technologies. Despite the overall positive reaction, robots were thought to be of restricted use. That is, when asked to take into account use cases, robots were particularly favoured in labour-intense domains like manufacturing or in settings that could potentially threaten humans' safety, for example, search and rescue, the military or space exploration. With regard to preferences for using robots in education, respondents appeared to be reserved. One problem with evidence from the Eurobarometer study concerns, however, the fact that respondents were not asked about specific robot prototypes, like educational robots, but rather had to report attitudes towards robots in general.

To overcome this problem, researchers have also adapted the available research instruments in order to investigate attitudes towards specific types of (educational) robots (Reich and Eyssel, 2013; Reich-Stiebert and Eyssel, 2015, 2016). This way, we can understand how people think and feel about particular robot types.

To illustrate, Reich and Eyssel (2013) explored attitudes toward service robots in the home environment in German respondents, showing that German people reported moderately positive attitudes and moderate levels of robot anxiety, while they were less inclined to potentially use such systems in their home. Personality traits that play a role in the attribution of human-like traits in non-human entities, for instance a person's need for cognition (i.e., an individual's disposition to enjoy engaging in cognitive tasks) or his or her dispositional loneliness, predicted positive attitudes towards service robots, above and beyond demographic variables such as gender or occupation. Reich and Eyssel (2013) furthermore found that males and professionals employed in non-social domains reported more positive attitudes toward robots in the service domain. Now, what are the attitudes towards educational robots like, you might wonder? We will provide some answers reflecting upon various findings from international research groups in the US, Asia, and Europe.

9.2.1 *Attitudes Towards Educational Robots*

Despite the vast amount of research on educational robots and their use (Benitti, 2012; Toh et al., 2016; Spolaôr and Benitti, 2017; Mubin et al., 2013b; Belpaeme et al., 2018a), fewer researchers have actually examined potential user attitudes in large-scale surveys with most efforts restricted to interviews with a select group of users in focus group type settings. Attitudes towards robots in educational settings have been researched through a range of mostly qualitative research (Choi et al., 2008; Han et al., 2009; Lee et al., 2008; Liu, 2010; Serholt et al., 2014; Shin and Kim, 2007).

To illustrate, in a study conducted in Korea, Shin and Kim (2007) have investigated primary and high school students' attitudes towards robots and found that these respondents deemed it important to be able to use robots because of their assumption that robots would constitute an important part of future T&L scenarios. Participants in this study evaluated the competence dimension of robots positively, with robots being able to avoid mistakes and potentially being more intelligent than human teachers. At the same time, they expressed worries about the fact that robot teaching assistants are not capable of experiencing and expressing emotions, which would have an impact on the social relationships in the educational context. In terms of attitudes towards learning with educational robots, attitudes were negative in that students did not want to be observed by robots in the classroom during their learning process[1].

Further, Korean Data by Lee et al. (2008) data were gathered from teachers, students, and parents. This evidence revealed positive attitudes towards using robots in schools, however, negative attitudes towards the idea of using robots as teachers. Teachers, in particular, worried about being replaced, so that they were not so much in favour of using robots in educational settings. Comparing Korean data with data from Spanish parents, Choi et al. (2008) reported that Spanish parents were much more sceptical towards the use of educational robots, viewing them as "machines". Korean parents, on the other hand, valued the idea of robots as companions. Han et al. (2009) revealed analogous findings regarding the purchase and use of robotic tutors, comparing Spanish, Korean, and Japanese respondents' attitudes. Korean parents were most open to the use of tutoring robots.

Serholt et al. (2014) interviewed a small set of European teachers on their inclination to use educational robots and their concerns in this regard. All interviewees acknowledged the added value of tutor robots potentially reducing their workload in the context of student assessment and documentation, particularly in group learning contexts. At the same time, tutor robots were deemed less useful in the context of larger groups of students that would require individual learning support. Moreover, teachers reported concerns with regard to extra work associated with the deployment of robots in the classroom, technical issues with the robots during use, and regarding their disruptive potential during T&L scenarios (such as the inability to maintain discipline). Other important overviews in the area of perception of educational robots have discussed the element of safety and privacy (Sharkey, 2016) in settings where robots and students interact in the classroom.

Other research focusing on survey-based perception of educational robots has also revealed interesting findings across various regions of the world. Lin et al. (2009) conducted interviews with Taiwanese fifth-graders to explore what they think about robots in general and robots in the classroom, as well as the children's design preferences for robots. Results of this qualitative research revealed that attitudes towards robots were generally positive, including inclinations to work with robots in school settings. Some children, however, expressed worries with regards to being potentially distracted by robots in their classroom, and thus, they were more in favour of traditional frontal instruction methods involving a human teacher. Liu (2010) has also studied young adolescents in Taiwan in a qualitative interview study, with a particular focus on young adolescents who were familiar with robotics and had previous experience with robots. This subgroup perceived educational robots positively, in terms of entertainment, and clearly acknowledged the added value of knowledge on robotics for the advancement of society and the potential for future employment.

In the German context, Reich-Stiebert and Eyssel (2015) have studied attitudes towards educational robots in university students, particularly taking into account predictors of positive attitudes and willingness to use robots. Importantly, it revealed that attitudes towards robots were moderately positive and intentions to use educational robots in the classroom were low. Robots were accepted in the classroom setting mainly as assistants to the teacher or tutors, primarily in individual learning contexts. They were preferred less to solitary manage a whole classroom nor as a replacement teacher. University students were inclined to use robots particularly in science and technology, not so much in the arts and humanities. Their attitudes and behavioural intentions to use educational robots were predicted by their gender and age as well as by inter-individual differences of their commitment towards technology. That is, females were less inclined to robots, so too were older students and those who did not like to engage in deep thinking and showed low affinity for technology in terms of personality traits.

In further research on teachers' attitudes towards educational robots in Germany (Reich-Stiebert and Eyssel, 2016), a similar picture arose, with technology commitment being a key predictor of positive attitudes and intentions to use robots in the classroom. Concerning the type of school, primary school teachers in comparison with secondary or tertiary school teachers, were particularly reluctant to use robots in their professional routines. Obviously, the available empirical evidence reveals a mixed picture with regards to attitudes and inclinations to use on the part of both learners and teachers. The general value of advanced teaching technologies is clearly appreciated, however, worries about the adequate handling of such technologies pose a threat to users' perceived self-efficacy. Equally important, the social implications of introducing robots in T&L settings have to be addressed, changing attitudes in a way that robots will not be viewed as disrupting learning and human relationships in classrooms of the future.

An overview of the research presented indicates that a certain disparity in views amongst teachers and students emerges when it comes to educational robots (Ahmad et al., 2016). The primary worries that most prominently affect personal and professional outcomes of teachers themselves revolve around job replacement and job loss (Reich-Stiebert and Eyssel, 2016). The fear is that the availability of new robots might reduce the number of positions available to human teachers, thereby decreasing the professional services offered by teachers more generally. This worry does not seem to be supported by evidence, as today's robots are clearly unable to replace teachers and researchers in educational robots do not intend to replace teachers with robots. In addition, the above mentioned scenarios and studies and the assumptions held by the participants therein are based on traditional T&L scenarios; leading to possible reluctance to readily adopt robots in the classroom. In digital T&L, where content delivery is digital and the in-class deepening phases are competence-oriented, highly interactive, and collaborative, we are no longer talking about the classical teacher role but about that of a learning guide. In such settings, robots acting as assistants to the teacher, as tutors or as tools, generate an enormous benefit by taking over technically-oriented and content-related tasks as described in Chapters 1 and 8.

Further critical issues raised have nothing to do with the effectiveness of educational methods or the learning performance of the students, but focus on the ethical dilemmas that society has to face following the introduction of robots in classrooms. These dilemmas have to do with the impossibility for robots to navigate complex social settings with very nuanced moral implications, and the rights of the students, like privacy. These issues will be addressed in depth in the following chapter.

Learning more about the diverse attitudes behind key aspects of technology adoption is important in order to facilitate the deployment of robots in our classrooms in the long run.

Questions for you to think about:

- What are some problems associated with measuring attitudes towards robots?
- Discuss important demographic factors that influence robot-related attitudes (e.g., age, gender, profession). How do these impact user attitudes?
- Imagine the following scenario: A student and a robot interact in the classroom. The student holds negative attitudes towards the robot. What strategies could the robot use to change this?

Future reading:

- Maartje MA De Graaf and Somaya Ben Allouch.   Exploring influencing variables for the acceptance of social robots.   *Robotics and Autonomous Systems*, 61 (12):1476–1486, 2013.   10.1016/j.robot. 2013.07.007.   URL https://doi.org/10.1016/j.robot.2013.07.007.

Note

1. These findings are in line with the results of the evaluation of the students' responses in the context of the H.E.A.R.T. project: https://www.project-heart.de/research-eng/applications/

10 Ethics

Morality is simply the attitude we adopt towards people we personally dislike.

Oscar Wilde, *An Ideal Husband*

What is covered in this chapter:

- Can a robot teach me right or wrong?
- An overview about ethical concerns applied to robotics.
- Prospective scenarios and related challenges.

A discussion on ethics in education, and the role robots might play in it, needs to distinguish between two issues: On the one hand, formal education plays a crucial role in the moral development of learners. When robots are introduced to take over some of the roles of the teacher, they will also inevitably affect the formation of values and norms in the students. Can robots be good role models and effectively contribute to the moral maturation of the students? On the other hand, there is the obvious question of whether robots might ever be programmed to behave ethically and make appropriate ethical decisions in the classroom environment, complying with the many deontic norms and principles that professional educators are expected to fulfil: consider for example that instructors are often required to administer disciplinary actions while preserving respect, confidentiality, and professional distance in their interactions with their students. Can robots be equipped with the necessary ethical decision-making abilities? This is to a large extent the more pressing question, due to the risk that robots could behave in a socially inappropriate or even unethical manner if not appropriately programmed to deal with morally challenging scenarios. Let us nevertheless first look at the former issue, that is, how teachers are instrumental in the development of moral principles and values in young learners[1].

It is well known that the role played by teachers in the classroom is crucial in more than one way: Not only do they support the process through which students develop cognitive skills and acquire knowledge, but they also shape the moral and psychological development of their students. Crucially, as members of educational institutions, they mediate the process of personal and intellectual growth through which a student becomes a mature individual, a responsible professional, a good citizen, and a respected member of their society (Carr, 2005). That is why teachers have to comply with strict codes of practice which demand, for example, that they protect the privacy of their students and their right to freely express their individual views (Campbell, 2000). Regardless of the contents being taught, teachers and tutors provide the students with a normative framework that points to goals to be fulfilled and mistakes to be avoided. The normative influence of this framework extends beyond the classroom environment and represents a beacon for the students through their whole life. Learning always benefits from teachers with high moral standards because their example motivates students to better appreciate values, distinguish right from wrong, and make the efforts necessary to achieve excellence. Teachers serve in this transformative process as guides and role models (Lumpkin, 2008). As such, teachers inevitably have a considerable influence on the character development of the students and, importantly, contribute to the formation of their worldview and moral values, even when this influence is not explicit or recognized by the students.

Understanding the ethical and professional expectations bestowed on teachers is fundamental to defining the ethical guidelines that should regulate the use of robots in a classroom, where the robot's activities serve to enhance those of the teacher. Accordingly, introducing a robot in the classroom setting requires careful implementation of such ethical guidelines. To discuss how the notions of "right" and "wrong" are to be applied in the context of educational robotics, we first need to briefly summarize how normative ethics define these notions in general and then how these moral notions are to be applied in the education setting.

10.1   What Is Ethics?

Ethics is the branch of philosophy that deals with the principles and criteria necessary to distinguish right from wrong. Its millennia-long history is rich and encompasses different traditions, which originate from different intuitions about the fundamental nature of good and evil. We roughly distinguish between three main approaches to normative ethics: consequentialism, deontology, and virtue ethics (Graham, 2004).

10.1.1 Consequentialism and Deontology

Consequentialism and *deontology* represent the standard positions in most debates in applied ethics. Both approaches aim to provide prescriptive rules and normative principles to distinguish morally right actions or decisions from the morally wrong ones. According to the Sinnott-Armstrong (2019), consequentialism defines a good action (or decision) as the one that—compared to all the other options available—produces the greatest benefits for the largest number of people. According to the same source, Deontology defines an action or decision as good if it best fulfils the moral agent's duties and obligations while protecting the rights of moral patients, for example recognizing the absolute, non-negotiable value of their personal freedom. Consequentialism evaluates the moral value of an action on the basis of the utility created by the action's effects, as it aims to assess how the action was beneficial to people. Deontology, in turn, focuses on the intentions that motivated the action, as it aims to assess whether the agent acted out of the authentic good will to fulfil their obligations and respect the others' rights.

Imagine this: a group of people is held hostage and the hostage taker has threatened to kill them. You are a sniper and can shoot the hostage taker. According to consequentialism you should shoot, as this will keep the hostages safe from harm. But deontology would tell you not to shoot. Killing is wrong, no matter the consequences.

Consequentialism and deontology certainly impact education: for the former, educational institutions produce a public utility to provide the best education to the largest number of people; for the latter, education is a fundamental right of the individual, and schools have a duty to reduce inequalities in the access to knowledge. They also have different recommendations regarding pedagogy and the ethical role of teachers. Consequentialist thinking would emphasize that teachers should act in ways that are beneficial to students and society at large. For example, adopting teaching methods that produce better learning outcomes, higher educational performance, and more robust and diverse academic skills. On the other hand, the approach to education inspired by deontology prioritizes respect for human rights and entitlements, including liberties and identities, and commitment to duties and moral obligations. For example, teachers must protect the students' privacy and confidentiality, respect their freedom to express their critical opinion and develop their own in-dependent points of view, but also demand from them honesty, integrity, and dedication (Chapfika, 2008).

While both approaches have something important to say about the ethics of teaching, they might be insufficient to define value and flour-ishing in the context of education. This is due to the complex, transfor-mative relationship between students, teachers, and the institutions. As virtue ethics is concerned with the value of one's lifestyle and personal flourishing, not single actions or decisions, it is better positioned than the other two theories to provide fruitful recommendations for stakeholders in the educational setting (Arthur et al., 2016).

Virtue ethics is not only a prescriptive theory, but also a philosophy of self-fulfilment and personal accomplishment: it maintains that one's individual journey for self-improvement and continuous education, when followed with dedication, is the most reliable way to secure authentic happiness. Instead of focusing on what actions are right or wrong, virtue ethics focuses on "virtues" and "vices", that is, character traits that make a person either admirable or reprehensible. Virtues and vices are implicit dispositions to produce certain behaviours, thoughts, or feelings (Carr and Steutel, 2005).

Virtue ethics emphasizes that good conduct emerges spontaneously when one follows one's "good nature", that is, the positive dispositions embedded in the moral character. Good character is not necessarily in-nate and certainly is not instinctive, but it can be acquired as "second nature" by promoting virtuous behaviours and attitudes in oneself and others and by dedicating oneself to the kinds of activities and thought patterns that contribute to realize a commendable lifestyle. Hence, ac-cording to virtue ethics, the purpose of education is primarily to direct students towards a good lifestyle, rather than teaching them to blindly follow predefined sets of norms or rules. Thus, virtue ethics particularly emphasizes the role of lifelong learning for character development and the moral value of exemplary actions and role models. In the educational context, the virtues a teacher could promote in students are, for example, curiosity, dedication, respect, civic sense, compassion, discipline, and in-tegrity. Classically, moderation and self-regulation are considered central for the education of young people as they mediate the development of other virtues.

10.2   Ethics for Robots

While humans are well trained and accustomed to making ethical de-cisions with little cognitive effort, robots would need to be carefully programmed in order to do it correctly. In and of itself, this constitutes a challenge, as discussed in Chapter 1. Robots do not have any ethical intuition or feeling and lack the common sense necessary to interpret a complex moral context and realize all the implications of their actions in it. Every decision and action needs to be calculated by the robot and hence requires the developer to make the meaning of "good" and "bad" formally explicit.

Consequentialism and deontology both require that the good robot could execute the top-down processes that are relevant to make a correct ethical decision. According to consequentialism, such correct ethical decision-making should be guided by the robot's understanding of the actions that human interaction partners may consider beneficial and advantageous. According to deontology, ethical decision-making should be guided by the robot's understanding of what is usually considered disrespectful or unsafe for the lives, the freedom, and the dignity of humans. In fact, both approaches to ethical robot design face structural challenges, due, on the one hand, to the top-down nature and abstractness of their guiding principles, and, on the other hand, to the technological limitations that prevent robots from implementing such principles in real life scenarios: even when provided with very accurate sets of instructions and rich heuristics, current artificial agents are unable to understand the context or the consequences of their actions, which makes it impossible for them to generate decisions and behaviours that meet the relevant standards of consequentialism or deontology. It is extremely difficult for a robot to calculate the impact that its actions have on the world and how desirable the consequences are for all of the people affected.

In the face of these shortcomings, we suggest focusing on a rather different way of understanding the ethical role of social robots, inspired by virtue ethics. This approach, called "Virtuous Robotics", is systematically explored in the paper "Can robots make us better humans? Virtuous Robotics and the good life with artificial agents" (Cappuccio et al., 2020) and in the special issue of International Journal of Social Robotics in which it is published. According to this approach, the ethical design of social robots based on virtue ethics is more promising for one essential reason: programming a robot to help humans develop their own character while working for self-improvement is easier than programming a robot to make decisions concerning utilitarian benefits or personal rights.

Virtuous Robotics relies on the user's desire for self-improvement rather than the robots' capability to make appropriate decisions. Robots can aid humans to develop or consolidate their virtue by helping them recognize their own shortcomings and flaws and actively counteracting them (Cappuccio et al., 2020). This is not computationally demanding and does not require unrealistic amounts of structured information because the cognitive burden lies entirely on the human. The robot is merely a mediator and a facilitator for self-discovery and self-regulation. Robot teaching assistants designed in accordance with the Virtuous Robotics paradigm could be used to cultivate good habits, help students to manage negative emotions like anger and envy, refrain from cheating on an exam (Mubin et al., 2020), and practise positive attitudes towards others, such as respect, care, and friendliness (Vallor, 2016). Robots can remind humans that they are indulging in bad habits such as smoking, excessive alcohol consumption, or abusive behaviour. Robots can make them realize that their manners and language are vulgar or offensive, or warn them of the shameful implications of their conduct such as how their anti-social behaviours could alienate their classmates.

10.2.1   Roles of Robots in Virtue Cultivation

A robot can play various roles to solicit responsible reactions in humans and guide them through a path of virtue cultivation and character formation. Here are some examples:

Confidant   The robot invites the human user to narrate their everyday experiences and, in doing so, promotes self-reflection. Through sentiment analysis techniques, the robot can select the most relevant questions to help the user identify trends and patterns in their own journey for moral development, suggesting corrections or providing encouragement as necessary.

Assistant coach and motivator   Following a personalized, predefined timetable, the robot reminds the user of daily routines. The robot supervises the execution of required activities, which can be physical, intellectual, or social. The robot evaluates the user's performance based on real-time feedback from the user, adapting interventions according to the user's current needs.

Reverse role model   Robots may solicit growth in students by inviting them to take the role of teachers and tutors. In this case, the robot would "play dumb", eliciting explanations and interventions from the human. This induces reflection on the values necessary to behave correctly and is likely to help the students develop a sense of responsibility.

Taken together, these examples highlight the potential of robots as cultivators of virtuous behaviour, demonstrating their impact on the moral development of their human interaction partners.

10.3 Ethical Concerns in the Classroom

The previously discussed ethical issues set fundamental constraints on what we can expect of a robot. But there are further, more applied and rather speculative ethical issues that might arise when robots operate in the classroom. Sharkey and Sharkey (2010, p. 161) argued that although there are currently no plans for a full-time replacement of human caretakers by robots, it would be "certainly on the cards". The main ethical concerns raised are:

Privacy Robots might infringe on the privacy rights granted by Articles 16 and 40 of the UN Convention on Child Rights. Differentiating between private and public information requires a level of common sense and understanding of social norms that robots lack by default.

Restraint A robot might be required to restrain a child in order to protect it from self-harm and/or harm to others. Restraining a human requires considerable ethical reasoning abilities and motor control. Robots might have neither. To make things worse, we predict that a robot would struggle distinguishing rough play from bullying. Hence, the robot would not even be able to alert the human teacher and ask for help.

Deception A robot expressing emotions without experiencing emotions could be considered a deception and could mislead the student into believing that the nature of their relationship is personal. We discuss this problem of inappropriate attachment in more detail below.

Accountability Caretakers have a legal responsibility for the children entrusted to them. If a robot is left alone with a group of students, then it becomes unclear who would be accountable. Is it the manufacturer of the robot, the organization that owns the robot or the robot itself? We envision the robot to be used only as an assistant to the teacher and hence the responsibility would remain with the human teachers.

Psychological Damage Using a robot to assist children with special needs may turn out harmful, due to the fact that the robot would not be equipped to provide adequate care. Sharkey and Sharkey (2010) admitted that very few, if any, empirical studies are available to shed light on these important issues because doing research in this area comes with a variety of challenges for research ethics.

Complementing the issues raised by Sharkey and Sharkey (2010), the following aspects require careful ethical consideration:

10.3.1   Authority

Granting robots authority and power would make many users uncomfortable (Zlotowski et al., 2017). At the same time, because of their limited capabilities, robots may lack the inherent authority necessary to discipline individuals (Brščiundefined et al., 2015). As a consequence, a robot seems more suitable for adopting the role of an assistant, proxy, or support to the human who is accepted and acknowledged as the key authority figure.

10.3.2   Attachment

Children might grow attached to robots they are interacting with. Thus, they even grow expectations about having a social relationship with them. Due to the empathic limitations of robots in general, such a bond would remain uni-directional (Sharkey and Sharkey, 2010; Scheutz, 2011). Huber et al. (2016) also identified attachment as one of the main concerns in human-robot interaction. One of the potential dangers is that the bond between a human and a robot could result in outcomes which are not in the interest of the human, whether by accident or by the robot exploiting the bond.

10.3.3   Identity

A robot might be unable to appropriately recognize and value the socio-cultural specificity of the students and their background, such as their ethnicity, gender, tradition, or religion. Apart from eliciting frustration and disappointment in the students, this might create misunderstandings and conflicts, and the students or their families could have reason to think that this failure was offensive or disrespectful.

10.3.4   De-socialization

Even if robots were able to perfectly coordinate students' intellectual activities and cognitive work in the classroom environment, they might be unable to coordinate social activities. The presence of the robots might inhibit the social abilities of the students, conducing them to overlook collaborative interactions with the other children and preventing the normal development of social traits like empathy and compassion. The opposite risk is also possible: that the robot, when perceived by the students as a toy or entertaining attraction, could dis-inhibit their social pulses, becoming a distracting element, and a trigger for undisciplined chat and play without the instructor's approval.

10.3.5 De-skilling

In a world in which machines increasingly take over tasks from humans, humans might lose essential skills. This also holds true for the educational context. A robot that takes over certain tasks could lead to teachers increasingly losing practise in those specific tasks. The worst-case scenario would be that the teachers' roles would be reduced, so to speak, to finding the on/off switch of the educational robot. Since we consider the robot to be an assistant and not a replacement for the teacher, we may assume that such a scenario is unlikely to become reality. But it is not only the teachers that might lose skills: also the students might experience de-skilling. Being able to verbally ask the robot any question and, at least for simple factual information, receive a direct response, inhibits critical research skills. The students might take the information provided by the robot at face value and not consider different sources and their respective validity. However, this potential risk concerns all digital technologies and is not specific of interactive robots.

10.3.6 Lack of Affective Intelligence

Robots are incapable of actually experiencing emotions. This has implications for communication and social bonding in general. To illustrate, students cannot be efficaciously coordinated or directed if the robot's mental states are opaque. Teaching empathy, compassion, and respect arguably requires a very nuanced sensitivity to emotional tones and personal motivations, which robots inevitably lack.

At the same time, if a robot is able to perceive (Zhang et al., 2013), process (Paiva et al., 2014), and express synthesized emotions (Bartneck and Reichenbach, 2005), does it matter at all if it experiences emotions in the same way humans do? Is it necessary for a robot to actually experience emotions in order to be emotionally competent? And following from that, how could an ethical robot teach the virtue of compassion if it cannot feel emotions? This problem does not only apply to emotions, but to other skills of the robot that seem to presuppose a first-person familiarity with the qualitative details of conscious experience.

These moral concerns build on the assumption that the robot's incapability to experience the emotional life of others implies moral incompetence, because moral competence requires the ability to predict and explain what emotions or feelings other sentient beings are likely to experience in one situation or another (including what they experience as beneficial, detrimental, and offensive). Explaining or predicting another's lived experience, in turn, cannot be done by inferential or intellectual processes alone, because it strictly requires either (1) having shared similar experiences in similar situations, or (2) having interpretive capabilities that can be developed only by participating in inter-subjective experiences that closely relate to a similar situation (Gallagher, 2012).

For example, to predict or explain what other humans feel when they live an embarrassing situation (including its qualitative and moral aspects), one needs to have experienced a similar embarrassment or one must have participated in intense situations in which that embarrassment was experienced by others, which feels close enough to empathize with. Robots are unaware of the qualitative component of that feeling (including nuances of shame, humiliation, degradation, and mortification), or of the situations in which humans experience it, because they do not have conscious experience in the first place. Robots remain incompetent regarding the moral implications associated with embarrassment, shame, humiliation, etc. because, even if they are given very rich descriptions of the objective facts associated with that embarrassment, they cannot just rationally infer the moral and experiential implications associated with it.

10.4   Conclusion

Typically, educational roboticists do not envision robots as replacements for human teachers. If they are right, then many of the concerns discussed in this chapter might not directly apply to the education context, because such concerns are serious only if the robot is left alone, unsupervised, to interact with the students. Nevertheless, discussing these concerns increases our preventive awareness of the potential ethical challenges deriving from the massive deployment of robots in society and provides developers with useful indications to design better and more sophisticated robots.

In this section, we suggest a number of heuristic strategies to deal with the aforementioned issues, minimizing possible distress for students and reducing unwanted liabilities for the teachers and their institutions.

1 The amount of trust educators put in a robot should be based on a realistic assessment of its characteristics and abilities. School management and teachers need to be equally aware of the limitations of the robot regarding tasks that are considered routine by a human. They should tailor their expectations to this awareness. Nowadays, robots can detect emotions in human users and recognize certain categories of goal-oriented behaviour, but robots do not have the capability to easily infer mental states, including desires and motivations, or interpret complex social situations. This makes it difficult for them to

make socially and morally acceptable decisions, and it is even unlikely that they can safely navigate potentially controversial etiquette issues.

2 Any morally significant decision should be left to the teacher, as the teacher is the only moral agent responsible for the educational value of teaching. Of course, the teacher should make sure that, at any time, decisions comply with the deontological standards of the profession or the policies of the institution. Robots used in the classroom and their specific capabilities should be factored into such decisions. For example, if the robot offers auxiliary functionalities of surveillance and conflict management, these should be taken into account in any scenario in which they might possibly become useful. However, despite such functionalities, the teacher should not be led to think that the robot could deal with a problematic classroom situation autonomously. A teacher thus should be co-present with the robot in the classroom, particularly when morally sensitive issues arise. This is because robots are not considered liable for the negative consequences of their actions, and ultimately, the teacher could be to blame.

3 The formative role played by the robot in the classroom should be compatible with the robot's perceived authority. Robot features, such as size, (human-like) appearance, tone of voice, or facial expression, are among the factors that impact the robot's perceived authority. Assuming that a robot could have sufficient authority to successfully carry out the tasks assigned to it, the question arises as to what are the psycho-social, cultural, and legal implications of a robot exerting authority.

4 Robots need to use their cameras and microphones to respond to students at all times and hence they might need to continuously record the classroom. This might compromise the privacy of the teachers and students. Information recording and sharing needs to comply to the local legal frameworks, such as the General Data Protection Regulation (GDPR) in the EU. Seeking consent from parents and teachers for using robots in the classroom is essential and should include full disclosures of how the data is recorded, processed, stored, and shared. The robot should also clearly indicate when it is recording, such as by using a red blinking light.

Questions for you to think about:

• What is the difference between consequentialism and deontology? How does it apply to educational robotics? Why is implementation of virtuous robotics more practical?

- How could one address the ethical concerns mentioned with regards to the implementation of robots in the classroom through the design of interaction and learning scenarios? Show examples of each.
- Give examples of different applications of virtuous robots in the classroom, referring to different roles and tasks that a robot can take in the classroom.
- What are some of the moral limitations of a robot that a human teacher should monitor?

Future reading:

- Massimiliano Cappuccio, Eduardo Benitez Sandoval, Omar Mubin, Mohammad Obaid, and Mari Velonaki. *Virtuous Robots: Artificial Agent and Good Life*. Special Issue in the International Journal of Social Robotics, 2021.
- C. Bartneck, Christoph Lütge, Alan Wagner, and Sean Welsh. *An Introduction to Ethics in Robotics and AI*. SpringerBriefs in Ethics. Springer, 2020a. ISBN 9783030511098. 10.1007/978-3-030-51110-4. URL https://www.springer.com/gp/book/9783030511098

Note

1. Today, the term "teacher" should be replaced by "educator" to enable a distinction between the role as a teacher in traditional T&L settings and a learning guide on the side in digital T&L settings.

11 Research Methods in Educational Robotics

Science is magic that works.

Kurt Vonnegut, *Cat's Cradle*

What is covered in this chapter:

- Different methods for different research questions;
- On the long road of scientific research: steps and challenges;
- New answers lead to further questions: publication a starting point.

The field of Human-Robot Interaction (HRI) gained prominence with the advent of the so called "Human-Robot Interaction" conference in 2006, which to date represents the flagship conference in the field. HRI as a discipline is closely related to Human-Computer Interaction (HCI) and, as such, most work published in this area is empirical research involving user studies with robots (Bethel and Murphy, 2010). Other types of research outcomes in the area of robotics can include models, frameworks or software implementations (Mubin et al., 2017). However, in order to integrate the human user into the perspective, empirical user studies are required (Bartneck, 2011). Such user studies could provide empirical answers to research questions regarding the use and efficiency of robotic systems in teaching scenarios, providing insights by means of systematic evaluation. To illustrate, potential end users, such as teachers, may wonder about the specific roles of the robot in the learning context, about the domain in which a robot could be useful, and about the specific behaviours it should display. For instance, to ascertain optimal learning outcomes, should the robot serve as a companion to the student or as an assistant to the teacher? Should it provide support in STEM education or the humanities and do so by providing friendly, constructive feedback or rather by applying simple "drill and repeat" rules instead?

The answers to these research questions are ideally determined through empirical investigation. This is research based on data collected through the observation and/or perception of human participants. These participants could be children, adults, teachers or learners, parents or peers, alike. Quantitative data is usually collected through questionnaires, surveys, by observing participants' behaviour in lab experiments or by observing them in the field, such as in their schools or within their families. Data can also be obtained by using a qualitative approach, that is by gathering responses through open-ended questions, for example, administered in focus groups, in interview settings or by making use of other qualitative methods. Going beyond measurements by means of self-report scales, qualitative methods have the potential to complement a quantitative view by providing insights into deep discussions and interrogations, as demonstrated by Serholt et al. (2014). Here, teachers were engaged to understand their views on the wider implications of robots in education. Such insights based on qualitative data can be used as a basis for hypothesis formation and testing that is characteristic of the usually quantitative laboratory studies.

11.1   Short-Term and Long-Term Investigations

Depending on the research question, empirical studies can vary dramatically in terms of complexity and duration. While research questions can be targeted by means of a brief online survey or cross-sectional laboratory experiments, other research endeavours entail longitudinal studies that run for decades, studying a particular group of people over time (such as Gonnella et al., 2004). Whether a certain intervention, for instance, a teaching method, is effective in improving teaching quality, student performance, or motivation, might only become visible after continued and sustained exposure. We also observe issues of saturation in HRI and educational robots, with students reporting an element of boredom after only a few sessions (Kanda et al., 2004). Therefore, longitudinal studies "when possible" are a true measure of the success of the implemented system or manipulation. The student would need to experience a new teaching method several times before any differences could be observed. For this purpose, longitudinal research studies can run over extended periods of time, ranging from multiple sessions, to across multiple weeks, months, or even years. Such studies often test effects of an intervention by measuring attitudes and behaviours of the same group of research participants multiple times across the whole duration of the study. Additionally, longitudinal studies are important to outline differences in participants' response or behaviour as a function of age, thus outlining the underlying psychological mechanisms that may be at play in specific phases of intellectual maturation. In short-term studies, measurements would only be collected in a single instance or a single data point. For both short-term or long-term studies, the learning success needs to be compared with a control group, that is, a group of participants who has not undergone the intervention treatment.

Logistical requirements such as those mentioned in Chapter 7 determine what is and what is not possible in terms of the experimental set-up. Availability of, and access to, research participants represents a key aspect; for example, running experiments in educational institutions can involve a long sequence of approvals from the government, ministries, school head offices, the teachers, and legal guardian of a student, if the student is not old enough to provide informed consent to participate in the research study. Furthermore, school administrators might be concerned about having their students participate in research for fear that the research activities may disturb the curriculum and the students' learning process. These are just a few examples of problems one faces when aiming to run experimental studies with students in educational settings— independent from actual robot use in that context. The use of robots in HRI research in the field comes with additional challenges (i.e., a lack of robust robot technology that can survive a day of experimentation without technical failure), particularly in longitudinal studies. Maintaining the research set-up, including the robot and the experiment room, and acquiring long-term commitment from participants is yet another challenge in longitudinal research. A high drop-out rate during the course of a field experiment might make it difficult to conclude a research with a reasonable sample size. These practical challenges in doing longitudinal research also contribute to the fact that there are only a few longitudinal studies which focus on studying and evaluating robot-assisted teaching and learning in individual and group settings (Kanda et al., 2007; Tanaka and Ghosh, 2011).

11.2   Research Process

The most common approach taken by researchers in social robotics and in educational robotics, in particular, are research studies that are typically conducted in the laboratory setting in the laboratory setting. In such a context, research participants are exposed to a T&L scenario that may involve dyadic face-to-face interactions between a human and the robot. Typically, a lab experiment in educational robotics involves recruitment, obtaining consent, explaining the procedure, carrying out the experiment with the participant interacting with the robot, an element of debriefing, and, lastly, departing from the setting.

The spectrum of research methods in HRI in general and education is extensive and it would go beyond the scope of this book to provide a complete overview. The interested reader might consult dedicated literature, such as Bethel and Murphy (2010), Check and Schutt (2011), or Wiersma (2008). We will thus only briefly outline the research process for the empirical investigation of research questions in educational robotics:

1 Literature review
2 Definition of research questions
3 Definition of method
4 Ethical approval and study registration
5 Data collection
6 Analysis
7 Writing
8 Publication

11.2.1   Literature Review

One of the foundations of innovative research is originality. Tackling a research question to which the answer is already known adds little to the growth of knowledge. It can still be useful to replicate and extend existing research to validate and confirm previous findings. Notably, the status of replication studies has dramatically increased with the arrival of the replication crisis (Makel and Plucker, 2014).

The replication crisis is based on the fact that many studies cannot successfully be replicated. Meaning that if an experiment is repeated following the instructions available in the method section of the original study, different results are obtained. Open Science Collaboration estimates that only one-third to one-half of studies in the area of psychology produce results that can be replicated.

It is good practice to consult the ever growing body of research literature before conducting an experiment. A good literature review will summarize what work has already been done in the area of interest and what gaps in the knowledge may exist. Educational robots research in particular should also look into literature in the field of educational technology to ascertain the gaps in techniques that do not involve robots but may utilize other smart artefacts. Most literature in the field of educational robots is published in the Human-Robot Interaction conference or other social robotics conferences such as RO-MAN, Human-Agent Interaction, International Conference of Social Robotics, and more. Popular journals that may publish educational robotics research include the International Journal of Social Robotics and a number of Educational Technology Journals, such as the top-ranked British Journal of Educational Technology, the Journal of Computers in Education, or the Computers in Human Behavior journal. Readers should note that accessing papers from conferences and journals normally requires a paid subscription. Contacting the authors themselves or searching papers on specialized searching engines like Google Scholar may provide the interested reader with a free PDF.

11.2.2   Definition of Research Questions

Defining novel and interesting questions is one of the hardest tasks in research. Not only does the ever growing body of scientific literature make it increasingly difficult to define truly novel questions, but also, a good research question is defined by not being able to predict its answer. Good arguments for and against the potential outcome would be plausible and ideally backed up by previous studies.

Research questions to which an answer seems certain could be considered trivial. Only in the rare cases in which a widely held belief is disproved (or the opposite) do these potentially trivial questions unfold their value. After all, these types of questions have unleashed the replication crisis. Ideally, experimental research is replicated, that is, repeated by other researchers to establish that specific findings bear validity beyond the walls of a particular research laboratory in a particular national or cultural context. Some conferences and journals that promote empirical research may demand hypotheses grounded in literature rather than open-ended research aims. Hypotheses in the field of educational robots will be stated as such to indicate expected outcomes or trends in learning outcomes or improvements. For example, a hypothesis may be that a particular robot intervention will lead to increased social engagement and/or higher test scores.

11.2.3   *Definition of Method*

An appropriate research method serves to produce valid answers to given research questions of interest. In case of inconclusive evidence based on inappropriate operationalization of measured constructs or other flaws in the research design, we do not evidence for or against our research hypotheses at hand. Naturally, which research method is used depends heavily on the type of research question asked: Earlier, we have described the difference between longitudinal and short-term experiments and also briefly introduced quantitative and qualitative data types. Typically a research method in HRI broadly or educational robots will include a description of:

1 The manipulation
2 The measurements
3 The research participants
4 The set-up
5 The procedure of the experiment

11.2.3.1   *Manipulation*

By manipulating a factor in the experiment it is possible to consider a potentially causal relationship between the manipulation and the measurements. To illustrate, in order to determine that the height of a robot has an impact on how much authority a student ascribes to it, it is necessary to expose participants to robots of different heights. The participants would be split into groups and each group would interact with a robot of just one size. Similarly, in an educational robot setting, we could have two variations of learning scenarios or pedagogy and evaluate which one serves the purpose better.

Another typical set-up is to divide the participants into a "treatment" group and a "control" group. The treatment group would be exposed to a robot exhibiting a certain behaviour, while the participants in the control group would interact with a robot that does not have that specific behaviour. For example, in Ahmad et al. (2019), since the manipulation was adaptive behaviour, the control group was a robot that did not employ adaptive behaviour with both conditions across an educational setting of learning vocabulary.

Using a correlational approach, researchers would use a survey to gather data on the relationship between a set of variables. For instance, we could measure the age of the participant, academic grades, etc. and his/her negative attitude towards the robot. However, such a correlational approach brings along certain limitations. The biggest limitation concerns the fact that correlational evidence can only provide insights into the relationship between a set of variables and the direction of this relationship. For instance, correlational survey data may reveal that willingness to use a robot in an educational setting correlates moderately positive with attitudes towards technology in general. That is, the more positive people are about technology in general, the more inclined they are to use robots in educational settings and vice versa. Thus, through this technique we learn something about the strength and direction of the relationship between the aforementioned variables, but we get no information about what causes it.

11.2.3.2   *Measurements*

Conducting empirical research implies collecting various types of data from research participants. Broadly, data can be categorized into objective or subjective types. Objective data is measurable data that is not subject to personal interpretation or bias, such as physiological data. Subjective data comprises personalized opinions and responses which are individual and hence open to interpretation.

Examples of objective data are skin conductivity, heart rate, administrative data (e.g., school grades), and observations done through video and audio recordings. The most common form of subjective data are responses received through self-report surveys (Bethel and Murphy, 2010).

In sum, empirical data gathered from research participants are considered as either subjective or objective; which can also be termed as qualitative or quantitative, respectively. For instance, the number of times a student provides a correct response to a teacher's question can be counted objectively. This assumes that a right answer can be easily defined. On the other hand, an interview with the student about why he or she chose that particular response would yield rich unstructured data which are more complex in terms of its analysis and interpretation. Responses from semi-structured interviews cannot easily be objectively counted and it will always be interpreted by the experimenter. Many statistical methods that enable researchers to summarize data and to draw conclusions from them require quantitative data. Qualitative data can also be analyzed through a variety of techniques which rely on categorizing sentiments and perceptions emerging from the data. These include grounded theory or content analysis. The challenge in analysing qualitative data is that it is subject to bias and interpretation. Relying on two or more researchers to interpret the data allows for control of such emerging biases.

Most educational robot studies rely on children as participants. Clearly, children cannot reliably and accurately fill in complex questionnaires. Customized and tailored self-reporting for children is hence an option, such as card sorting. Often, for an interesting case study, nonverbal behaviour of children is analysed through video analysis as a means of answering the research questions. Social engagement or particular emotions, such as surprise or fear, can be counted by viewing the video recording. Yet again, although video data may be quantitative in nature, it is initiated through a qualitative interpretation of video coders, that is, members of the research team who manually sift through the video and mark points where certain key events occur. As mentioned above, including multiple coders and computing inter-rater reliability can help identify personal biases. Furthermore, psychological measures (i.e., intellectual quotient, language or reading abilities), can be taken into account, and associated with behavioural responses to enrich results with explanatory sources.

The advantages and disadvantages of the variety of data collection approaches have been a standing discussion point between researchers and the debate can at times become heated. We will refrain from taking a side and recommend a mix of both quantitative and qualitative data collection and analysis, considering logistical constraints. Taking advantage of the best of both approaches seems a fruitful way to acquire valid and relevant knowledge. All participants' responses, once measured, are typically stored electronically in databases or spreadsheets.

11.2.3.3   Participants

It is important to consider the characteristics of the participants in the study. Arguably the age of the participants will have one of the biggest impacts on the results of an educational research study due to the developmental variations in age groups of children. It is therefore necessary to precisely define who will participate in the study. This will automatically constrain the generalizability of the results. A study that was conducted with 10- to 12-year-olds will only give knowledge about children in this specific age group. To minimize the impact of coincidental biases, it is useful to sample a large number of participants. The freely available G*Power software[1] allows experimenters to estimate the number of participants they need given an expected effect size. An increase in the number of observations is rewarded with the measured random noise cancelling each other out. Many journals expect accepted papers to showcase power analysis of their studies, that is how many participants are required to generate the expected effect.

11.2.3.4   Set-up

Experiments are often set up in a laboratory to be able to exclude as many coincidental biases as possible. The lab experimental setting comprises a somewhat simulated and artificial reality that sometimes appears removed from an actual realistic setting which we usually encounter in everyday school life. That is, the experimental procedure is standardized and controlled and is—except for the manipulation—identical for all research participants. This assures internal validity, enabling researchers to establish that only changes in one variable causes differences in another. At the same time, this of course limits the generalizability of the experimental findings. This constraint is often referred to as ecological validity. The results of a lab study only apply to the exact settings of the study and thus the experimental evidence has to be interpreted with caution when applied to settings in the real world or other labs. Its ecological validity is therefore low.

Conducting experiments in the actual T&L environment does improve the ecological validity of the study, but it may introduce a lot of noise in the measurements. Events may, for example, happen during the study that have nothing to do with the study itself but nonetheless influence the measurements, such as a fire drill.

Logistically, both approaches, the lab versus "in the wild", have their own challenges. As we have elucidated at the start of this chapter, running HRI experiments in a school requires a series of approvals and synchronization with school timetables, curriculum matters, and student availability. Similarly, conducting HRI experiments of an educational nature in a lab means children would need to be transported to and hosted at the research lab environment. In both cases, proper precautions needs to be taken in relation to ethics and safety.

The effort necessary to prepare the robot for an experiment should not be underestimated. Programming all the necessary behaviours and interactions requires substantial effort by a competent programmer. This involves several iterative cycles of development and testing. While some robotic software platforms, such as SoftBank Robotics's Choregraphe, utilize a visual programming paradigm that appeals to non-programmers, the fundamental challenges of robotics and software engineering remain. Making sense of sensor data, deciding what action to take, and executing the selection actions requires careful planning and control. It is wise to collaborate with a robotics expert to ensure that the robot's functions work sufficiently well to complete the experiment. Any observational data lost due to malfunctions of the robot is an avoidable risk. This is precisely why researchers conduct pilots, mock-ups, or rehearsals of their experiments to ascertain any unexpected errors or loopholes that may appear within the experimental set-up and robot behaviour.

At times, the robot requires skills that go beyond what is possible with a typical amount of software development. If a robot is, for example, expected to operate in an actual classroom, then the robot's ability to recognize the utterances of a specific child will be compromised by the surrounding noise of all the other children. While there are some advanced technologies available, such as microphone arrays embedded in the environment, this might go beyond the financial resources available to the project. In such cases, it is often easier to have a person in another room remotely listening through the microphones in the robot and to trigger the appropriate actions. The robot would then not be completely autonomous, but this difference would be invisible to the participants in the experiment. Such studies are often referred to as WoZ studies, named after the movie in which a person controls a large illusion behind a curtain (Riek, 2012). It is imperative to mention here that the participant in this HRI experiment would be unaware of this set-up and essentially be deceived. This is usually acknowledged by the researchers at the end of the experiment session by debriefing the participants. The use of deception does need to be explicitly mentioned in the ethics applications of the study (see section below).

Commonly, participants get rewarded for their effort. An appropriate remuneration for their effort depends on the social norms of the specific environment. At times non-monetary acknowledgements can work well to not only reward participants, but also to prevent the participant feeling obliged to comply with the experiment.

11.2.3.5 Procedure

The procedure section will describe the most important steps that each participant will go through. This includes welcoming the participants to the study, the administration of the manipulation (if applicable), the collection of responses, and the debriefing of the participants. The purpose of detailing each step in the protocol is mainly to allow replication of the experiment by other researchers. This will help to reduce the replication crisis (see box above).

11.2.4 Ethics Approval and Study Registration

Any study that includes human participants requires the approval of an institution's board of ethics. The purpose of the institutional review process is to ensure that the risks that participants are exposed to during a study are in proportion to the expected gains in knowledge. It also ensures that participants are not exposed to unnecessary risks. Conducting experiments with minors and/or vulnerable groups requires the utmost care and is likely to involve seeking consent from the legal guardians. Getting ethical approval for studies on HRI with children may require an expedited review to assure that consent, safety, and the children's welfare is sustained during the experiment.

It has also become good practice to pre-register studies. This typically involves publishing research questions, the method, the planned statistical analysis, and the expected results prior to executing the experiment. This safeguards researchers against accusations of misconduct, such as p-hacking (Head et al., 2015). Popular pre-registration services include AsPredicted[2] and the Center for Open Science[3].

11.2.5   Analysis

The structure of the experiment defined by the manipulation, process, and measurements determines what statistical analysis is appropriate. The main goal of any statistical analysis is to exclude the possibility that the differences in the measurements observed are due to chance alone. There is A wide spectrum of statistical methods are available and the interested reader might consult dedicated books on this topic such as Field (2017). A variety of software suites are available to analyse quantitative data once it is placed in spreadsheets. These spreadsheets are easily imported into statistical packages of which SPSS and R Studio[4] are the most commonly used. SPSS is provided by IBM but it requires an expensive licence which may not be available through the educational institution. R Studio is open source but requires programming knowledge as it is based on the R programming language. Jamovi[5] is an open source statistical program that makes the data and the analysis process completely transparent and it can be shared in one file.

11.2.6   Writing and Publishing

Sharing knowledge is in the essence of scientific progress and hence, no study is complete without it being reported. There are several writing tools available that help scientists to prepare their manuscripts. This includes free systems, such as LaTeX, but also commercial solutions, such as Microsoft Word and Endnote. Using such tools will dramatically reduce the workload and increase the consistency. Going through several iterations of writing and review are essential and a professional copy editor will increase the quality of the manuscript.

Most reporting of empirical research in HRI and consequently Educational Robots is inspired by the American Psychological Association (APA) style of reporting experiments (Association, 2020). This standardized style of reporting experiments allows for easy replication and comprehension for readers and reviewers alike.

The manuscript is then submitted to scientific journals or conferences for consideration. It should be reviewed by peer experts in a double-blind or, at least, single-blind process in which at least the reviewers are unknown to the authors. Upon passing the review process, the manuscript gets published. It is desirable to have the paper published following the open-access policy, so that its content is not hidden behind a pay wall and can be received by a larger audience in the scientific community and beyond.

It has also become good practice to make the data collected in the study and all materials used in running the experiment available to other researchers. This can be done using open and free platforms such as the Open Science Foundation[6] or Figshare[7]. This enables other researchers to not only verify the statistical analysis conducted, but also to include the data in meta-analyses that try to combine the knowledge gained from several experiments.

Questions for you to think about:

- What are the pros and cons of conducting research in the area of Educational Robots either in the lab or "in the wild"?
- What are the types of data that can be collected in experiments concentrating on Educational Robots?
- What aspects need to be considered before conducting experiments with children within the context of Educational Robots?

Future reading:

- Guy Hoffman and Xuan Zhao (2020). A Primer for Conducting Experiments in Human–Robot Interaction. ACM Transactions on Human-Robot Interaction (THRI), 10(1), 1-31. https://doi.org/10.1145/3412374
- Cindy L. Bethel and Robin R. Murphy. Review of human studies methods in HRI and recommendations. *International Journal of Social Robotics*, 2(4):347–359, 2010. 10.1007/s12369-010-0064-9. URL https://doi.org/10.1007/s12369-010-0064-9

- Jonathan Lazar, Jinjuan Heidi Feng, and Harry Hochheiser. *Research Methods in Human-Computer Interaction*. Morgan Kaufmann, 2017. ISBN 978-0-12-805390-4

Notes

1. https://www.psychologie.hhu.de/arbeitsgruppen/allgemeine-psychologie-und-arbeitspsychologie/gpower.html
2. https://aspredicted.org/
3. https://www.cos.io/our-services/prereg
4. https://rstudio.com/
5. https://www.jamovi.org/
6. https://osf.io/
7. https://figshare.com/

Bibliography

Evan Ackerman. Jibo is probably totally dead now. *IEEE Spectrum*, 2018. URL https://spectrum.ieee.org/automaton/robotics/home-robots/jibo-is-probably-totally-dead-now.

Henny Admoni and Brian Scassellati. Social eye gaze in human-robot interaction: A review. *Journal of Human-Robot Interaction*, 6(1):25–63, May 2017. ISSN 2163-0364. 10.5898/JHRI.6.1.Admoni. URL https://doi.org/10.5898/JHRI.6.1.Admoni.

Muneeb Imtiaz Ahmad, Omar Mubin, and Joanne Orlando. Children views' on social robot's adaptations in education. In *Proceedings of the 28th Australian Conference on Computer-Human Interaction*, pages 145–149, 2016. URL https://doi.org/10.1145/3010915.3010977.

Muneeb Imtiaz Ahmad, Omar Mubin, Suleman Shahid, and Joanne Orlando. Robot's adaptive emotional feedback sustains children's social engagement and promotes their vocabulary learning: a long-term child–robot interaction study. *Adaptive Behavior*, 27(4):243–266, 2019. URL https://doi.org/10.1177/1059712319844182.

I. Ajzen and M. Fishbein. *Understanding Attitudes and Predicting Social Behaviour*. Pearson, 1980.

Maija Aksela and Outi Haatainen. Project-based learning (PBL) in practise: Active teachers' views of its' advantages and challenges. In *Integrated Education for the Real World*, pages 9–16, Australia, 2019. Queensland University of Technology.

Moza Alahbabi, Fatima Almazroei, Mariam Almarzoqi, Aysha Almeheri, Mariam Alkabi, A. Al Nuaimi, Massimiliano Cappuccio, and Fady Alnajjar. Avatar based interaction therapy: A potential therapeutic approach for children with autism. In *International Conference on Mechatronics and Automation (ICMA)*. IEEE, August 2017. 10.1109/icma.2017.8015864. URL https://doi.org/10.1109%2Ficma.2017.8015864.

Minoo Alemi, Ali Meghdari, and Maryam Ghazisaedy. Employing humanoid robots for teaching English language in Iranian junior high-schools. *International Journal of Humanoid Robotics*, 11(03): 1450022, 2014. https://doi.org/10.1142/S0219843614500224. URL https://doi.org/10.1142/S0219843614500224.

Wadee Alhalabi. Virtual reality systems enhance students' achievements in engineering education. *Behaviour & Information Technology*, 35(11):919–925, 2016. 10.1080/0144929X.2016.1212931. URL https://doi.org/10.1080/0144929X.2016.1212931.

Walter Sinnott-Armstrong. Consequentialism. Stanford Encyclopedia of Philosophy, retrieved online 4/1/2021, https://plato.stanford.edu/entries/consequentialism/

Dimitris Alimisis. Educational robotics: Open questions and new challenges. *Themes in Science and Technology Education*, 6(1):63–71, 2013.

Dimitris Alimisis and George Boulougaris. Robotics in physics education: Fostering graphing abilities in kinematics. In *Proceedings of 4th International Workshop Teaching Robotics, Teaching with Robotics & 5th International Conference Robotics in Education*, pages 2–10, 2014.

Atheer Alkhalifah, Bashayer Alsalman, Deema Alnuhait, Ohoud Meldah, Sara Aloud, Hend S. Al-Khalifa, and Hind M. Al-Otaibi. Using NAO humanoid robot in kindergarten: a proposed system. In *The 15th International Conference on Advanced Learning Technologies*, pages 166–167. IEEE, 2015.

Fady Alnajjar, Sumayya Khalid, Alstair Vogan, Rui Nouchi, Ryuta Kawashima, et al. Emerging cognitive intervention technologies to meet the needs of an aging population: A systematic review. *Frontiers in Aging Neuroscience*, 11:291, 2019a. URL https://doi.org/10.3389/fnagi.2019.00291.

Fady Alnajjar, Massimiliano Cappuccio, Abdulrahman Renawi, Omar Mubin, and Chu Kiong Loo. Personalized robot interventions for autistic children: An automated methodology for attention assessment. *International Journal of Social Robotics*, March 2020. 10.1007/s12369-020-00639-8. URL https://doi.org/10.1007%2Fs12369-020-00639-8.

Fady S. Alnajjar, Abdulrahman Majed Renawi, Massimiliano Cappuccio, and Omar Mubin. A low-cost autonomous attention assessment system for robot intervention with autistic children. In *The Tenth IEEE Global Engineering Education Conference*, pages 787–792. IEEE, 2019b. URL https://doi.org/10.1109/EDUCON.2019.8725132.

Fady Alnajjar, Hassan Umari, Waleed K. Ahmed, Munkhjargal Gochoo, Alistair A. Vogan, Adel Aljumaily, Peer Mohamad, Shingo Shimoda, CHAD: Compact Hand-Assistive Device for enhancement of function in hand impairments, *Robotics and Autonomous Systems*, Volume 142, 2021, 103784, https://doi.org/10.1016/j.robot.2021.103784.

Patrícia Alves-Oliveira, Pedro Sequeira, and Ana Paiva. The role that an educational robot plays. In *2016 25th IEEE International Symposium on Robot and Human Interactive Communication (RO-MAN)*, pages 817–822. IEEE, 2016. URL https://doi.org/10.1145/2909824.3020231.

Patrícia Alves-Oliveira, Pedro Sequeira, Francisco S. Melo, Ginevra Castellano, and Ana Paiva. Empathic robot for group learning: A field study. *ACM Transactions on Human-Robot Interaction*, March 2019. 10.1145/3300188. URL https://doi.org/10.1145/3300188.

Sean Andrist, Xiang Zhi Tan, Michael Gleicher, and Bilge Mutlu. Conversational gaze aversion for humanlike robots. In *Proceedings of the 9th ACM/IEEE International Conference on Human-Robot Interaction*, HRI '14, pages 25–32, New York, NY, USA, 2014. Association for Computing Machinery. ISBN 9781450326582. 10.1145/2559636.2559666. URL https://doi.org/10.1145/2559636.2559666.

Saira Anwar, Nicholas Alexander Bascou, Muhsin Menekse, and Asefeh Kardgar. A systematic review of studies on educational robotics. *Journal of Pre-College Engineering Education Research (J-PEER)*, 9(2):2, 2019. 10.7771/2157-9288.1223. URL https://doi.org/10.7771/2157-9288.1223.

Julie Archer-Kath, David W. Johnson, and Roger T. Johnson. Individual versus group feedback in cooperative groups. *The Journal of Social Psychology*, 134(5):681–694, 1994.

Kai O Arras and Daniela Cerqui. Do we want to share our lives and bodies with robots? A 2000 people survey: A 2000-people survey. *Technical Report*, 605(1), 2005. 10.3929/ethz-a-010113633. URL https://doi.org/10.3929/ethz-a-010113633.

James Arthur, Kristján Kristjánsson, Tom Harrison, Wouter Sanderse, and Daniel Wright. *Teaching Character and Virtue in Schools*. Routledge, London, 2016. 10.4324/9781315695013.

Isaac Asimov. The Fun They Had in "Boys and Girls Page". *NEA service Inc*, 1951.

Thibault Asselborn, Wafa Johal, and Pierre Dillenbourg. Keep on moving! exploring anthropomorphic effects of motion during idle moments. In *The 26th IEEE International Symposium on Robot and Human Interactive Communication*, pages 897–902. IEEE, 2017.

American Psychological Association. *Publication Manual of the American Psychological Association*. American Psychological Association, 7th edition, 2020. ISBN 9781433832161.

Richard C. Atkinson and Richard M. Shiffrin. Human memory: A proposed system and its control processes. In Kenneth W. Spence and Janet Taylor Spence, editors, *Psychology of Learning and Motivation*, volume 2, pages 89–195. Academic Press, New York, 1968. https://doi.org/10.1016/S0079-7421(08)60422-3. URL http://www.sciencedirect.com/science/article/pii/S0079742108604223.

Ronald T. Azuma. A survey of augmented reality. *Presence: Teleoperators & Virtual Environments*, 6(4):355–385, 1997. 10.1162/pres.1997.6.4.355. URL https://doi.org/10.1162/pres.1997.6.4.355.

Uba Backonja, Amanda K. Hall, Ian Painter, Laura Kneale, Amanda Lazar, Maya Cakmak, Hilaire J. Thompson, and George Demiris. Comfort and attitudes towards robots among young, middle-aged, and older adults: A cross-sectional study. *Journal of Nursing Scholarship*, 50(6):623–633, 2018. URL https://doi.org/10.1111/jnu.12430.

A. Baddeley. Working memory. *Science*, 255(5044):556–559, 1992. ISSN 0036-8075. 10.1126/science.1736359. URL https://science.sciencemag.org/content/255/5044/556.

Il-han Bae and Jeong-hye Han. Analysis on teacher's height and authority in robot-assisted learning. *Journal of Digital Contents Society*, 18(8):1501–1507, 2017a. URL http://www.dbpia.co.kr/Journal/articleDetail?nodeId=NODE07293508.

Ilhan Bae and Jeonghye Han. Does height affect the strictness of robot assisted teacher? In *Proceedings of the Companion of the ACM/IEEE International Conference on Human-Robot Interaction*, pages 73–74, 2017b. URL https://doi.org/10.1145/3029798.3038401.

J. Wesley Baker. The "classroom flip": Using web course management tools to become the guide on the side. *Selected Papers from the 11th International Conference on College Teaching and Learning*, pages 9–17, 01 2000.

Albert Bandura. Social learning theory of aggression. *Journal of Communication*, 28(3):12–29, 1978.

Albert Bandura, Dorothea Ross, and Sheila A. Ross. Imitation of film-mediated aggressive models. *The Journal of Abnormal and Social Psychology*, 66(1):3, 1963a.

Albert Bandura, Dorothea Ross, and Sheila A. Ross. Vicarious reinforcement and imitative learning. *The Journal of Abnormal and Social Psychology*, 67(6):601, 1963b.

C. Bartneck and Merel Keijsers. The morality of abusing a robot. *Paladyn—Journal of Behavioral Robotics (submitted)*, 2020.

C. Bartneck, Christoph Lütge, Alan Wagner, and Sean Welsh. *An Introduction to Ethics in Robotics and AI*. SpringerBriefs in Ethics. Springer, 2020a. ISBN 9783030511098. 10.1007/978-3-030-51110-4. URL https://www.springer.com/gp/book/9783030511098.

Christoph Bartneck. The end of the beginning: A reflection on the first five years of the HRI conference. *Scientometrics*, 86(2):487–504, 2011. 10.1007/s11192-010-0281-x. URL https://doi.org/10.1007/s11192-010-0281-x.

Christoph Bartneck and Juliane Reichenbach. Subtle emotional expressions of synthetic characters. *The International Journal of Human-Computer Studies*, 62(2):179–192, 2005. 10.1016/j.ijhcs.2004.11.006. URL http://www.bartneck.de/publications/2005/subtleEmotional ExpressionsSyntheticCharacters/bartneckReichenbachIJHCS2005.pdf.

Christoph Bartneck, Takayuki Kanda, Hiroshi Ishiguro, and Norihiro Hagita. Is the uncanny valley an uncanny cliff? In *The 16th IEEE International Symposium on Robot and Human Interactive Communication*, pages 368–373. IEEE, 2007a. 10.1109/ROMAN.2007. 4415111.

Christoph Bartneck, Tomohiro Suzuki, Takayuki Kanda, and Tatsuya Nomura. The influence of people's culture and prior experiences with Aibo on their attitude towards robots. *Ai & Society*, 21(1-2):217–230, 2007b. 10.1007/s00146-006-0052-7. URL https://doi.org/10.1007/s00146-006-0052-7.

Christoph Bartneck, Tony Belpaeme, Friederike Eyssel, Takayuki Kanda, Merel Keijsers, and Selma Šabanović. *Human-Robot Interaction: An Introduction*. Cambridge University Press, Cambridge, 2020b. URL https://doi.org/10.1017/9781108676649.

Paul Baxter, Emily Ashurst, Robin Read, James Kennedy, and Tony Belpaeme. Robot Education Peers in a Situated Primary School Study: Personalisation Promotes Child Learning. *PLOS ONE*, 12(5):e0178126, 2017. 10.1371/journal.pone.0178126. URL http://journals.plos.org/plosone/article?id=10.1371/journal.pone.0178126.

Jenay M. Beer, Arthur D. Fisk, and Wendy A. Rogers. Toward a framework for levels of robot autonomy in human-robot interaction. *Journal of Human-Robot Interaction*, 3(2):74–99, 2014. 10.5898/JHRI.3.2.Beer. URL https://doi.org/10.5898/JHRI.3.2.Beer.

John Bell, William Cain, Amy Peterson, and Cui Cheng. From 2D to Kubi to Doubles: Designs for student telepresence in synchronous hybrid classrooms. *International Journal of Designs for Learning*, 7(3): 19–33, 2016. URL https://www.learntechlib.org/p/209594/.

Tony Belpaeme, Paul Baxter, Robin Read, Rachel Wood, Heriberto Cuayáhuitl, Bernd Kiefer, Stefania Racioppa, Ivana Kruijff-Korbayová, Georgios Athanasopoulos, Valentin Enescu, et al. Multimodal child-robot interaction: Building social bonds. *Journal of Human-Robot Interaction*, 1(2):33–53, 2013. 10.5555/3109688.3109691. URL https://dl.acm.org/doi/abs/10.5555/3109688.3109691.

Tony Belpaeme, James Kennedy, Aditi Ramachandran, Brian Scassellati, and Fumihide Tanaka. Social robots for education: A review. *Science Robotics*, 3(21):eaat5954, 2018a.

Tony Belpaeme, Paul Vogt, Rianne Van den Berghe, Kirsten Bergmann, Tilbe Göksun, Mirjam De Haas, Junko Kanero, James Kennedy, Aylin C Küntay, Ora Oudgenoeg-Paz, et al. Guidelines for designing social robots as second language tutors. *International Journal of Social Robotics*, 10(3):325–341, 2018b. 10.1007/s12369-018-0467-6. URL https://doi.org/10.1007/s12369-018-0467-6.

Fabiane Barreto Vavassori Benitti. Exploring the educational potential of robotics in schools: A systematic review. *Computers & Education*, 58(3):978–988, 2012. 10.1016/j.compedu.2011.10.006. URL https://doi.org/10.1016/j.compedu.2011.10.006.

Cindy L. Bethel and Robin R. Murphy. Review of human studies methods in HRI and recommendations. *International Journal of Social Robotics*, 2(4):347–359, 2010. 10.1007/s12369-010-0064-9. URL https://doi.org/10.1007/s12369-010-0064-9.

Frank Biocca. Communication within virtual reality: Creating a space for research. *Journal of Communication*, 42(4):5–22, 1992. 10.1111/j.1460-2466.1992.tb00810.x. URL https://psycnet.apa.org/doi/10.1111/j.1460-2466.1992.tb00810.x.

Christopher M. Bishop. *Pattern Recognition and Machine Learning*. Springer, 2006. ISBN 0387310738.

Olivier Blanson-Henkemans, Vera Hoondert, Femke Schrama-Groot, Rosemarijn Looije, Laurence Alpay, and Mark Neerincx. "I just have diabetes": children's need for diabetes self-management support and how a social robot can accommodate their needs. *Patient Intelligence*, 4:51–61, 2012. 10.2147/PI.S30847.

Benjamin S. Bloom. The 2 sigma problem: The search for methods of group instruction as effective as one-to-one tutoring. *Educational Researcher*, 13(6):4–16, 1984. 10.3102/0013189X013006004. URL https://doi.org/10.3102/0013189X013006004.

Jason Borenstein and Ronald C. Arkin. Nudging for good: Robots and the ethical appropriateness of nurturing empathy and charitable behavior. *AI & Society*, 32(4):499–507, 2017. 10.1007/s00146-016-0684-1. URL https://doi.org/10.1007/s00146-016-0684-1.

Sofiane Boucenna, David Cohen, Andrew N. Meltzoff, Philippe Gaussier, and Mohamed Chetouani. Robots learn to recognize individuals from imitative encounters with people and avatars. *Scientific Reports*, 6: 19908, 2016.

Matt Bower, Cathie Howe, Nerida McCredie, Austin Robinson, and David Grover. Augmented reality in education–cases, places and potentials. *Educational Media International*, 51(1):1–15, 2014. 10.1080/

09523987.2014.889400. URL https://doi.org/10.1080/09523987.2014.
889400.

Neil A. Bradbury. Attention span during lectures: 8 seconds, 10 minutes,
or more? *Advances in Physiology Education*, 40:509–513, 2016.

J. Brandstetter, P. Rácz, C. Beckner, E. B. Sandoval, J. Hay, and C. Bartneck. A peer pressure experiment: Recreation of the Asch conformity
experiment with robots. In *The IEEE/RSJ International Conference
on Intelligent Robots and Systems*, pages 1335–1340, September 2014.
10.1109/IROS.2014.6942730.

Cynthia Breazeal. Socially intelligent robots. *Interactions*, 12(2):19–22,
2005.

John Bridgeland, Mary Bruce, and Arya Hariharan. The missing piece:
A national teacher survey on how social and emotional learning can
empower children and transform schools. a report for CASEL. *Civic
Enterprises*, 2013.

Dražen Brščiundefined, Hiroyuki Kidokoro, Yoshitaka Suehiro, and
Takayuki Kanda. Escaping from children's abuse of social robots.
In *Proceedings of the Tenth Annual ACM/IEEE International Conference on Human-Robot Interaction*, HRI '15, pages 59–66, New
York, NY, USA, 2015. Association for Computing Machinery. ISBN
9781450328838. 10.1145/2696454.2696468. URL https://doi.org/
10.1145/2696454.2696468.

George Butterworth. *Principles of Developmental Psychology: An Introduction*. Psychology Press, 2014.

Elizabeth Campbell. Professional ethics in teaching: Towards the development of a code of practice. *Cambridge Journal of Education*, 30(2):
203–221, 2000. 10.1080/03057640050075198. URL https://doi.org/
10.1080/03057640050075198.

Angelo Cangelosi and Matthew Schlesinger. From babies to robots: The
contribution of developmental robotics to developmental psychology.
Child Development Perspectives, 12(3):183–188, 2018. 10.1111/
cdep.12282. URL https://srcd.onlinelibrary.wiley.com/doi/abs/10.1111/
cdep.12282.

Massimiliano Cappuccio, Eduardo Benitez Sandoval, Omar Mubin, Mohammad Obaid, and Mari Velonaki. *Virtuous Robots: Artificial Agent
and Good Life*. Special Issue in the International Journal of Social
Robotics, 2021.

Massimiliano L. Cappuccio and Stephen V. Shepherd. 13 pointing hand:
Joint attention and embodied symbols. *The Hand, an Organ of the
Mind: What the Manual Tells the Mental*, page 303, 2013.

Massimiliano L. Cappuccio, Anco Peeters, and William McDonald. Sym-
pathy for Dolores: Moral consideration for robots based on virtue
and recognition. *Philosophy and Technology*, 33(1):9–31, 2019.
10.1007/s13347-019-0341-y.

Julie Carpenter, Matt Eliot, and Daniel Schultheis. Machine or friend: Understanding users' preferences for and expectations of a humanoid robot companion. In *Proceedings of the 5th Conference on Design and Emotion 2006*, 2006. ISBN 9197507954.

Stefano Carpin, Mike Lewis, Jijun Wang, Stephen Balakirsky, and Chris Scrapper. USARSim: A robot simulator for research and education. In *IEEE International Conference on Robotics and Automation*, pages 1400–1405. IEEE, 2007. 10.1109/ROBOT.2007.363180. URL https://doi.org/10.1109/ROBOT.2007.363180.

David Carr. *Professionalism and Ethics in Teaching*. Routledge, London, 2005.

David Carr and Jan Steutel. *Virtue Ethics and Moral Education*. Routledge, London, 2005.

Jonathan Casas, Bahar Irfan, Emmanuel Senft, Luisa Gutiérrez, Monica Rincon-Roncancio, Marcela Munera, Tony Belpaeme, and Carlos A Cifuentes. Social assistive robot for cardiac rehabilitation: A pilot study with patients with angioplasty. In *Companion of the 13th ACM/IEEE International Conference on Human-Robot Interaction*, pages 79–80. Association for Computing Machinery, 2018. 10.1145/3173386.3177052. URL https://doi.org/10.1145/3173386.3177052.

Chris Caswell and Sean Neill. *Body Language for Competent Teachers*. Routledge, 2003.

Albert Causo, Giang Truong Vo, I-Ming Chen, and Song Huat Yeo. Design of robots used as education companion and tutor. In *Robotics and Mechatronics*, pages 75–84. Springer, 2016.

Elizabeth Cha, Samantha Chen, and Maja J. Mataric. Designing telepresence robots for k-12 education. In *Proceedings of the 26th IEEE International Symposium on Robot and Human Interactive Communication*, pages 683–688. IEEE, 2017. 10.1109/ROMAN.2017.8172377. URL https://ieeexplore.ieee.org/abstract/document/8172377.

Chih-Wei Chang, Jih-Hsien Lee, Po-Yao Chao, Chin-Yeh Wang, and Gwo-Dong Chen. Exploring the possibility of using humanoid robots as instructional tools for teaching a second language in primary school. *Journal of Educational Technology & Society*, 13(2):13–24, 2010. URL https://www.learntechlib.org/p/75345/.

Blessing Chapfika. The role of integrity in higher education. *International Journal for Educational Integrity*, 4(1), 2008.

Catherine C. Chase, Doris B. Chin, Marily A. Oppezzo, and Daniel L. Schwartz. Teachable agents and the protégé effect: Increasing the effort towards learning. *Journal of Science Education and Technology*, 18(4):334–352, 2009. 10.1007/s10956-009-9180-4. URL https://doi.org/10.1007/s10956-009-9180-4.

Vidushi Chaudhary, Vishnu Agrawal, Pragya Sureka, and Ashish Sureka. An experience report on teaching programming and computational thinking to elementary level children using lego robotics education kit. In *The Eighth International Conference on Technology for Education (T4E)*, pages 38–41. IEEE, 2016. URL https://doi.org/10.1109/T4E.2016.016.

Joseph Check and Russell K. Schutt. *Research Methods in Education*. Sage Publications, 2011.

Selene Chew, Willie Tay, Danielle Smit, and Christoph Bartneck. Do social robots walk or roll? In Shuzhi Sam Ge, Haizhou Li, John-John Cabibihan, and Yeow Kee Tan, editors, *Social Robotics*, pages 355–361, Berlin, Heidelberg, 2010. Springer Berlin Heidelberg. ISBN 978-3-642-17248-9. 10.1007/978-3-642-17248-9_37. URL https://doi.org/10.1007/978-3-642-17248-9_37.

Hsu Chincheng, Alexander Schmitz, Kosuke Kusayanagi, and Shigeki Sugano. Continuous sensing ability of robot finger joints with tactile sensors. In *Proceedings of the IEEE/ASME International Conference on Advanced Intelligent Mechatronics (AIM)*, pages 1440–1444. IEEE, 2019.

Jong-Hong Choi, Jong-Yun Lee, and Jeong-Hye Han. Comparison of cultural acceptability for educational robots between Europe and Korea. *Journal of Information Processing Systems*, 4(3):97–102, 2008. 10.3745/JIPS.2008.4.3.97. URL https://doi.org/10.3745/JIPS.2008.4.3.97.

Alexandre Coninx, Paul Baxter, Elettra Oleari, Sara Bellini, Bert Bierman, Olivier Blanson Henkemans, Lola Canamero, Piero Cosi, Valentin Enescu, Raquel Ros Espinoza, Antoine Hiolle, Remi Humbert, Bernd Kiefer, Ivana Kruijff-korbayova, Rosemarijn Looije, Marco Mosconi, Mark Neerincx, Giulio Paci, Georgios Patsis, Clara Pozzi, Francesca Sacchitelli, Hichem Sahli, Alberto Sanna, Giacomo Sommavilla, Fabio Tesser, Yiannis Demiris, and Tony Belpaeme. Towards long-term social child-robot interaction: Using multi-activity switching to engage young users. *Journal of Human-Robot Interaction*, 5(1):32–67, 2016. 10.5898/JHRI.5.1.Coninx.

Carolina Cruz-Neira, Daniel J. Sandin, Thomas A. DeFanti, Robert V. Kenyon, and John C. Hart. The cave: Audio visual experience automatic virtual environment. *Communications of the ACM*, 35 (6):64–73, 1992. 10.1145/129888.129892. URL https://doi.org/10.1145/129888.129892.

Adam Csapo, Emer Gilmartin, Jonathan Grizou, JingGuang Han, Raveesh Meena, Dimitra Anastasiou, Kristiina Jokinen, and Graham Wilcock. Multimodal conversational interaction with a humanoid robot. In *The 3rd IEEE International Conference on Cognitive Infocommunications (CogInfoCom)*, pages 667–672. IEEE, 2012.

William Damon. Peer education: The untapped potential. *Journal of Applied Developmental Psychology*, 5(4):331–343, 1984.

Chandan Datta, Chandimal Jayawardena, I Han Kuo, and Bruce A Mac-Donald. Robostudio: A visual programming environment for rapid authoring and customization of complex services on a personal service robot. In *The IEEE/RSJ International Conference on Intelligent Robots and Systems*, pages 2352–2357. IEEE, 2012. URL https://doi.org/10.1109/IROS.2012.6386105.

Kerstin Dautenhahn and Iain Werry. Towards interactive robots in autism therapy: Background, motivation and challenges. *Pragmatics & Cognition*, 12(1):1–35, 2004. 10.1075/pc.12.1.03dau. URL https://doi.org/10.1075/pc.12.1.03dau.

Daniel O. David, Cristina A. Costescu, Silviu Matu, Aurora Szentagotai, and Anca Dobrean. Developing joint attention for children with autism in robot-enhanced therapy. *International Journal of Social Robotics*, 10(5):595–605, November 2018. ISSN 1875-4805. 10.1007/s12369-017-0457-0. URL https://doi.org/10.1007/s12369-017-0457-0.

E Roy Davies. *Computer Vision: Principles, Algorithms, Applications, Learning*. Academic Press, 2017. ISBN 978-0-12-809284-2.

Maartje de Graaf, Somaya Allouch, and Jan A.G.M. Van Dijk. Why would I use this in my home?: A model of domestic social robot acceptance. *Human-Computer Interaction*, 04 2017. 10.1080/07370024.2017.1312406.

Maartje MA De Graaf and Somaya Ben Allouch. Exploring influencing variables for the acceptance of social robots. *Robotics and Autonomous Systems*, 61(12):1476–1486, 2013. 10.1016/j.robot.2013.07.007. URL https://doi.org/10.1016/j.robot.2013.07.007.

Hanne De Jaegher. Social understanding through direct perception? Yes, by interacting. *Consciousness and Cognition*, 18(2):535–542, 2009. ISSN 1053-8100. https://doi.org/10.1016/j.concog.2008.10.007. URL http://www.sciencedirect.com/science/article/pii/S1053810008001438.

Hanne De Jaegher, Ezequiel Di Paolo, and Shaun Gallagher. Can social interaction constitute social cognition? *Trends in Cognitive Sciences*, 14(10):441–447, 2010. ISSN 1364-6613. https://doi.org/10.1016/j.tics.2010.06.009. URL http://www.sciencedirect.com/science/article/pii/S1364661310001464.

Jean Decety. The neural pathways, development and functions of empathy. *Current Opinion in Behavioral Sciences*, 3:1–6, 2015. ISSN 2352-1546. https://doi.org/10.1016/j.cobeha.2014.12.001. URL http://www.sciencedirect.com/science/article/pii/S2352154614000321.

Dennis J. Delprato and Bryan D. Midgley. Some fundamentals of B.F. Skinner's behaviorism. *American Psychologist*, 47(11):1507–1520, 1992. 10.1037/0003-066X.47.11.1507. URL https://doi.org/10.1037/0003-066X.47.11.1507.

Peter J Denning and Matti Tedre. *Computational Thinking*. MIT Press Ltd, Cambridge, Massachusetts, 2019.

Mark D'Esposito. From cognitive to neural models of working memory. *Philosophical Transactions of the Royal Society of London. Series B, Biological Sciences*, 362(1481):761–72, may 2007. ISSN 0962-8436. 10.1098/rstb.2007.2086. URL http://www.pubmedcentral.nih.gov/articlerender.fcgi?artid=2429995{&}tool=pmcentrez{&}rendertype=abstract.

Morton Deutsch. A theory of co-operation and competition. *Human Relations*, 2(2):129–152, 1949. 10.1177/001872674900200204. URL https://doi.org/10.1177/001872674900200204.

Morton Deutsch. Cooperation and trust: Some theoretical notes. In M. R. Jones, editor, *Nebraska Symposium on Motivation*, pages 275–320. University of Nebraska Press, 1962. URL https://psycnet.apa.org/record/1964-01869-002.

Giuseppe Di Cesare, Giancarlo Valente, Cinzia Di Dio, Emanuele Ruffaldi, Massimo Bergamasco, Rainer Goebel, and Giacomo Rizzolatti. Vitality forms processing in the insula during action observation: A multivoxel pattern analysis. *Frontiers in Human Neuroscience*, 10:267, 2016. 10.3389/fnhum.2016.00267. URL https://doi.org/10.3389/fnhum.2016.00267.

Cinzia Di Dio, Sara Isernia, Chiara Ceolaro, Antonella Marchetti, and Davide Massaro. Growing up thinking of god's beliefs: Theory of mind and ontological knowledge. *Sage Open*, 8(4):2158244018809874, 2018. 10.1177/2158244018809874. URL https://doi.org/10.1177/2158244018809874.

Cinzia Di Dio, Federico Manzi, S. Itakura, Takayuki Kanda, Hiroshi Ishiguro, Davide Massaro, and Antonella Marchetti. It does not matter who you are: Fairness in pre-schoolers interacting with human and robotic partners. *International Journal of Social Robotics*, pages 1–15, 2019. 10.1007/s12369-019-00528-9. URL https://doi.org/10.1007/s12369-019-00528-9.

Cinzia Di Dio, Federico Manzi, Giulia Peretti, Angelo Cangelosi, Paul L Harris, Davide Massaro, and Antonella Marchetti. How children think about the robot's mind. The role of attachment and theory of mind in the attribution of mental states to a robotic agent. *Sistemi Intelligenti*, 1:41–56, 2020a.

Cinzia Di Dio, Federico Manzi, Giulia Peretti, Angelo Cangelosi, Paul L

Harris, Davide Massaro, and Antonella Marchetti.   Shall I trust you? From child–robot interaction to trusting relationships. *Frontiers in Psychology*, 11:469, 2020b.   URL https://doi.org/10.1177/2158244018809874.

A. Diamond. Executive functions. *Annual Review of Psychology*, 64: 135–168, 2013. 10.1146/annurev-psych-113011-143750.

David Didau and Nick Rose.   *What Every Teacher Needs to Know about... Psychology.* John Catt Educational Limited, Melton, Woodbridge, 2016.

Pierre Dillenbourg. What do you mean by collaborative learning?, 1999.

James Diprose, Bruce MacDonald, John Hosking, and Beryl Plimmer. Designing an API at an appropriate abstraction level for programming social robot applications. *Journal of Visual Languages & Computing*, 39: 22–40, 2017. URL https://doi.org/10.1016/j.jvlc.2016.07.005.

Carl F. DiSalvo, Francine Gemperle, Jodi Forlizzi, and Sara Kiesler. All robots are not created equal: The design and perception of humanoid robot heads.   In *Proceedings of the 4th Conference on Designing Interactive Systems: Processes, Practices, Methods, and Techniques*, pages 321–326, 2002. 10.1145/778712.778756. URL https://doi.org/10.1145/778712.778756.

Brian R Duffy.   Anthropomorphism and the social robot.   *Robotics and Autonomous Systems*, 42(3-4):177–190, 2003. ISSN 0921-8890. https://doi.org/10.1016/S0921-8890(02)00374-3.   URL http://www.sciencedirect.com/science/article/pii/S0921889002003743.

Hugh Durrant-Whyte and Tim Bailey.   Simultaneous localization and mapping: part I.   *IEEE Robotics & Automation Magazine*, 13(2): 99–110, 2006.   10.1109/MRA.2006.1638022.   URL https://doi.org/10.1109/MRA.2006.1638022.

Thierry Dutoit. *An introduction to text-to-speech synthesis*, volume 3. Springer Science & Business Media, 1997. 10.1007/978-94-011-5730-8. URL https://link.springer.com/book/10.1007/978-94-011-5730-8.

Chad Edwards, Autumn Edwards, Patric R. Spence, and Xialing Lin. I, teacher: Using artificial intelligence (AI) and social robots in communication and instruction. *Communication Education*, 67(4):473–480, 2018.

David Efron. *Gesture and Environment.* King's Crown Press, 1941.

Amy Eguchi.   Educational robotics theories and practice: Tips for how to do it right. In *Robots in K-12 Education: A New Technology for Learning*, pages 1–30. IGI Global, 2012. 10.4018/978-1-4666-0182-6.

P. Ekman and W.V. Friesen. *Facial Action Coding System (FACS): Manual.* Palo Alto: Consulting Psychologists Press, 1978.

Paul Ekman. *Unmasking the Face.* Prentice Hall., 1975.

Paul Ekman and Wallace V. Friesen. The repertoire of nonverbal behavior: Categories, origins, usage, and coding. *Semiotica*, 1(1):49–98, 1969.

Nicholas Epley, Adam Waytz, and John T. Cacioppo. On seeing human: A three-factor theory of anthropomorphism. *Psychological Review*, 114 (4):864, 2007. URL https://doi.org/10.1037/0033-295X.114.4.864.

Peggy A. Ertmer and Timothy J. Newby. Behaviorism, cognitivism, constructivism: Comparing critical features from an instructional design perspective. *Performance Improvement Quarterly*, 6(4):50–72, 1993a. URL https://doi.org/10.1111/j.1937-8327.1993.tb00605.x.

Peggy A. Ertmer and Timothy J. Newby. Behaviorism, cognitivism, constructivism: Comparing critical features from an instructional design perspective. *Performance Improvement Quarterly*, 26 (2):43–71, 1993b. 10.1111/j.1937-8327.1993.tb00605.x. URL https://doi.org/10.1111/j.1937-8327.1993.tb00605.x.

Special Eurobarometer. Public attitudes towards robots. *European Commission*, 2012. URL https://www.ab.gov.tr/files/ardb/evt/Public_attitudes_toward_robots_2012.pdf.

Informatics Europe. Female Students in Informatics Bachelor's Programs. https://www.informatics-europe.org/data/higher-education/statistics/bachelor_all_semesters_percentage.html, 2020. Accessed: 2020-02-01.

Friederike Eyssel and Frank Hegel. (s) he's got the look: Gender stereotyping of robots 1. *Journal of Applied Social Psychology*, 42(9):2213–2230, 2012.

Francesco Ferrari and Friederike Eyssel. Toward a hybrid society. In Arvin Agah, John-John Cabibihan, Ayanna M. Howard, Miguel A. Salichs, and Hongsheng He, editors, *Social Robotics*, pages 909–918, Cham, 2016. Springer International Publishing.

Norma D Feshbach. Studies on empathic behavior in children. *Progress in Experimental Personality Research*, pages 1–47, 1978.

Andy Field. *Discovering Statistics using IBM SPSS Statistics (5th Edition).* Sage, 2017.

Julia Fink. Anthropomorphism and human likeness in the design of robots and human-robot interaction. In Shuzhi Sam Ge, Oussama Khatib, John-John Cabibihan, Reid Simmons, and Mary-Anne Williams, editors, *International Conference on Social Robotics*, pages 199–208, Berlin, Heidelberg, 2012. Springer Berlin Heidelberg. 10.1007/978-3-642-34103-8_20. URL https://doi.org/10.1007/978-3-642-34103-8_20.

Aaron J. Fischer, Bradley S. Bloomfield, Racheal R. Clark, Amelia L. McClelland, and William P. Erchul. Increasing student compliance with teacher instructions using telepresence robot problem-solving teleconsultation. *International Journal of School & Educational Psychology*, 7(sup1):158–172, 2019. 10.1080/21683603.2018.1470948. URL https://doi.org/10.1080/21683603.2018.1470948.

Susan T. Fiske. Stereotyping, prejudice, and discrimination. *The Handbook of Social Psychology*, 2(4):357–411, 1998.

Naomi T. Fitter, Nisha Raghunath, Elizabeth Cha, Christopher A. Sanchez, Leila Takayama, and Maja J. Matarić. Are we there yet? Comparing remote learning technologies in the university classroom. *IEEE Robotics and Automation Letters*, 5(2):2706–2713, 2020. 10.1109/LRA.2020.2970939. URL https://ieeexplore.ieee.org/abstract/document/8978487/.

Priska Flandorfer. Population ageing and socially assistive robots for elderly persons: the importance of sociodemographic factors for user acceptance. *International Journal of Population Research*, 2012, 2012.

Terrence Fong, Illah Nourbakhsh, and Kerstin Dautenhahn. A survey of socially interactive robots. *Robotics and Autonomous Systems*, 42(3-4):143–166, 2003. 10.1016/S0921-8890(02)00372-X. URL https://doi.org/10.1016/S0921-8890(02)00372-X.

Edgar Z. Friedenberg. Toward a theory of instruction by Jerome S. Bruner. Cambridge: Belknap Press, 1966. 177 pp. $3.95. *The Bulletin of the National Association of Secondary School Principals*, 50(309):304–312, 1966. 10.1177/019263656605030929. URL https://doi.org/10.1177/019263656605030929.

Joaquin M. Fuster. Network memory. *Trends in Neurosciences*, 20(10): 451–459, 1997.

Shaun Gallagher. Understanding others: Embodied social cognition. In Paco Calvo and Antoni Gomila, editors, *Handbook of Cognitive Science*, pages 437–452. Elsevier, San Diego, 2008. https://doi.org/10.1016/B978-0-08-046616-3.00022-0. URL http://www.sciencedirect.com/science/article/pii/B9780080466163000220.

Shaun Gallagher. *Social Cognition, the Chinese Room, and the Robot Replies*, pages 83–97. Palgrave Macmillan UK, London, 2012. ISBN 978-0-230-36806-4. 10.1057/9780230368064_5. URL https://doi.org/10.1057/9780230368064_5.

Shaun Gallagher and Daniel Schmicking. *Handbook of Phenomenology and Cognitive Science*. Springer Netherlands, 2010. 10.1007/978-90-481-2646-0.

Vittorio Gallese. Embodied simulation: From mirror neuron systems to interpersonal relations. In *Empathy and Fairness*, pages 3–19. John Wiley & Sons, Ltd, 2008. ISBN 9780470030585. 10.1002/9780470030585.ch2. URL https://onlinelibrary.wiley.com/doi/abs/10.1002/9780470030585.ch2.

Vittorio Gallese. Mirror neurons, embodied simulation and a second-person approach to mindreading. *Cortex*, 49(10):2954–2956, 2013. ISSN 0010-9452. https://doi.org/10.1016/j.cortex.2013.09.008. URL http://www.sciencedirect.com/science/article/pii/S0010945213002414.

Y. Gao, W. Barendregt, M. Obaid, and G. Castellano. When robot personalisation does not help: Insights from a robot-supported learning study. In *The 27th IEEE International Symposium on Robot and Human Interactive Communication*, pages 705–712. IEEE, Aug 2018. 10.1109/ROMAN.2018.8525832.

Alberto Giaretta, Michele De Donno, and Nicola Dragoni. Adding salt to pepper: A structured security assessment over a humanoid robot. In *Proceedings of the 13th International Conference on Availability, Reliability and Security*, pages 1–8, 08 2018. ISBN 978-1-4503-6448-5. 10.1145/3230833.3232807. URL http://dx.doi.org/10.1145/3230833.3232807.

Pablo Gomez Esteban, Paul Baxter, Tony Belpaeme, Erik Billing, Haibin Cai, Hoang-Long Cao, Mark Coeckelbergh, Cristina Costescu, Daniel David, Albert De Beir, Yinfeng Fang, Zhaojie Ju, James Kennedy, Honghai Liu, Alexandre Mazel, Amit Pandey, Kathleen Richardson, Emmanuel Senft, Serge Thill, Greet Van De Perre, Bram Vanderborght, David Vernon, Yu Hui, and Tom Ziemke. How to build a Supervised autonomous system for robot-enhanced therapy for children with autism spectrum disorder. *Paladyn Journal of Behavioral Robotics*, 8(1):18–38, 2017. 10.1515/pjbr-2017-0002. URL https://www.degruyter.com/view/j/pjbr.2017.8.issue-1/pjbr-2017-0002/pjbr-2017-0002.xml?format=INT.

Joseph S. Gonnella, James B. Erdmann, and Mohammadreza Hojat. An empirical study of the predictive validity of number grades in medical school using 3 decades of longitudinal data: implications for a grading system. *Medical Education*, 38(4):425–434, 2004. 10.1111/j.1365-2923.2004.01774.x. URL https://onlinelibrary.wiley.com/doi/abs/10.1111/j.1365-2923.2004.01774.x.

Goren Gordon, Samuel Spaulding, Jacqueline Kory Westlund, Jin Joo Lee, Luke Plummer, Marayna Martinez, Madhurima Das, and Cynthia Breazeal. Affective personalization of a social robot tutor for children's second language skills. In *Thirtieth AAAI Conference on Artificial Intelligence*, 2016.

Michal Gordon, Edith Ackermann, and Cynthia Breazeal. Social robot toolkit: Tangible programming for young children. In *Proceedings of the Tenth Annual ACM/IEEE International Conference on Human-Robot Interaction Extended Abstracts*, HRI'15 Extended Abstracts, pages 67–68, New York, NY, USA, 2015a. Association for Computing Machinery. ISBN 9781450333184. 10.1145/2701973.2702001. URL https://doi.org/10.1145/2701973.2702001.

Michal Gordon, Eileen Rivera, Edith Ackermann, and Cynthia Breazeal. Designing a relational social robot toolkit for preschool children to explore computational concepts. In *Proceedings of the 14th International Conference on Interaction Design and Children*, IDC '15, pages 355–358, New York, NY, USA, 2015b. Association for Computing Machinery. ISBN 9781450335904. 10.1145/2771839.2771915. URL https://doi.org/10.1145/2771839.2771915.

Javi F. Gorostiza and Miguel A. Salichs. End-user programming of a social robot by dialog. *Robotics and Autonomous Systems*, 59(12): 1102–1114, 2011. URL https://doi.org/10.1016/j.robot.2011.07.009.

Gordon Graham. *Eight Theories of Ethics*. Routledge, London, 2004.

Raffaele Grandi, Riccardo Falconi, and Claudio Melchiorri. Robotic competitions: Teaching robotics and real-time programming with lego mindstorms. *IFAC Proceedings Volumes*, 47(3):10598 – 10603, 2014. ISSN 1474-6670. https://doi.org/10.3182/20140824-6-ZA-1003. 00222. URL http://www.sciencedirect.com/science/article/pii/ S1474667016432970. 19th IFAC World Congress.

Jillian Greczek, Katelyn Swift-Spong, and Maja Matarić. Using eye shape to improve affect recognition on a humanoid robot with limited expression. *Technical Report*, 2011.

Edward T. Hall. *The Hidden Dimension*. Doubleday, 1966.

Jaap Ham and Cees J.H. Midden. A persuasive robot to stimulate energy conservation: The influence of positive and negative social feedback and task similarity on energy-consumption behavior. *International Journal of Social Robotics*, 6(2):163–171, 2014. 10.1007/s12369-013-0205-z. URL https://doi.org/10.1007/s12369-013-0205-z.

Jaap Ham and Andreas Spahn. Shall I show you some other shirts too? the psychology and ethics of persuasive robots. In *A Construction Manual for Robots' Ethical Systems*, pages 63–81. Springer, 2015. 10.1007/978-3-319-21548-8_4. URL https://doi.org/10.1007/978-3-319-21548-8_4.

Jeonghye Han. Emerging technologies: Robot assisted language learning. *Language Learning & Technology*, 16(3):1–9, 2012.

Jeonghye Han, Eunja Hyun, Miryang Kim, Hyekyung Cho, Takayuki Kanda, and Tatsuya Nomura. The cross-cultural acceptance of tutoring robots with augmented reality services. *International Journal of Digital Content Technology and its Applications*, 3(2):95–102, 2009.

JingGuang Han, Nick Campbell, Kristiina Jokinen, and Graham Wilcock. Investigating the use of non-verbal cues in human-robot interaction with a NAO robot. In *The 3rd IEEE International Conference on*

Cognitive Infocommunications (CogInfoCom), pages 679–683. IEEE, 2012.

Jürgen Handke. *1 Gelingensbedingungen für den Inverted Classroom: Lehren und Lernen im 21. Jahrhundert*, pages 1–14. Tectum, Baden-Baden, 01 2017. ISBN 9783828867826. 10.5771/9783828867826-1. URL http://dx.doi.org/10.5771/9783828867826-1.

Jürgen Handke and Peter Franke. xMOOCs im virtual linguistics campus. *Schulmeister R, Herausgeber. MOOCs-Massive Open Online Courses: Offene Bildung oder Geschäftsmodell*, pages 101–126, 2013.

Markus Häring, Nikolaus Bee, and Elisabeth André. Creation and evaluation of emotion expression with body movement, sound and eye color for humanoid robots. In *The 20th International Symposium on Robot and Human Interactive Communication*, pages 204–209. IEEE, 2011.

Mark Haselgrove. *Learning: A Very Short Introduction*. Oxford University Press, Oxford, 2016.

Megan L. Head, Luke Holman, Rob Lanfear, Andrew T. Kahn, and Michael D. Jennions. The extent and consequences of p-hacking in science. *PLOS Biology*, 13(3):1–15, 03 2015. 10.1371/journal. pbio.1002106. URL https://doi.org/10.1371/journal.pbio.1002106.

Fritz Heider and Marianne Simmel. An experimental study of apparent behavior. *The American Journal of Psychology*, 57(2):243–259, 1944.

Kate Highfield, Joanne Mulligan, and John Hedberg. Early mathematics learning through exploration with programmable toys. In *Proceedings of the Joint Meeting of PME*, volume 32, pages 169–176. Citeseer, 2008.

Martin L Hoffman. Interaction of affect and cognition in empathy. *Emotions, Cognition, and Behavior*, pages 103–131, 1984.

Devayani Hollands, Fiona M. ; Tirthali. Resource requirements and costs of developing and delivering MOOCs. *International Review of Research in Open and Distributed Learning*, 15(5):113–133, 2014. 10.19173/irrodl.v15i5.1901.

Deanna Hood, Séverin Lemaignan, and Pierre Dillenbourg. When children teach a robot to write: An autonomous teachable humanoid which uses simulated handwriting. In *Proceedings of the Tenth Annual ACM/IEEE International Conference on Human-Robot Interaction*, pages 83–90, New York, NY, USA, 2015. Association for Computing Machinery. ISBN 9781450328838. 10.1145/2696454.2696479. URL https://doi.org/10.1145/2696454.2696479.

Andreas Huber, Astrid Weiss, and Marjo Rauhala. The ethical risk of attachment: How to identify, investigate and predict potential ethical risks in the development of social companion robots. In *The Eleventh ACM/IEEE International Conference on Human Robot Interaction*,

HRI '16, pages 367–374. IEEE Press, 2016. ISBN 9781467383707.

Carl J Hughes, Michael Beverley, and Juliet Whitehead. Using precision teaching to increase the fluency of word reading with problem readers. *European Journal of Behavior Analysis*, 8(2):221–238, 2007. 10.1080/15021149.2007.11434284. URL https://doi.org/10.1080/15021149.2007.11434284.

Hiroshi Ishiguro, Tetsuo Ono, Michita Imai, and Takayuki Kanda. Development of an interactive humanoid robot "Robovie"—an interdisciplinary approach. In *Robotics Research*, pages 179–191. Springer, 2003. 10.1007/3-540-36460-9_12. URL https://link.springer.com/chapter/10.1007/3-540-36460-9_12.

Shoji Itakura. Development of mentalizing and communication: From viewpoint of developmental cybernetics and developmental cognitive neuroscience. *IEICE Transactions on Communications*, 91(7): 2109–2117, 2008. 10.1093/ietcom/e91-b.7.210. URL https://search.ieice.org/bin/summary.php?id=e91-b_7_2109.

Shoji Itakura, Hiraku Ishida, Takayuki Kanda, Yohko Shimada, Hiroshi Ishiguro, and Kang Lee. How to build an intentional android: Infants' imitation of a robot's goal-directed actions. *Infancy*, 13(5):519–532, 2008.

Jesin James, Catherine Inez Watson, and Bruce MacDonald. Artificial empathy in social robots: An analysis of emotions in speech. In *The 27th IEEE International Symposium on Robot and Human Interactive Communication*, pages 632–637. IEEE, 2018.

Joris B Janssen, Chrissy C van der Wal, Mark A Neerincx, and Rosemarijn Looije. Motivating children to learn arithmetic with an adaptive robot game. In *Proceedings of the Third International Conference on Social Robotics*, ICSR'11, pages 153–162, Berlin, Heidelberg, 2011. Springer-Verlag. ISBN 978-3-642-25503-8. 10.1007/978-3-642-25504-5_16. URL http://dx.doi.org/10.1007/978-3-642-25504-5{_}16.

David Johnson and Roger Johnson. An educational psychology success story: Social interdependence theory and cooperative learning. *Educational Researcher*, 38, 06 2009. 10.3102/0013189X09339057.

David W. Johnson and Roger T. Johnson. *Reducing School Violence Through Conflict Resolution*. ASCD, 1995.

David W. Johnson, Roger T. Johnson, Ann E. Ortiz, and Marybeth Stanne. The impact of positive goal and resource interdependence on achievement, interaction, and attitudes. *The Journal of General Psychology*, 118(4):341–347, 1991. 10.1080/00221309.1991.9917795. URL https://doi.org/10.1080/00221309.1991.9917795.

David W. Johnson, Roger T. Johnson, and Karl A. Smith. Cooperative learning returns to college what evidence is there that it works? *Change: The Magazine of Higher Learning*, 30(4):26–35, 1998. 10.1080/00091389809602629. URL https://doi.org/10.1080/00091389809602629.

David W. Johnson, Roger T. Johnson, and Karl Smith. The state of co-operative learning in postsecondary and professional settings. *Educational Psychology Review*, 19(1):15–29, 2007.

David W. Johnson, Roger T. Johnson, and Karl A. Smith. Cooperative learning: Improving university instruction by basing practice on validated theory. *Journal on Excellence in University Teaching*, 25(4): 1–26, 2014.

Sung Eun Jung and Eun-sok Won. Systematic review of research trends in robotics education for young children. *Sustainability*, 10 (4):905, 2018. ISSN 2071-1050. 10.3390/su10040905. URL https://www.mdpi.com/2071-1050/10/4/905.

Peter H. Kahn, Nathan G. Freier, Takayuki Kanda, Hiroshi Ishiguro, Jolina H. Ruckert, Rachel L. Severson, and Shaun K. Kane. Design patterns for sociality in human-robot interaction. In *Proceedings of the 3rd ACM/IEEE International Conference on Human Robot Interaction*, pages 97–104, 2008. URL https://doi.org/10.1145/1349822.1349836.

Peter H. Kahn Jr, Takayuki Kanda, Hiroshi Ishiguro, Nathan G. Freier, Rachel L. Severson, Brian T. Gill, Jolina H. Ruckert, and Solace Shen. "Robovie, you'll have to go into the closet now": Children's social and moral relationships with a humanoid robot. *Developmental Psychology*, 48(2):303, 2012. URL https://psycnet.apa.org/doi/10.1037/a0027033.

Hiroko Kamide, Yasushi Mae, Koji Kawabe, Satoshi Shigemi, Masato Hirose, and Tatsuo Arai. New measurement of psychological safety for humanoid. In *Proceedings of the 7th ACM/IEEE International Conference on Human-Robot Interaction*, pages 49–56. IEEE, 2012. 10.1145/2157689.2157698. URL https://ieeexplore.ieee.org/abstract/document/6249614.

T. Kanda, R. Sato, N. Saiwaki, and H. Ishiguro. A two-month field trial in an elementary school for long-term human–robot interaction. *IEEE Transactions on Robotics*, 23(5):962–971, Oct 2007. ISSN 1941-0468. 10.1109/TRO.2007.904904.

Takayuki Kanda, Takayuki Hirano, Daniel Eaton, and Hiroshi Ishiguro. Interactive robots as social partners and peer tutors for children: A field trial. *Human–Computer Interaction*, 19(1–2):61–84, 2004. 10.1080/07370024.2004.9667340. URL https://www.tandfonline.com/doi/abs/10.1080/07370024.2004.9667340.

Mohammad Ehsanul Karim, Séverin Lemaignan, and Francesco Mondada. A review: Can robots reshape k-12 stem education? In *The IEEE*

International Workshop on Advanced Robotics and its Social Impacts (ARSO), pages 1–8. IEEE, 2015. 10.1109/ARSO.2015.7428217. URL https://doi.org/10.1109/ARSO.2015.7428217.

Kenneth A. Kavale and Mark P. Mostert. Social skills interventions for individuals with learning disabilities. *Learning Disability Quarterly*, 27(1):31–43, 2004. 10.2307/1593630. URL https://doi.org/10.2307/1593630.

Birte Keller, Janine Baleis, Christopher Starke, and Frank Marcinkowski. Machine learning and artificial intelligence in higher education: A state-oftheart report on the German university landscape. In V.W. Stiftung, 31 pages. Springer Verlag, Berlin, 2020.

James Kennedy, Paul Baxter, and Tony Belpaeme. The robot who tried too hard: Social behaviour of a robot tutor can negatively affect child learning. In *Proceedings of the 10th Annual ACM/IEEE International Conference on Human-Robot Interaction*, pages 67–74, Portland, Oregon, USA, 2015. ACM Press. ISBN 9781450328838. 10.1145/2696454.2696457.

James Kennedy, Paul Baxter, Emmanuel Senft, and Tony Belpaeme. Social robot tutoring for child second language learning. In *Proceedings of the 11th ACM/IEEE International Conference on Human-Robot Interaction*, pages 231–238, March 2016. 10.1109/HRI.2016.7451757. URL http://dx.doi.org/10.1109/HRI.2016.7451757.

James Kennedy, Paul Baxter, and Tony Belpaeme. Nonverbal Immediacy as a Characterisation of Social Behaviour for Human-Robot Interaction. *International Journal of Social Robotics*, 9(1):109–128, 2017a. 10.1007/s12369-016-0378-3.

James Kennedy, Paul Baxter, and Tony Belpaeme. The impact of robot tutor nonverbal social behavior on child learning. *Frontiers in ICT*, 4:6, 2017b. ISSN 2297-198X. 10.3389/fict.2017.00006. URL https://www.frontiersin.org/article/10.3389/fict.2017.00006.

James Kennedy, Séverin Lemaignan, Caroline Montassier, Pauline Lavalade, Bahar Irfan, Fotios Papadopoulos, Emmanuel Senft, and Tony Belpaeme. Child speech recognition in human-robot interaction: Evaluations and recommendations. In *Proceedings of the 12th ACM/IEEE International Conference on Human-Robot Interaction*, pages 82–90, New York, NY, USA, 2017c. Association for Computing Machinery. ISBN 9781450343367. 10.1145/2909824.3020229. URL https://doi.org/10.1145/2909824.3020229.

Hanan Khalil and Martin Ebner. MOOCs completion rates and possible methods to improve retention—A literature review. *Proceedings of the World Conference on Educational Multimedia, Hypermedia and Telecommunications*, pages 1236–1244, 01 2014. URL https://www.learntechlib.org/p/147656.

Negar Khojasteh, Cathy Liu, and Susan R. Fussell. Understanding undergraduate students' experiences of telepresence robots on campus. In *Conference Companion Publication of the 2019 on Computer Supported Cooperative Work and Social Computing*, pages 241–246, 2019. 10.1145/3311957.3359450. URL https://doi.org/10.1145/3311957.3359450.

Alison King. From sage on the stage to guide on the side. *College Teaching*, 41(1):30–35, 1993. 10.1080/87567555.1993.9926781. URL https://doi.org/10.1080/87567555.1993.9926781.

Wolfgang Kohler, Kurt Koffka, and Friedrich Sander. Psicología de la forma, 1973.

Dimitra Kokotsaki, Victoria Menzies, and Andy Wiggins. Project-based learning: A review of the literature. *Improving Schools*, 19(3): 267–277, 2016. 10.1177/1365480216659733. URL https://doi.org/10.1177/1365480216659733.

Hideki Kozima, Marek P. Michalowski, and Cocoro Nakagawa. Keepon. *International Journal of Social Robotics*, 1(1):3–18, 2009. 10.1007/s12369-008-0009-8. URL https://doi.org/10.1007/s12369-008-0009-8.

Annica Kristoffersson, Silvia Coradeschi, and Amy Loutfi. A review of mobile robotic telepresence. *Advances in Human-Computer Interaction*, 2013:1–17, 2013. 10.1155/2013/902316. URL https://doi.org/10.1155/2013/902316.

Svetlana Kubilinskiene, Inga Zilinskiene, Valentina Dagiene, and Vytenis Sinkevièius. Applying robotics in school education: A systematic review. *Baltic journal of modern computing*, 5(1):50–69, 2017.

Kwon, Oh-Hun, Koo, Seong-Yong, Kim, Young-Geun, and Kwon, Dong-Soo. Telepresence robot system for English tutoring. In *IEEE Workshop on Advanced Robotics and its Social Impacts*, pages 152–155. IEEE, 2010. 10.1109/ARSO.2010.5679999.

Linda la Velle and Jan Georgeson. Developing teacher confidence in robotics and computation: Case studies from a collaborative European project. In *European Conference on Educational Research (ECER)*, August 2017. URL http://researchspace.bathspa.ac.uk/11944/.

Maureen Lage, Glenn Platt, and Michael Treglia. Inverting the classroom: A gateway to creating an inclusive learning environment. *Journal of Economic Education*, 31:30–43, 12 2000. 10.1080/00220480009596759. URL http://dx.doi.org/10.1080/00220480009596759.

Victor Lavy and Edith Sand. On the origins of gender human capital gaps: Short and long term consequences of teachers' stereotypical biases. Technical report, National Bureau of Economic Research, 2015. URL https://www.nber.org/papers/w20909.

Pamela B. Lawhead, Michaele E. Duncan, Constance G. Bland, Michael Goldweber, Madeleine Schep, David J. Barnes, and Ralph G. Hollingsworth. A road map for teaching introductory programming using lego© mindstorms robots. *ACM SIGCSE Bulletin*, 35(2):191–201, 2002. URL https://doi.org/10.1145/782941.783002.

Jonathan Lazar, Jinjuan Heidi Feng, and Harry Hochheiser. *Research Methods in Human-Computer Interaction*. Morgan Kaufmann, 2017. ISBN 978-0-12-805390-4.

Serena Lecce, Marcella Caputi, and Claire Hughes. Does sensitivity to criticism mediate the relationship between theory of mind and academic achievement? *Journal of Experimental Child Psychology*, 110 (3):313–331, 2011.

Serena Lecce, Marcella Caputi, and Adriano Pagnin. Long-term effect of theory of mind on school achievement: The role of sensitivity to criticism. *European Journal of Developmental Psychology*, 11(3):305–318, 2014.

EunKyoung Lee, YoungJun Lee, Bokyung Kye, and Beomseog Ko. Elementary and middle school teachers', students' and parents' perception of robot-aided education in Korea. In *Proceedings of ED-MEDIA 2008 World Conference on Educational Multimedia, Hypermedia & Telecommunications*, pages 175–183. Association for the Advancement of Computing in Education (AACE), 2008. URL https://www.learntechlib.org/p/28391/.

Séverin Lemaignan, Alexis Jacq, Deanna Hood, Fernando Garcia, Ana Paiva, and Pierre Dillenbourg. Learning by teaching a robot: The case of handwriting. *IEEE Robotics & Automation Magazine*, 23(2):56–66, 2016. ISSN 1558-223X. 10.1109/MRA.2016.2546700.

Mark L. Lester. Class of 1999, 1990. URL https://www.imdb.com/title/tt0099277/.

Daniel Leyzberg, Aditi Ramachandran, and Brian Scassellati. The effect of personalization in longer-term robot tutoring. *Journal of Human-Robot Interaction*, 7(3), December 2018. 10.1145/3283453. URL https://doi.org/10.1145/3283453.

Yi-Chun Lin, Tzu-Chien Liu, Maiga Chang, and Shiau-Ping Yeh. Exploring children's perceptions of the robots. In *International Conference on Technologies for E-Learning and Digital Entertainment*, pages 512–517. Springer, 2009. 10.1007/978-3-642-03364-3_63. URL https://doi.org/10.1007/978-3-642-03364-3_63.

Eric Zhi-Feng Liu. Early adolescents' perceptions of educational robots and learning of robotics. *British Journal of Educational Technology*, 41(3):E44–E47, 2010. 10.1111/j.1467-8535.2009.00944.x. URL https://doi.org/10.1111/j.1467-8535.2009.00944.x.

Angela Lumpkin. Teachers as role models teaching character and moral virtues. *Journal of Physical Education, Recreation & Dance*, 79(2):45–50, 2008. 10.1080/07303084.2008.10598134. URL https://doi.org/10.1080/07303084.2008.10598134.

Matthew C. Makel and Jonathan A. Plucker. Facts are more important than novelty: Replication in the education sciences. *Educational Researcher*, 43(6):304–316, 2014. 10.3102/0013189X14545513. URL https://doi.org/10.3102/0013189X14545513.

Guido Makransky and Lau Lilleholt. A structural equation modeling investigation of the emotional value of immersive virtual reality in education. *Educational Technology Research and Development*, 66(5):1141–1164, 2018. 10.1007/s11423-018-9581-2. URL https://doi.org/10.1007/s11423-018-9581-2.

Federico Manzi, M. Ishikawa, Cinzia Di Dio, S Itakura, T. Kanda, H. Ishiguro, Davide Massaro, and Antonella Marchetti. The understanding of congruent and incongruent referential gaze in 17-month-old infants: An eye-tracking study comparing human and robot. *Scientific Reports*, 10(1):1–10, 2020a. URL https://doi.org/10.1038/s41598-020-69140-6.

Federico Manzi, Giulia Peretti, Cinzia Di Dio, Angelo Cangelosi, Shoji Itakura, Takayuki Kanda, Hiroshi Ishiguro, Davide Massaro, and Antonella Marchetti. A robot is not worth another: Exploring children's mental state attribution to different humanoid robots. *Frontiers in Psychology*, 11:2011, 2020b.

Antonella Marchetti, Federico Manzi, Shoji Itakura, and Davide Massaro. Theory of mind and humanoid robots from a lifespan perspective. *Zeitschrift für Psychologie*, 226:98–109, 2018. URL https://doi.org/10.1027/2151-2604/a000326.

Antonella Marchetti, Laura Miraglia, and Cinzia Di Dio. Toward a socio-material approach to cognitive empathy in autistic spectrum disorder. *Frontiers in Psychology*, 10:2965, 2019. 10.3389/fpsyg.2019.02965. URL https://www.frontiersin.org/articles/10.3389/fnhum.2016.00267/full.

Fred Martin, Bakhtiar Mikhak, Mitchel Resnick, Brian Silverman, and Robbie Berg. *To Mindstorms and Beyond: Evolution of a Construction Kit for Magical Machines*, pages 9–33. Morgan Kaufmann Publishers Inc., San Francisco, CA, USA, 2000. ISBN 1558605975.

Maja J. Matarić. *The Robotics Primer*. MIT Press, Cambridge, MA, 2007. ISBN 9780262633543. URL http://www.worldcat.org/oclc/604083625.

Susan McDonald and Jennifer Howell. Watching, creating and achieving: Creative technologies as a conduit for learning in the early years. *British Journal of Educational Technology*, 43(4):641–651, 2012. 10.1111/j.1467-8535.2011.01231.x. URL https://onlinelibrary. wiley.com/doi/abs/10.1111/j.1467-8535.2011.01231.x.

William McDougall. *An Introduction to Social Psychology*. Psychology Press, 2015.

David McNeill. So you think gestures are nonverbal? *Psychological Review*, 92(3):350, 1985.

David McNeill. *Hand and Mind: What Gestures Reveal about Thought*. University of Chicago Press, 1992.

Andrew N. Meltzoff. Imitation as a mechanism of social cognition: Origins of empathy, theory of mind, and the representation of action. *Blackwell Handbook of Childhood Cognitive Development*, pages 6–25, 2002. 10.1002/9780470996652.ch1. URL https://onlinelibrary. wiley.com/doi/abs/10.1002/9780470996652.ch1.

Andrew N. Meltzoff and Rechele Brooks. "Like me" as a building block for understanding other minds: Bodily acts, attention, and intention. *Intentions and Intentionality: Foundations of Social Cognition*, 171191, 2001.

Andrew N. Meltzoff and Jean Decety. What imitation tells us about social cognition: A rapprochement between developmental psychology and cognitive neuroscience. *Philosophical Transactions of the Royal Society of London. Series B: Biological Sciences*, 358(1431):491–500, 2003. 10.1098/rstb.2002.1261. URL https://royalsocietypublishing.org/doi/ abs/10.1098/rstb.2002.1261.

Andrew N. Meltzoff and M. Keith Moore. Imitation of facial and manual gestures by human neonates. *Science*, 198(4312):75–78, 1977.

Giorgio Metta, Giulio Sandini, Lorenzo Natale, Laila Craighero, and Luciano Fadiga. Understanding mirror neurons: A bio-robotic approach. *Interaction Studies: Social Behaviour and Communication in Biological and Artificial Systems*, 7(2):197–232, 2006. 10.1075/is.7.2.06met.

David P. Miller and Illah Nourbakhsh. Robotics for education. In Bruno Siciliano and Oussama Khatib, editors, *Springer Handbook of Robotics*, pages 2115–2134. Springer International Publishing, Cham, 2016. ISBN 978-3-319-32552-1. 10.1007/978-3-319-32552-1_79. URL https://doi.org/10.1007/978-3-319-32552-1_79.

George A. Miller. The magical number seven, plus or minus two: Some limits on our capacity for processing information. *Psychological Review*, 63(2):81–97, 1956.

Lauren R. Milne and Richard E. Ladner. Blocks4all: Overcoming accessibility barriers to blocks programming for children with visual impairments. In *Proceedings of the CHI Conference on Human Factors in Computing Systems*, pages 1–10, 2018. URL https://doi.org/ 10.1145/3173574.3173643.

Rubén Mitnik, Matías Recabarren, Miguel Nussbaum, and Alvaro Soto. Collaborative robotic instruction: A graph teaching experience. *Computers & Education*, 53(2):330–342, 2009. 10.1016/j.compedu. 2009.02.010. URL https://doi.org/10.1016/j.compedu.2009.02.010.

Masahiro Mori et al. The uncanny valley. *Energy*, 7(4):33–35, 1970.

Yusuke Moriguchi, Takayuki Kanda, Hiroshi Ishiguro, Yoko Shimada, and Shoji Itakura. Can young children learn words from a robot? *Interaction Studies*, 12(1):107–118, 2011.

Omar Mubin, Christoph Bartneck, Loe Feijs, Hanneke Hooft van Huysduynen, Jun Hu, and Jerry Muelver. Improving speech recognition with the robot interaction language. *Disruptive Science and Technology*, 1 (2):79–88, 2012.

Omar Mubin, Joshua Henderson, and Christoph Bartneck. Talk ROILA to your robot. In *Proceedings of the 15th ACM International Conference on Multimodal Interaction*, pages 317–318, 2013a. 10.1145/2522848.2531752. URL https://doi.org/10.1145/2522848.2531752.

Omar Mubin, Suleman Shahid, and Christoph Bartneck. Robot assisted language learning through games: A comparison of two case studies. *Australian Journal of Intelligent Information Processing Systems*, 13 (3):9–14, 2013b.

Omar Mubin, Catherine J. Stevens, Suleman Shahid, Abdullah Al Mahmud, and Jian-Jie Dong. A review of the applicability of robots in education. *Journal of Technology in Education and Learning*, 1 (209-0015):13, 2013c. URL http://dx.doi.org/10.2316/Journal.209.2013.1.209-0015.

Omar Mubin, Joshua Henderson, and Christoph Bartneck. You just do not understand me! speech recognition in human robot interaction. In *The 23rd IEEE International Symposium on Robot and Human Interactive Communication*, pages 637–642. IEEE, 2014.

Omar Mubin, Mohammad Obaid, Philipp Jordan, Patricia Alves-Oliveria, Thommy Eriksson, Wolmet Barendregt, Daniel Sjolle, Morten Fjeld, Simeon Simoff, and Mark Billinghurst. Towards an agenda for sci-fi inspired HCI research. In *Proceedings of the 13th International Conference on Advances in Computer Entertainment Technology*, pages 1–6, 2016. 10.1145/3001773.3001786. URL https://doi.org/10.1145/3001773.3001786.

Omar Mubin, Max Manalo, Muneeb Ahmad, and Mohammad Obaid. Scientometric analysis of the HAI conference. In *Proceedings of the 5th International Conference on Human Agent Interaction*, pages 45–51, 2017. 10.1145/3125739.3125747. URL https://doi.org/10.1145/3125739.3125747.

Omar Mubin, Mariam Alhashmi, Rama Baroud, and Fady S Alnajjar. Humanoid robots as teaching assistants in an Arab school. In
*Proceedings of the 31st Australian Conference on Human-Computer-
Interaction*, pages 462–466, 2019a. URL https://doi.org/10.1145/
3369457.3369517.

Omar Mubin, Kewal Wadibhasme, Philipp Jordan, and Mohammad
Obaid. Reflecting on the presence of science fiction robots in computing
literature. ACM *Transactions on Human-Robot Interaction*, 8(1):1–25,
2019b. 10.1145/3303706. URL https://doi.org/10.1145/3303706.

Omar Mubin, Max Cappuccio, Fady Alnajjar, Muneeb Ahmad, and
Shahid. Shahid. Can a robot invigilator prevent cheating? *AI and
Society - To Appear*, 2020. URL https://doi.org/10.1007/s00146-020-
00954-8.

Kristina Neubök, Michael Kopp, and Martin Ebner. What do we know
about typical MOOC participants? first insights from the field. In *European MOOCs Stakeholders Summit*, 05 2015.

Veronica Ahumada Newhart and Judith S. Olson. My student is a robot:
How schools manage telepresence experiences for students. In *Proceedings of the CHI Conference on Human Factors in Computing
Systems*, pages 342–347, 2017. 10.1145/3025453.3025809. URL
https://doi.org/10.1145/3025453.3025809.

Veronica Ahumada Newhart, Mark Warschauer, and Leonard Sender.
Virtual inclusion via telepresence robots in the classroom: An exploratory case study. *The International Journal of Technologies in Learning*, 23(4):9–25, 2016. URL https://escholarship.org/
uc/item/9zm4h7nf.

Shuichi Nishio, Hiroshi Ishiguro, and Norihiro Hagita. *Geminoid: Teleoperated Android of an Existing Person*, chapter 20. IntechOpen, Ri-
jeka, 2007. 10.5772/4876. URL https://doi.org/10.5772/4876.

T. Nomura and T. Kanda. On proposing the concept of robot anxiety and
considering measurement of it. In *Proceedings of the 12th IEEE International Workshop on Robot and Human Interactive Communication*,
pages 373–378. IEEE, 2003. 10.1109/ROMAN.2003.1251874. URL
https://doi.org/10.1109/ROMAN.2003.1251874.

Tatsuya Nomura. Robots and gender. In Marianne J. Legato, editor,
Principles of Gender-Specific Medicine (Third Edition), pages 695 –
703. Academic Press, San Diego, third edition, 2017. ISBN 978-0-12-
803506-1. 10.1016/B978-0-12-803506-1.00042-5. URL http://www.
sciencedirect.com/science/article/pii/B9780128035061000425.

Tatsuya Nomura, Tomohiro Suzuki, Takayuki Kanda, and Kensuke Kato.
Measurement of anxiety toward robots. In *The 15th IEEE International Symposium on Robot and Human Interactive Communication*,

pages 372–377. IEEE, 2006a. 10.1109/ROMAN.2006.314462. URL https://doi.org/10.1109/ROMAN.2006.314462.

Tatsuya Nomura, Tomohiro Suzuki, Takayuki Kanda, and Kensuke Kato. Measurement of negative attitudes toward robots. *Interaction Studies*, 7(3):437–454, 2006b. 10.1075/is.7.3.14nom. URL https://doi.org/10.1075/is.7.3.14nom.

Tatsuya Nomura, Takayuki Kanda, Tomohiro Suzuki, and Kensuke Kato. Prediction of human behavior in human–robot interaction using psychological scales for anxiety and negative attitudes toward robots. *IEEE Transactions on Robotics*, 24(2):442–451, 2008. 10.1109/TRO.2007.914004. URL https://doi.org/10.1109/TRO.2007.914004.

M. Obaid, E. B. Sandoval, J. Złotowski, E. Moltchanova, C. A. Basedow, and C. Bartneck. Stop! that is close enough. how body postures influence human-robot proximity. In *The 25th IEEE International Symposium on Robot and Human Interactive Communication*, pages 354–361, Aug 2016. 10.1109/ROMAN.2016.7745155.

Mohammad Obaid, Radosław Niewiadomski, and Catherine Pelachaud. Perception of spatial relations and of coexistence with virtual agents. In Hannes Högni Vilhjálmsson, Stefan Kopp, Stacy Marsella, and Kristinn R. Thórisson, editors, *Intelligent Virtual Agents*, pages 363–369, Berlin, Heidelberg, 2011. Springer Berlin Heidelberg. ISBN 978-3-642-23974-8. URL https://doi.org/10.1007/978-3-642-23974-8_39.

Mohammad Obaid, Felix Kistler, Markus Häring, René Bühling, and Elisabeth André. A framework for user-defined body gestures to control a humanoid robot. *International Journal of Social Robotics*, 6(3): 383–396, 2014.

Mohammad Obaid, Felix Kistler, Gabrielė Kasparavičiūtė, Asim Evren Yantaç, and Morten Fjeld. How would you gesture navigate a drone?: a user-centered approach to control a drone. In *Proceedings of the 20th International Academic Mindtrek Conference*, pages 113–121. ACM, 2016a.

Mohammad Obaid, Maha Salem, Micheline Ziadee, Halim Boukaram, Elena Moltchanova, and Majd Sakr. Investigating effects of professional status and ethnicity in human-agent interaction. In *Proceedings of the Fourth International Conference on Human Agent Interaction*, HAI '16, pages 179–186, New York, NY, USA, 2016b. Association for Computing Machinery. ISBN 9781450345088. 10.1145/2974804.2974813. URL https://doi.org/10.1145/2974804.2974813.

Mohammad Obaid, Yuan Gao, Wolmet Barendregt, and Ginevra Castellano. Exploring users' reactions towards tangible implicit probes for measuring human-robot engagement. In Abderrahmane Kheddar, Eiichi Yoshida, Shuzhi Sam Ge, Kenji Suzuki, John-John Cabibihan,

Friederike Eyssel, and Hongsheng He, editors, *Social Robotics*, pages 402–412, Cham, 2017. Springer International Publishing. ISBN 978-3-319-70022-9.

Mohammad Obaid, Ruth Aylett, Wolmet Barendregt, Christina Basedow, Lee J. Corrigan, Lynne Hall, Aidan Jones, Arvid Kappas, Dennis Küster, Ana Paiva, Fotios Papadopoulos, Sofia Serholt, and Ginevra Castellano. Endowing a robotic tutor with empathic qualities: Design and pilot evaluation. *International Journal of Humanoid Robotics*, 15(06):1850025, 2018.   10.1142/S0219843618500251. URL https://doi.org/10.1142/S0219843618500251.

Shotaro Okajima, Fady S Alnajjar, Hiroshi Yamasaki, Matti Itkonen, Álvaro Costa García, Yasuhisa Hasegawa, and Shingo Shimoda. Grasp-training robot to activate neural control loop for reflex and experimental verification. In *The IEEE International Conference on Robotics and Automation*, pages 1849–1854. IEEE, 2018.   URL https://doi.org/10.1109/ICRA.2018.8461114.

Open Science Collaboration. Estimating the reproducibility of psychological science. *Science*, 349(6251), 2015. ISSN 0036-8075. 10.1126/science.aac4716.   URL https://science.sciencemag.org/content/349/6251/aac4716.

Ayberk Özgür, Séverin Lemaignan, Wafa Johal, Maria Beltran, Manon Briod, Léa Pereyre, Francesco Mondada, and Pierre Dillenbourg. Cellulo: Versatile handheld robots for education. In *Proceedings of the 12th ACM/IEEE International Conference on Human-Robot Interaction*, pages 119–127, New York, NY, USA, 2017. Association for Computing Machinery. ISBN 9781450343367.   10.1145/2909824.3020247. URL https://doi.org/10.1145/2909824.3020247.

Ana Paiva, Iolanda Leite, and Tiago Ribeiro. Emotion modeling for social robots. In Rafael Calvo, Sidney D'Mello, Jonathan Gratch, and Arvid Kappas, editors, *The Oxford Handbook of Affective Computing*, pages 296–308. Oxford University Press, 2014. 10.1093/oxfordhb/9780199942237.013.029.

Ana Paiva, Iolanda Leite, Hana Boukricha, and Ipke Wachsmuth. Empathy in Virtual Agents and Robots: A Survey. *ACM Transactions on Interactive Intelligent Systems*, 7(3), September 2017. ISSN 2160-6455. 10.1145/2912150. URL https://doi.org/10.1145/2912150.

Seymour Papert. *Mindstorms: Children, Computers and Powerful Ideas.* Basic Book, New York, 1980.

Robert Ezra Park. The concept of social distance as applied to the study of racial attitudes and racial relations. *Journal of Applied Sociology*, 8: 339–344, 1924.

Bjarke Kristian Maigaard Kjær Pedersen, Jørgen Christian Larsen, and Jacob Nielsen. The effect of commercially available educational robotics:

A systematic review. In Munir Merdan, Wilfried Lepuschitz, Gottfried Koppensteiner, Richard Balogh, and David Obdržálek, editors, *Robotics in Education*, pages 14–27, Cham, 2020. Springer International Publishing. ISBN 978-3-030-26945-6. 10.1007/978-3-030-26945-6_2. URL https://doi.org/10.1007/978-3-030-26945-6_2.

Josef Perner and Heinz Wimmer. "john thinks that Mary thinks that..." attribution of second-order beliefs by 5-to 10-year-old children. *Journal of Experimental Child Psychology*, 39(3):437–471, 1985.

Denis Phillips and Jonas F Soltis. *Perspectives on Learning*. Teachers College Press, New York, 2015.

Jean Piaget. The child's conception of the world (J. Tomlinson & A. Tomlinson, trans.). *St. Albans: Granada*, 1929.

Jean Piaget. The language and thought of the child (M. Gabain, trans.). *New York*, 1959.

David Premack and Guy Woodruff. Does the chimpanzee have a theory of mind? *Behavioral and Brain Sciences*, 1(4):515–526, 1978.

Irene Rae, Leila Takayama, and Bilge Mutlu. The influence of height in robot-mediated communication. *ACM/IEEE International Conference on Human-Robot Interaction*, pages 1–8, 2013. ISSN 21672148. 10.1109/HRI.2013.6483495.

Natasha Randall. A survey of robot-assisted language learning (RALL). *ACM Transactions on Human-Robot Interaction*, 9(1):1–36, 2019. 10.1145/3345506. URL https://doi.org/10.1145/3345506.

Byron Reeves and Clifford Ivar Nass. *The Media Equation: How People Treat Computers, Television, and New Media Like Real People and Places*. Cambridge University Press, 1996.

Natalia Reich and Friederike Eyssel. Attitudes towards service robots in domestic environments: The role of personality characteristics, individual interests, and demographic variables. *Journal of Behavioral Robotics*, 2(2):123–130, 2013. doi:10.2478/pjbr-2013-0014.

Natalia Reich-Stiebert. *Acceptance and Applicability of Educational Robots. Evaluating Factors Contributing to a Successful Introduction of Social Robots into Education*. PhD thesis, Universität Bielefeld, 2019. URL urn:nbn:de:0070-pub-29366422.

Natalia Reich-Stiebert and Friederike Eyssel. Learning with educational companion robots? Toward attitudes on education robots, predictors of attitudes, and application potentials for education robots. *International Journal of Social Robotics*, 7(5):875–888, 2015. 10.1007/s12369-015-0308-9. URL https://doi.org/10.1007/s12369-015-0308-9.

Natalia Reich-Stiebert and Friederike Eyssel. Robots in the classroom: What teachers think about teaching and learning with education robots. In *International Conference on Social Robotics*, pages 671–680. Springer, 2016. 10.1007/978-3-319-47437-3_66. URL https://doi.org/10.1007/978-3-319-47437-3_66.

Natalia Reich-Stiebert, Friederike Eyssel, and Charlotte Hohnemann. Exploring university students' preferences for educational robot design by means of a user-centered design approach. *International Journal of Social Robotics*, pages 1–11, 2019. URL https://doi.org/10.1007/s12369-019-00554-7.

Daniel Reisberg. *The Oxford Handbook of Cognitive Psychology*. Oxford University Press, 2013. ISBN 978-0-19-537674-6.

A. Fernando Ribeiro and Gil Lopes. Learning robotics: A review. *Current Robotics Reports*, pages 1–11, 2020. 10.1007/s43154-020-00002-9. URL https://doi.org/10.1007/s43154-020-00002-9.

Paul Ricoeur and Gwendoline Jarczyk. Soi-même comme un autre, 1991.

Fanny Riedo, Philippe Rétornaz, Luc Bergeron, Nathalie Nyffeler, and Francesco Mondada. A two years informal learning experience using the Thymio robot. In *Advances in Autonomous Mini Robots*, pages 37–48. Springer, 2012. 10.1007/978-3-642-27482-4_7. URL https://doi.org/10.1007/978-3-642-27482-4_7.

Fanny Riedo, Morgane Chevalier, Stéphane Magnenat, and Francesco Mondada. Thymio II, a robot that grows wiser with children. In *The IEEE Workshop on Advanced Robotics and its Social Impacts*, pages 187–193. IEEE, 2013. URL https://doi.org/10.1109/ARSO.2013.6705527.

Laurel D Riek. Wizard of Oz studies in HRI: a systematic review and new reporting guidelines. *Journal of Human-Robot Interaction*, 1(1): 119–136, 2012.

Nina Riether, Frank Hegel, Britta Wrede, and Gernot Horstmann. Social facilitation with social robots? In *The 7th ACM/IEEE International Conference on Human-Robot Interaction*, pages 41–47. IEEE, 2012. URL https://doi.org/10.1145/2157689.2157697.

Giacomo Rizzolatti, Luciano Fadiga, Vittorio Gallese, and Leonardo Fogassi. Premotor cortex and the recognition of motor actions. *Cognitive Brain Research*, 3(2):131–141, 1996.

J. Jill Rogers, Marylin Lisowski, and Amy A. Rogers. Girls, robots, and science education. *Science Scope*, page 62, 2006.

Barbara Rogoff. *Cognition as a Collaborative Process*. John Wiley & Sons Inc, New York, 1998.

Raquel Ros, Elettra Oleari, Clara Pozzi, Francesca Sacchitelli, Daniele Baranzini, Anahita Bagherzadhalimi, Alberto Sanna, and Yiannis Demiris. A motivational approach to support healthy habits in long-term child–robot interaction. *International Journal of Social*

Robotics, 2016. ISSN 1875-4791. 10.1007/s12369-016-0356-9. URL http://link.springer.com/10.1007/s12369-016-0356-9.

Evgenia Roussou and Maria Rangoussi. On the use of robotics for the development of computational thinking in kindergarten: Educational intervention and evaluation. In Munir Merdan, Wilfried Lepuschitz, Gottfried Koppensteiner, Richard Balogh, and David Obdržálek, editors, *International Conference on Robotics and Education (RiE 2017)*, pages 31–44, Cham, 2019. Springer, Springer International Publishing. 10.1007/978-3-030-26945-6_3. URL https://doi.org/10.1007/978-3-030-26945-6_3.

Martin Saerbeck, Tom Schut, Christoph Bartneck, and Maddy D. Janse. Expressive robots in education: Varying the degree of social supportive behavior of a robotic tutor. In *Proceedings of the SIGCHI Conference on Human Factors in Computing Systems*, pages 1613–1622, 2010. 10.1145/1753326.1753567. URL https://doi.org/10.1145/1753326.1753567.

Eduardo Benitez Sandoval, Omar Mubin, and Mohammad Obaid. Human robot interaction and fiction: A contradiction. In *International Conference on Social Robotics*, pages 54–63. Springer, 2014. 10.1007/978-3-319-11973-1_6. URL https://doi.org/10.1007/978-3-319-11973-1_6.

Beatriz Sousa Santos, Paulo Dias, Angela Pimentel, Jan-Willem Baggerman, Carlos Ferreira, Samuel Silva, and Joaquim Madeira. Head-mounted display versus desktop for 3D navigation in virtual reality: A user study. *Multimedia Tools and Applications*, 41(1):161, 2009. 10.1007/s11042-008-0223-2. URL https://doi.org/10.1007/s11042-008-0223-2.

Brian Scassellati, Henny Admoni, and Maja Matarić. Robots for use in autism research. *Annual Review of Biomedical Engineering*, 14:275–294, 2012. annurev-bioeng-071811-150036. URL https://doi.org/10.1146/annurev-bioeng-071811-150036.

B.R. Schadenberg, M.A. Neerincx, F. Cnossen, and R. Looije. Personalising game difficulty to keep children motivated to play with a social robot: A Bayesian approach. *Cognitive Systems Research*, 43:222 – 231, 2017. ISSN 1389-0417. https://doi.org/10.1016/j.cogsys.2016.08.003. URL http://www.sciencedirect.com/science/article/pii/S1389041716300523.

Matthias Scheutz. The inherent dangers of unidirectional emotional bonds between humans and social robots. In Patrick Lin, Keith Abney, and George A. Bekey, editors, *Robot Ethics: The Ethical and Social Implications of Robotics*, page 205. MIT Press, 2011.

Marc Schröder and Jürgen Trouvain. The German text-to-speech synthesis system Mary: A tool for research, development and teaching.

International Journal of Speech Technology, 6(4):365–377, 2003. 10.1023/A:1025708916924.   URL https://link.springer.com/article/ 10.1023/A:1025708916924.

Laura Screpanti, Lorenzo Cesaretti, Laura Marchetti, Angelica Baione, I.N. Natalucci, and David Scaradozzi. An educational robotics activity to promote gender equality in stem education. In *Proceedings of the Eighteenth International Conference on Information, Communication Technologies in Education (ICICTE 2018)*, pages 336–346, 2018.

Lucia Seminara, Paolo Gastaldo, Simon J. Watt, Kenneth F. Valyear, Fernando Zuher, and Fulvio Mastrogiovanni. Active haptic perception in robots: A review. *Frontiers in Neurorobotics*, 13:53, 2019. ISSN 1662-5218.   10.3389/fnbot.2019.00053.   URL https://www. frontiersin.org/article/10.3389/fnbot.2019.00053.

S. Serholt, C. A. Basedow, W. Barendregt, and M. Obaid. Comparing a humanoid tutor to a human tutor delivering an instructional task to children. In *The 14th IEEE-RAS International Conference on Humanoid Robots*, pages 1134–1141. IEEE, Nov 2014.   10.1109/HUMANOIDS.2014.7041511.

Sofia Serholt. Breakdowns in children's interactions with a robotic tutor: A longitudinal study. *Computers in Human Behavior*, 81(December): 250–264, 2018. ISSN 07475632. 10.1016/j.chb.2017.12.030.

Sofia Serholt, Wolmet Barendregt, Iolanda Leite, Helen Hastie, Aidan Jones, Ana Paiva, Asimina Vasalou, and Ginevra Castellano. Teachers' views on the use of empathic robotic tutors in the classroom. In *The 23rd IEEE International Symposium on Robot and Human Interactive Communication*, pages 955–960. IEEE, 2014. 10.1109/ROMAN.2014.6926376.   URL https://doi.org/10.1109/ROMAN.2014. 6926376.

Amanda J.C. Sharkey. Should we welcome robot teachers? *Ethics and Information Technology*, 18(4):283–297, 2016. URL https://doi.org/ 10.1007/s10676-016-9387-z.

Noel Sharkey and Amanda Sharkey.   The crying shame of robot nannies: An ethical appraisal. *Interaction Studies*, 11(2):161–190, 2010.   ISSN 1572-0373.   https://doi.org/10.1075/is.11.2.01sha. URL https://www.jbe-platform.com/content/journals/10.1075/is.11.2. 01sha.

Solace Shen, Petr Slovak, and Malte F. Jung. "Stop. I see a conflict happening." A robot mediator for young children's interpersonal conflict resolution. In *Proceedings of the 13th ACM/IEEE International Conference on Human-Robot Interaction*, pages 69–77, 2018.

S. Shepherd and M. Cappuccio. Sociality, attention, and the mind's eyes. *Joint attention: New developments in Psychology*, 2011.

Richard M. Shiffrin and Robert M. Nosofsky. Seven plus or minus two: a commentary on capacity limitations. *Psychological Review*, 101(2): 357–361, 1994.

Namin Shin and Sangah Kim.   Learning about, from, and with robots: Students' perspectives. In *The 16th IEEE International Symposium on Robot and Human Interactive Communication*, pages 1040–1045. IEEE, 2007.   10.1109/ROMAN.2007.4415235.   URL https://doi.org/10.1109/ROMAN.2007.4415235.

Elaine Short, Justin Hart, Michelle Vu, and Brian Scassellati. No fair!! An interaction with a cheating robot.   In *Proceedings of the 5th ACM/IEEE International Conference on Human-Robot Interaction*, pages 219–226. IEEE, 2010.   10.1109/HRI.2010.5453193.   URL https://ieeexplore.ieee.org/abstract/document/5453193.

Bruno Siciliano and Oussama Khatib. *Springer Handbook of Robotics*. Springer, 2016. ISBN 978-3-540-23957-4.

Burrhus Frederic Skinner. *Science and Human Behavior*. Simon and Schuster, 1965. 92904.

Robert E. Slavin.   Research on cooperative learning and achievement: What we know, what we need to know.   *Contemporary Educational Psychology*, 21(1):43–69, 1996. 10.1006/ceps.1996.0004. URL https://doi.org/10.1006/ceps.1996.0004.

Softbank Robotics.   Softbank Robotics Documentation.   http://doc. aldebaran.com/2-8/index.html, 2020. Accessed: 2020-02-02.

Newton Spolaôr and Fabiane B. Vavassori Benitti. Robotics applications grounded in learning theories on tertiary education: A systematic review. *Computers & Education*, 112:97–107, 2017. 10.1016/ j.compedu.2017.05.001. URL https://doi.org/10.1016/j.compedu.2017. 05.001.

Grant Sputore. I Am Mother, 2019. URL https://www.imdb.com/title/ tt6292852/.

Jonathan Steuer. Defining virtual reality: Dimensions determining telepresence. *Journal of Communication*, 42(4):73–93, 1992.   10.1111/ j.1460-2466.1992.tb00812.x.   URL https://doi.org/10.1111/j.1460-2466.1992.tb00812.x.

Laurie Stevahn. Integrating conflict resolution training into the curriculum. *Theory into Practice*, 43(1):50–58, 2004.

Laurie Stevahn, David W. Johnson, Roger T. Johnson, Katie Oberle, and Leslie Wahl.   Effects of conflict resolution training integrated into a kindergarten curriculum. *Child Development*, 71(3):772–784, 2000.

Jeff Stone, Christian I. Lynch, Mike Sjomeling, and John M. Darley. Stereotype threat effects on black and white athletic performance. *Journal of Personality and Social Psychology*, 77(6):1213, 1999.   URL https://doi.org/10.1037/0022-3514.77.6.1213.

Amanda Sullivan and Marina Umaschi Bers. Gender differences in kindergarteners' robotics and programming achievement. *International Journal of Technology and Design Education*, 23(3):691–702, 2013. 10.1007/s10798-012-9210-z. URL https://doi.org/10.1007/s10798-012-9210-z.

Fumihide Tanaka and Madhumita Ghosh. The implementation of care-receiving robot at an English learning school for children. In *Proceedings of the 6th International Conference on Human-Robot Interaction*, HRI '11, pages 265–266, New York, NY, USA, 2011. Association for Computing Machinery. ISBN 9781450305617. 10.1145/1957656.1957763. URL https://doi.org/10.1145/1957656.1957763.

Fumihide Tanaka, Toshimitsu Takahashi, Shizuko Matsuzoe, NAO Tazawa, and Masahiko Morita. Telepresence robot helps children in communicating with teachers who speak a different language. In *Proceedings of the 9th ACM/IEEE International Conference on Human-Robot Interaction*, pages 399–406. ACM, 2014. 10.1145/2559636.2559654. URL https://doi.org/10.1145/2559636.2559654.

Fumihide Tanaka, Kyosuke Isshiki, Fumiki Takahashi, Manabu Uekusa, Rumiko Sei, and Kaname Hayashi. Pepper learns together with children: Development of an educational application. In *The 15th International Conference on Humanoid Robots (Humanoids)*, pages 270–275. IEEE-RAS, 2015.

C. Tannenbaum, R. P. Ellis, F. Eyssel, J. Zou, and L. Schiebinger. Sex and gender analysis improves science and engineering. *Nature*, 575:137–146, Nov 2019. https://doi.org/10.1038/s41586-019-1657-6. URL https://doi.org/10.1038/s41586-019-1657-6.

Serge Thill, Cristina A. Pop, Tony Belpaeme, Tom Ziemke, and Bram Vanderborght. Robot-assisted therapy for autism spectrum disorders with (partially) autonomous control: Challenges and outlook. *Paladyn*, 3(4):209–217, 2012. 10.2478/s13230-013-0107-7. URL https://doi.org/10.2478/s13230-013-0107-7.

Gary Thomas. *Education: A Very Short Introduction*. Oxford University Press, Oxford, 2013.

Lai Poh Emily Toh, Albert Causo, Pei-Wen Tzuo, I-Ming Chen, and Song Huat Yeo. A review on the use of robots in education and young children. *Journal of Educational Technology & Society*, 19(2):148–163, 2016. URL https://www.jstor.org/stable/jeductechsoci.19.2.148.

Keith J Topping. Trends in peer learning. *Educational Psychology*, 25(6):631–645, 2005.

Colwyn Trevarthen. Communication and cooperation in early infancy: A description of primary intersubjectivity. *Before Speech: The Beginning of Interpersonal Communication*, 1:530–571, 1979.

Endel Tulving and Donald M. Thomson. Encoding specificity and retrieval processes in episodic memory. *Psychological Review*, 80(5):352,
1973. 10.1037/h0020071. URL https://doi.org/10.1037/h0020071.

Shannon Vallor. *Technology and the Virtues: A Philosophical Guide to a
Future Worth Wanting*. Oxford University Press, 2016.

Kurt VanLehn. The relative effectiveness of human tutoring, intelligent
tutoring systems, and other tutoring systems. *Educational Psychologist*, 46(4):197–221, 2011. 10.1080/00461520.2011.611369. URL
https://doi.org/10.1080/00461520.2011.611369.

Viswanath Venkatesh and Hillol Bala. Technology acceptance model
3 and a research agenda on interventions. *Decision Sciences*, 39(2):
273–315, 2008. 10.1111/j.1540-5915.2008.00192.x. URL https://
onlinelibrary.wiley.com/doi/abs/10.1111/j.1540-5915.2008.00192.x.

Samuele Vinanzi, Massimiliano Patacchiola, Antonio Chella, and Angelo
Cangelosi. Would a robot trust you? Developmental robotics model
of trust and theory of mind. *Philosophical Transactions of the Royal
Society B*, 374(1771):20180032, 2019. 10.1098/rstb.2018.0032. URL
https://doi.org/10.1098/rstb.2018.0032.

Alistair A. Vogan, Fady Alnajjar, Munkhjargal Gochoo, and Sumayya
Khalid. Robots, AI, and cognitive training in an era of mass age-related
cognitive decline: A systematic review. *IEEE Access*, 8:18284–18304,
2020. URL https://doi.org/10.1109/ACCESS.2020.2966819.

P. Vogt, R. van den Berghe, M. de Haas, L. Hoffman, J. Kanero, E. Mamus, J. Montanier, C. Oranç, O. Oudgenoeg-Paz, D. H. García, F. Papadopoulos, T. Schodde, J. Verhagen, C. D. Wallbridge, B. Willem-
sen, J. de Wit, T. Belpaeme, T. G oksun, S. Kopp, E. Krahmer, A. C.
K untay, P. Leseman, and A. K. Pandey. Second language tutoring
using social robots: A large-scale study. In *Proceedings of the 14th
ACM/IEEE International Conference on Human-Robot Interaction*,
pages 497–505, March 2019. 10.1109/HRI.2019.8673077. URL
http://dx.doi.org/10.1109/HRI.2019.8673077.

Paul Vogt, Rianne van den Berghe, Mirjam de Haas, Laura Hoffman, Junko Kanero, Ezgi Mamus, Jean-Marc Montanier, Cansu
Oranç, Ora Oudgenoeg-Paz, Daniel Hernández García, et al. Second language tutoring using social robots: A large-scale study. In
*Proceedings of the 14th ACM/IEEE International Conference on
Human-Robot Interaction*, pages 497–505. IEEE, 2019. URL
https://doi.org/10.1109/HRI.2019.8673077.

Anna-Lisa Vollmer, Robin Read, Dries Trippas, and Tony Belpaeme. Children conform, adults resist: A robot group induced peer pressure on
normative social conformity. *Science Robotics*, 3(21):eaat7111, 2018.
10.1126/scirobotics.aat7111.

Eleni Vrochidou, Aouatif Najoua, Chris Lytridis, Michail Salonidis, Vassilios Ferelis, and George A. Papakostas. Social robot NAO as a self-regulating didactic mediator: a case study of teaching/learning numeracy. In *Proceedings of the 26th International Conference on Software, Telecommunications and Computer Networks (SoftCOM)*, pages 1–5. IEEE, 2018. 0.23919/SOFTCOM.2018.8555764. URL https://ieeexplore.ieee.org/document/8555764.

Lev S. Vygotsky. *Thought and Language (Eugenia Hanfmann & Gertrude Vakar, translation)*. MIT Press, Cambridge, Massachusetts, 1962.

L.S. Vygotsky. Socio-cultural theory. *Mind in Society*, 1978.

Ying Wang, Yun-Hee Park, Shoji Itakura, Annette Margaret Elizabeth Henderson, Takayuki Kanda, Naoki Furuhata, and Hiroshi Ishiguro. Infants' perceptions of cooperation between a human and robot. *Infant and Child Development*, 29(2):e2161, 2020.

Gerard Way and Gabriel Ba. *The Umbrella Academy*. Dark Horse Books, 2008. ISBN 9781593079789.

Patrice L. Tamar Weiss, Carolynn P. Whiteley, Jutta Treviranus, and Deborah I. Fels. Pebbles: A personal technology for meeting educational, social and emotional needs of hospitalised children. *Personal and Ubiquitous Computing*, 5(3):157–168, 2001. 10.1007/s007790170006. URL https://doi.org/10.1007/s007790170006.

Henry M. Wellman. Theory of mind: The state of the art. *European Journal of Developmental Psychology*, 15(6):728–755, 2018.

Henry M. Wellman, David Cross, and Julanne Watson. Meta-analysis of theory-of-mind development: The truth about false belief. *Child Development*, 72(3):655–684, 2001.

Fred A. Westall, R. Denis Johnston, and Alwyn V. Lewis. *Speech Technology for Telecommunications*. Springer US, 1998. ISBN 9780412790805.

John White and John Gardner. *The Classroom x-factor: The Power of Body Language and Non-verbal Communication in Teaching*. Routledge, 2013.

William Wiersma. *Research Methods in Education: An Introduction (9th Edition)*. Pearson, 2008.

Janie H. Wilson and Lawrence Locker Jr. Immediacy scale represents four factors: Nonverbal and verbal components predict student outcomes. *The Journal of Classroom Interaction*, pages 4–10, 2007. URL www.jstor.org/stable/23869788.

Karen Wilson and James H. Korn. Attention during lectures: Beyond ten minutes. *Teaching of Psychology*, 34(2):85–89, 2007.

Heinz Wimmer and Josef Perner. Beliefs about beliefs: Representation and constraining function of wrong beliefs in young children's understanding of deception. *Cognition*, 13(1):103–128, 1983.

Jeannette M. Wing. Computational thinking. *Communications of the ACM*, 49(3):33–35, March 2006. ISSN 0001-0782. 10.1145/1118178.1118215. URL https://doi.org/10.1145/1118178.1118215.

Paul L. Witt, Lawrence R. Wheeless, and Mike Allen. A meta-analytical review of the relationship between teacher immediacy and student learning. *Communication Monographs*, 71(2):184–207, 2004. 10.1080/0362052042000228054. URL https://doi.org/10.1080/0362052042000228054.

David Wood and Heather Wood. Vygotsky, tutoring and learning. *Oxford review of Education*, 22(1):5–16, 1996. URL https://doi.org/10.1080/0305498960220101.

Luke J. Wood, Abolfazl Zaraki, Ben Robins, and Kerstin Dautenhahn. Developing Kaspar: A humanoid robot for children with autism. *International Journal of Social Robotics*, Jul 2019. ISSN 1875-4805. 10.1007/s12369-019-00563-6. URL https://doi.org/10.1007/s12369-019-00563-6.

Rachel Wood, Paul Baxter, and Tony Belpaeme. A review of long-term memory in natural and synthetic systems. *Adaptive Behavior*, 20(2):81–103, 2012.

Hsin-Kai Wu, Silvia Wen-Yu Lee, Hsin-Yi Chang, and Jyh-Chong Liang. Current status, opportunities and challenges of augmented reality in education. *Computers & Education*, 62:41–49, 2013. URL https://doi.org/10.1016/j.compedu.2012.10.024.

Agnieszka Wykowska, Thierry Chaminade, and Gordon Cheng. Embodied artificial agents for understanding human social cognition. *Philosophical Transactions of the Royal Society B: Biological Sciences*, 371(1693):20150375, 2016. 10.1098/rstb.2015.0375. URL https://doi.org/10.1098/rstb.2015.0375.

Satoshi Yamamoto, Toshiro Tetsui, Mitsuru Naganuma, and Ryuhei Kimura. Trial of using robotic pet as human interface of multimedia education system for pre-school aged child in kindergarten. In *Proceedings of the SICE-ICASE International Joint Conference*, pages 3398–3403, Oct 2006. 10.1109/SICE.2006.315079. URL http://dx.doi.org/10.1109/SICE.2006.315079.

Cristina Zaga, Manja Lohse, Khiet P. Truong, and Vanessa Evers. The effect of a robot's social character on children's task engagement: Peer versus tutor. In Adriana Tapus, Elisabeth André, Jean-Claude Martin, François Ferland, and Mehdi Ammi, editors, *Social Robotics*, pages 704–713, Cham, 2015. Springer International Publishing. ISBN 978-3-319-25554-5.

Dan Zahavi. Empathy, embodiment and interpersonal understanding: From Lipps to Schutz. *Inquiry*, 53(3):285–306, 2010. URL https://doi.org/10.1080/00201741003784663.

Dan Zahavi. Empathy and mirroring: Husserl and Gallese. In Roland Breeur and Ullrich Melle, editors, *Life, Subjectivity & Art*, pages 217–254. Springer Netherlands, Dordrecht, 2012. ISBN 978-94-007-2211-8. 10.1007/978-94-007-2211-8_9. URL https://doi.org/10.1007/978-94-007-2211-8_9.

Sabrina Zeaiter and Patrick Heinsch. Roboprax—Teaching and learning with humanoid robots. In *12th Annual International Conference of Education, Research and Innovation*, pages 918–925, 11 2019. 10.21125/iceri.2019.0287.

Li Zhang, Ming Jiang, Dewan Farid, and M.A. Hossain. Intelligent facial emotion recognition and semantic-based topic detection for a humanoid robot. *Expert Systems with Applications*, 40(13): 5160–5168, 2013. ISSN 0957-4174. https://doi.org/10.1016/j.eswa.2013.03.016. URL http://www.sciencedirect.com/science/article/pii/S0957417413001668.

Mingshao Zhang, Pengji Duan, Zhou Zhang, and Sven Esche. Development of telepresence teaching robots with social capabilities. In *ASME International Mechanical Engineering Congress and Exposition*, volume 52064, page V005T07A017. American Society of Mechanical Engineers, 2018. 10.1115/IMECE2018-86686. URL https://doi.org/10.1115/IMECE2018-86686.

Ning-Ning Zhou and Yu-Long Deng. Virtual reality: A state-of-the-art survey. *International Journal of Automation and Computing*, 6(4):319–325, 2009. 10.1007/s11633-009-0319-9. URL https://doi.org/10.1007/s11633-009-0319-9.

Jakub Zlotowski, Diane Proudfoot, and Christoph Bartneck. More human than human: Does the uncanny curve really matter? In *HRI2013 Workshop on Design of Humanlikeness in HRI from Uncanny Valley to Minimal Design*, pages 7–13, 2013. URL http://www.geminoid.jp/ws/Humanlikeness/index.php?plugin=attach&refer=Home&openfile=HL2013Proceedings.pdf.

Jakub Zlotowski, Hidenobu Sumioka, Shuichi Nishio, Dylan Glas, Christoph Bartneck, and Hiroshi Ishiguro. Persistence of the uncanny valley: the influence of repeated interactions and a robot's attitude on its perception. *Frontiers in Psychology*, 6:883, 2015. ISSN 1664-1078. 10.3389/fpsyg.2015.00883. URL https://www.frontiersin.org/article/10.3389/fpsyg.2015.00883.

Jakub Zlotowski, Kumar Yogeeswaran, and Christoph Bartneck. Can we control it? Autonomous robots threaten human identity, uniqueness, safety, and resources. *International Journal of Human-Computer Studies*, 100:48–54, 2017. ISSN 1071-5819. https://doi.org/10.1016/j.ijhcs.2016.12.008. URL http://www.sciencedirect.com/science/article/pii/S1071581916301768.

Jakub Zlotowski, Hidenobu Suminokar, Shuichi Nishio, C. Bartneck, Friederike Eyssel, and Hiroshi Ishiguro. Model of dual anthropomorphism: The relationship between the media equation effect and implicit anthropomorphism. *International Journal of Social Robotics*, 10(5): 701–714, 2018. 10.1007/s12369-018-0476-5.

Index

3D-printing, 118

actuator, 51
age, 45
agency, 41, 61
Aibo, 8
Aldebaran Robotics, 8
ALIZ-E, 138
anthropomorphism, 35, 41, 61
    animism, 41
    determinants, 42
    pareidolia, 41
applications, 116
Arduino, 6
    controller, 82
Artificial Intelligence, 66, 88
Asimov, Isaac, 11
attitude, 149
    behaviour control, 150
    Eurobarometer, 151
    hedonic, 150
    social norms, 150
    utilitarian, 150
Autism Spectrum Disorder, 135
Avatar Robot, 137

Bandura, Albert
    model learning, 23
    vicarious learning, 23
    vicarious reinforcement, 23
Blockly, 75

Bloom, Benjamin, 23
Bobo, 22
Boston Dynamics, 12
BrickPi, 79
BuSaif, 118

Cellulo, 131
Choregraphe, 62, 76, 84, 126,
    133, 177
Classroom Application Package,
    103, 141, 142
cloud computing, 88
cognitive psychology, 30
    attention, 31, 61
    chunking, 33
    executive functions, 34
        cognitive flexibility, 34
    memory, 31
        long-term memory, 32
        short-term memory, 32
        working memory, 33
cognitive science, 30
    cognitive systems, 30
collaborative learning, 24
    project-based learning, 26
    settings, 24
communication, 55
    speech recognition, 56
    speech synthesis, 56
computational thinking, 74, 87,
    132

computer vision, 56
    algorithms, 57
construction kit, 72, 75, 78, 81, 88
constructionism, 21, 71, 73, 78, 87
cooperative learning, 24, 25
customization, 117

demographics, 44
Developmental Cybernetics, 41
developmental psychology, 30
Developmental Robotics, 41, 48

educational robots, 6
educational tool, 71, 72, 86
embodiment, 36, 38, 51, 59, 93
EMOTE, 134
empathy, 35
    affective empathy, 36
    cognitive empathy, 36
Ethics, 157
    Consequentialism, 159
    Deontology, 159
    ethical concerns, 163
    Virtue Ethics, 160
ethnicity, 46
exoskeleton, 137

Facial Action Coding System, 43
Flipped Classroom, 103, 126

gender, 45, 73

H.E.A.R.T., 145, 155
hardware, 54, 75, 76
    battery technology, 54
    custom, 81
    electronics, 55
    micro-controller, 54, 59
    open source, 82
HRI, 26, 27, 169
    experiments, 177
    research methods, 172

IBM Watson, 68
imitation, 35, 37
    mutual imitation, 39
inMoov, 82
Integrated Development
        Environments, 62
inverted teaching, 4
iRobiQ, 139

Java, 74

KeepOn, 107

L2TOR, 139
lab experiment, 172
learning
    learning analytics, 108, 144
    machine learning, 67
    online learning, 67
    peer learning, 99
LEGO Mindstorms, 6, 21, 62, 63,
        65, 75, 79, 84–86, 89,
        116, 132
Logo, 21, 71, 74
    body-syntonic reasoning, 21
    programming, 21

MaryTTS, 56
Massive Open Online Course, 3,
        125, 143
mBot, 81
middleware, 63
mirror neurons, 37
Moravec's paradox, 112

NAO, 8, 26, 47, 58, 61, 62, 76,
        85, 89, 102, 116, 120,
        126, 133, 134
    battery runtime, 123
    development, 125
    transport, 121
    tutor, 24, 97

non-verbal social cues, 42, 59
    body posture, 44
    eye gaze, 43, 57, 60, 61
    facial expressions, 43, 57
    gestures, 43
    proxemics, 42, 44

odometry, 65
Opsoro, 88
Ozobot, 78

Papert, Seymour, 21, 73
    algorithmic thinking, 21
    LEGO Mindstorms, 21
Pedagogy, 15
Pepper, 8, 53, 56, 58, 61, 62, 103,
        108, 116, 120, 126, 133,
        143, 144
    battery runtime, 123
    development, 125
    transport, 121
personalization, 95, 96, 99
    features, 100
persuasive robotics, 138
Piaget, Jean, 16, 18, 41, 73
    accommodation, 18
    assimilation, 18
PiStorms, 79
pre-recorded sounds, 60
protégé effect, 101
Python, 62, 74, 76, 84, 126

QR-Code identification, 145
Quizmaster App, 143

RALL, *see* Robot-Assisted
        Language, learning
Raspberry Pi, 6, 64, 79, 81, 82
ready-to-run, 88
ready-to-run robots, 77
    Aibo, 77
    Ozobot, 78
    Tiny, 78

replication crisis, 172
RoboBase, 125, 134
Robocup, 85
RoboPraX, 125, 133
Robot
    android, 93
    autonomy, 53
    etymology, 149
    geminoid, 8, 93
    humanoid robot, 8, 13, 53, 93
    leasing, 118
    mobility, 65
    Opsoro, 88
    tele-presence, 8
    wheeled robot, 53
    zoomorphic robot, 8, 53, 77,
        78
Robot-Assisted Language
    L2TOR, 97
    learning, 96, 138
    NAO, 97
Robotikum, 121, 134
ROILA, 26

Scratch, 75
sensor, 51
    conductivity, 58
    infrared, 57
    physiological, 58
    proximity, 57
    Q-sensor, 59
    sonar, 57
    touch, 58
sex, 45
simulation, 84
Skinner, Burrhus F., 17
social cognition, 34
social psychology, 29
social robot, 88, 94
    status, 99
Softbank Robotics, 8, 62, 64, 120
    online forum, 125

software, 83
    platforms, 84
    programming, 84
speakers, 60
speech recognition, 140
Sphinx, 64
STEAM education, 72
STEM, 26, 45, 72, 73, 85, 130,
        170
Student Advisor App, 144

tele-operation, 53
The Turtle, 71
theories of learning
    behaviourism, 16
    cognitivism, 17
    constructivism, 18, 22, 73,
        99, 132
Theory of Mind, 39, 47
Thymio, 79, 131
Toki Pona, 140
Turtlebot, 81
tutoring, 23, 95, 102
    limitations, 96
    research, 95
    strength, 96

uncanny valley, 42

visual programming environment,
        75, 76
Vygotsky, Lew, 16, 18, 106
    scaffolding, 19
    ZPD, 19

Wizard-of-Oz, 56